Routledge Revivals

Systematic Aesthetics

First published in 1995, this work aims at rehabilitating systematic aesthetics. To this end, it attempts to show how metaphysical, transcendental, and systematic aesthetics comprise the fundamental options for the philosophy of art, how metaphysical and transcendental aesthetics internally undermine themselves, and, finally, how their dilemmas are overcome by systematic aesthetics.

It discusses themes like critique of metaphysical aesthetics; impasse of transcendental aesthetics; individuality of beauty; the existence of beauty in the work of art; the extreme reality of the work of art and the reception of art. This is a must read for scholars and researchers of philosophy of art and philosophy in general.

Systematic Aesthetics

Richard Dien Winfield

First published in 1995
by University Press of Florida

This edition first published in 2024 by Routledge
4 Park Square, Milton Park, Abingdon, Oxon, OX14 4RN

and by Routledge
605 Third Avenue, New York, NY 10017

Routledge is an imprint of the Taylor & Francis Group, an informa business

© 1995 Richard Dien Winfield

All rights reserved. No part of this book may be reprinted or reproduced or utilised in any form or by any electronic, mechanical, or other means, now known or hereafter invented, including photocopying and recording, or in any information storage or retrieval system, without permission in writing from the publishers.

Publisher's Note
The publisher has gone to great lengths to ensure the quality of this reprint but points out that some imperfections in the original copies may be apparent.

Disclaimer
The publisher has made every effort to trace copyright holders and welcomes correspondence from those they have been unable to contact.

A Library of Congress record exists under ISBN: 0813013682

ISBN: 978-1-032-78168-6 (hbk)
ISBN: 978-1-003-48688-6 (ebk)
ISBN: 978-1-032-78230-0 (pbk)

Book DOI 10.4324/9781003486886

Systematic Aesthetics

Richard Dien Winfield

University Press of Florida
Gainesville / Tallahassee / Tampa / Boca Raton
Pensacola / Orlando / Miami / Jacksonville

Copyright 1995 by the Board of Regents of the State of Florida
Printed in the United States of America on acid-free paper
All rights reserved

00 99 98 97 96 95 6 5 4 3 2 1

Library of Congress Cataloging-in-Publication Data

Winfield, Richard Dien, 1950–
Systematic Aesthetics / Richard Dien Winfield.
  p. cm.
Includes bibliographical references and index.
ISBN 0-8130-1368-2
1. Aesthetics. 2. Art—Philosophy. I. Title.
BH39.W56 1995
111'.85—dc20   95-8153

The University Press of Florida is the scholarly publishing agency for the State University System of Florida, comprised of Florida A & M University, Florida Atlantic University, Florida International University, Florida State University, University of Central Florida, University of Florida, University of North Florida, University of South Florida, and University of West Florida.

University Press of Florida
15 Northwest 15th Street
Gainesville, FL 32611

To Kenley Royce Dove
for rehabilitating the project of
systematic philosophy without foundations

Contents

Introduction 1

Part 1: *The Dilemmas of Metaphysical and Transcendental Aesthetics* 13

Chapter 1: The Immanent Critique of Metaphysical Aesthetics 15
  The Rationale for Metaphysical Aesthetics 15
  Art as Artifact 17
  Art as Imitative Artifact 20
  Edification as the Rationale for Imitative Art 23
  The Self-Transcendence of Imitative Craft 26

Chapter 2: The Impasse of Transcendental Aesthetics 34
  The Rationale for Transcendental Aesthetics 34
  Aesthetics as an Empirical Theory of Taste 39
  The A Priori Critique of Taste 43
  The Fundamental Dilemmas of Transcendental Aesthetics 55

Part 2: *Systematic Aesthetics* 59

Chapter 3: The Mandate of Systematic Aesthetics 61
  The Rationale for Systematic Aesthetics 61
  The Rational Reconstruction of Aesthetics 63
  Appropriating Hegel for the Rational Reconstruction of Aesthetics 66
  With What Must Aesthetics Begin? 67
  Truth, Individuality, and the Minimal Determination of Beauty 71

Chapter 4: The Individuality of Beauty   78
  The Constitutive Connection of Universality, Particularity,
    and Individuality   78
  Individuality and the Forms of Universality   80
  Beauty and the Concrete Universal   83
  Beauty as a Display of Objective, Concrete Universality   90

Chapter 5: Beauty as Such and Natural Beauty   92
  The Challenge of Natural Beauty   93
  Natural Beauty and the Philosophy of Nature   94
  The Limits of Natural Beauty   95

Chapter 6: Beauty as Artistic Beauty   106
  The Truth Ingredient in Beauty   106
  Ethics, Religion, and Science as Domains for Beauty   112
  Can the Concept of Beauty Legitimately Refer to Religion
    and Science?   113
  The Exemplary Meaning of Beauty   114
  The Freedom in Artistic Beauty   117
  Two Tests for Confirming the Minimal Determinacy of Beauty   120

Chapter 7: The Existence of Beauty in the Work of Art   122
  Conceiving Aesthetic Value as Artistic Beauty   122
  Content and Expression in the Work of Fine Art   124
  Beyond Mimesis to the Minimal Content of Artistic Beauty   126
  The Divine as an Object of Fine Art   129
  The Transition to Ethical Action as an Object of Artistic Beauty   131
  Preliminary Suspicions Regarding Ethical Action as an Object
    of Artistic Beauty   132

Chapter 8: Conduct as an Object of Artistic Beauty   134
  The General Background of Conduct as an Object of Artistic
    Beauty   135
  The Precipitating Situation of Conduct as an Object of Art   146
  Conduct and Agency as Contents of Artistic Beauty   153
  Anticipatory Response to the Charge of Literary Bias   160

Chapter 9: The External Reality of the Work of Art   162
  The Work of Art as an External Thing   163
  The External Reality of the Work of Art as Determined in
    Its Relation to the Audience   167

Chapter 10: Artistic Creation   176
   The Place of Artistic Creation in Systematic Aesthetics   176
   The Challenge of Purely Formal Artistic Creation: The Cases
      of "Found," "Primitive," and "Industrial" Art   178
   The Question of Creativity in the Performing Arts   180
   The Constitutive Aspects of Artistic Creation   181
   The Subjective Side of Artistic Creation: The Imaginative
      Inspiration of Genius   183
   The Objectivity of Artistic Creation   187
   The Originality of Artistic Creation   187

Chapter 11: The Reception of Art   191
   The Place of Aesthetic Judgment in Systematic Aesthetics   191
   The Abiding Truths of Catharsis   192
   The Recovery of Aesthetic Judgment   194
   Interpretation and Aesthetic Judgment   197

Postscript: The Abiding Tasks of Systematic Aesthetics   202
Notes   205
Bibliography   231
Index   235

Introduction

Despite the long history aesthetics enjoys, the possibility of the philosophy of art remains embroiled in controversy. Pretenders have not been wanting, but whether any have conquered the challenge that art presents to reason is another matter.

The Problematic Character of a Philosophy of Art

Today the borders of aesthetics have become more obscure than ever, as much for those theorizing about art as for those practicing artistic creation. Increasingly, the difficulties of laying hold of what art is explicitly inform the creations of contemporary artists, whose work so often aims at overturning traditional boundaries. They, like their critics, confront a perennial dilemma of drawing lines both descriptive and prescriptive. Not only must some determination be made of what qualifies as art, but some norm must be provided to decide what qualifies as good art. Otherwise, prospective artists and art critics alike must question the direction, let alone the reality, of their own vocations.

Compounding the difficulty is controversy over the method for philosophizing about art. Granted that there is such a thing as art, it is far from clear how it should be philosophically conceived. Indeed, it is debatable whether philosophy can deal with art at all. Might not the descriptive limits distinguishing art from nonart and the prescriptive norms differentiating good art from bad be equally opaque to reason, as matters determined either by personal taste or cultural convention?

Complicating the issue of method is quandary over where the treatment of art falls within philosophical investigation. Can art be subjected to philosophical analysis without further preliminaries, or are there philosophical issues that must be resolved before aesthetics can proceed with any rigor? And if the conception of art must rest on prior theoretical labors, what problems must be settled before addressing art? Here the whole issue of the relation between philosophy and art comes to the fore, with one extreme bewailing the intractable quarrel between philosophy and art and the other embracing the art of language as a paradigm of speculative reason.

To some degree, such problems are endemic to any particular area of philosophical inquiry, since any specific topic already carries with it certain defining assumptions for which philosophy must account if dogmatism is to be overcome. Yet in the case of art, the difficulties seem particularly acute. Almost without exception, art is acknowledged to be marked by features traditionally considered opaque to reason. Whether in an object of sense or in literary imagination, the work of art presents a sensuous configuration seemingly incongruous with the concepts of reason. Moreover, the work of art possesses an original individuality appearing to escape the generality of thought. Similarly, artistic creation seems governed by its own individual genius, irreducible to any rules or patterns that reason could capture or mandate. And even the appreciation of the work of art seems undecidable by philosophical argument, leaving aesthetic judgment hostage to taste, from which arbitrariness cannot be removed. Furthermore, the prescriptive dimension of art, involving the comparative aesthetic value of artistic creations, invites skeptical challenges paralleling those besetting ethics, whose rationality is so commonly contested. And, as if to add insult to injury, one need only survey the latest creations to be reminded how the limits and standards of art have become problematic within art itself.

All this confronts any philosophy of art with the need to answer two basic questions: first, can reason determine what art is? and second, can reason prescribe what art should be? Of course, whether these are really separable questions is itself a matter of controversy. Just as the whole enterprise of metaethics rests on the debatable formalist assumption that the distinction between the ethical and the nonethical can be drawn without differentiating the ethical and the unethical, so too those who radically separate the descriptive and prescriptive dimensions of aesthetics presume that determining the nature of art does not of itself dictate any standard for evaluating artistic creations.

Efforts to answer these questions have perennially addressed three basic dimensions of art, each fostering controversy in its own sphere. First of these is the nature of the work of art in itself and in relation to other factors. On both accounts, artistic creations can be addressed descriptively or prescriptively. Taking the work of art in itself, one can address what is generic to it, however artistically successful it may be, while prescriptively, one can seek the ideal standard against which the aesthetic value of creations should be judged. Regarding the work of art in relation to other factors, there is the descriptive problem of whether art is autonomous or conditioned by psychological, sociological, historical, or other external factors, whereas prescriptively, it warrants investigating whether aesthetically successful art must accord with political, religious, scientific, or other concerns. The second dimension is the character of artistic creation, something seemingly predicated on the character of the work of art. Once again, descriptive and prescriptive avenues beckon, on the one hand, concerning the nature of artistic production, and, on the other hand, addressing the aesthetic norms of creativity, which for their part might be thought autonomous or instrumental. Third comes the character of aesthetic judgment, entailing its own descriptive and prescriptive dimensions revolving around how the audience for art can and should appreciate artistic creations.

A common source of dispute regarding each of these aspects lies in the tendency to isolate certain factors ingredient in art, which are then given a privileged role at the expense of others. Taken in isolation, such disputes appear to arise from wholly arbitrary judgments of no inherent appeal. Yet, controversy in aesthetic theory has a deeper, unavoidable origin rooted in the basic logic of justification.

Justification and the Three Fundamental Forms of Aesthetic Theory

Beauty, goodness, and truth must not be conflated, and one of the primary tasks of aesthetics consists in differentiating art from the themes of epistemology and ethics. Nevertheless, to the degree that beauty comprises the ideal of aesthetic value, it involves a normative dimension like the true and the good. As a consequence, attempts to conceive beauty in art inevitably fall into three groups, reflecting the fundamental strategies of normative argumentation that equally distinguish the varieties of epistemology and ethics.

Normative theory can construe validity in three basic ways. It can locate justification in an appeal to privileged givens, which serve as ultimate standards in virtue of their prior, putatively nonderivative, unconditioned content. This is the strategy shared by metaphysical philosophy and teleological ethics, both of which aim at uncovering first principles in whose self-evident immediacy normative validity is enshrined. However, whether any given can provide ultimate justification owing to its content alone can readily be cast into doubt. Not only can immediacy be ascribed indifferently to competing candidates for first principle, but any attempt to justify the primacy of some given either undercuts its privileged immediacy by appealing to some other foundation or fails to establish that all else rests on the putative first principle by taking for granted what comprises the derivative totality as well as what counts as its grounding.

It thus becomes natural to abandon the metaphysical appeal to privileged givens and turn instead to some privileged determiner, which permits other terms to enjoy legitimacy based not on their own content, but in their derivation from the privileged determiner that confers validity on them. In this way, the metaphysical search for passively contemplated first principles of what is gets supplanted with the transcendental search for conditions of knowing by which objectivity is constructed. Similarly, liberal theory rejects the authority of teleological conceptions of the good and invests practical legitimacy in whatever norms and institutions are determined according to some sanctioned choice procedure. In this way, the strategy of treating normative validity as something to be found is supplanted by one in which the true and good possess their validity in virtue of being made by the proper determiner. Once, however, the content and special role of such a privileged determiner is called into question, it becomes evident that appealing to one is tantamount to appealing to a privileged given. Owing to their role as ultimate sources of validity, transcendental conditions, like the choice procedures of liberal ethics, cannot help but be asserted in just as immediate a fashion as metaphysical first principles of reality and knowing or teleological highest goods. The entailed discrepancy between what has normative validity conferred on it and what confers normative validity presents anew the fundamental stumbling block of any foundationalism. Whereas transcendental conditions of knowing constitute epistemic validity, they cannot possess the same authority they bestow unless they be determined by themselves, something precluded by their defining role as antecedent conditions of knowledge. By the same token, privileged procedures of ethical construction cannot enjoy the normative legitimacy they establish as the outcome of their operation unless they somehow determine themselves, undermining their own function as privileged determiners of derivative institutions.

These difficulties have filled the sails of the postmodern variation on the transcendental turn, leading many to take the failures of the metaphysical and transcendental strategies as condemning reason to impotence, testifying to how all normative domains must rest on unjustifiable foundations, providing the privileged vocabularies without which no claims of normative validity can be advanced in knowing, conduct, or art. Whether these allegedly irremovable foundations be described as empirically given language games, historically variable cultural standpoints, or posits of a will to power, those who advance them commit two blunders that undermine their own positions: first they make immediate reference to these sources of privileged terms, reverting to the dogmatic reading off of the given of metaphysical reference, and then they elevate these sources to determining conditions of knowing and conduct, reverting to the transcendental moves whose failure is to be avoided. Thus, Wittgenstein cannot authoritatively characterize language games and ascribe to them the privileged role of determining meaning and truth without stepping outside them all. If instead he abides by his own edicts, leaving his claims relative to the particular language games in which they gain expression, they forfeit their juridical role and cease to undercut competing positions.[1] Similarly, Foucault can hardly diagnose how historical epistemic frameworks constitute dominating horizons of knowledge and value without inexplicably freeing his own discourse of these very limits. For if his diagnosis is equally predicated on an interest-laden *episteme*, it becomes but one more transient ideology, with no more privileged validity than any of its counterparts.[2]

Accordingly, if dogmatism is to be overcome, the postmodern

resignation to arbitrary foundations must be cast aside. In the face of the breakdown of the metaphysical and transcendental strategies, one alternative remains, the option of a systematic philosophy without foundations. It abandons the foundationalist appeal to privileged givens and privileged determiners, recognizing normativity to reside neither in what is found nor in what is made, but rather in self-determination. Self-determination affords the very logic of normativity in two correlative ways, which together allow it to overcome the dilemmas of foundationalism and postmodern "anti-foundationalism" alike. On the one hand, self-determination involves a liberation from the given, be it construed as nature in itself or as the privileged conditions of validity in knowledge and conduct. Only if reason and conduct are undetermined by independently given factors can they escape being conditioned by unjustified terms. On the other hand, reason and conduct can complement this purely negative liberation from bondage to the given and attain a positive yet nondogmatic determination only if it arises in a presuppositionless, self-grounding way. If reason and conduct can be radically self-determined, they obtain a content that rests on no antecedent givens, for what they are as self-determined is what they have determined themselves to be. Whereas the true cannot be defined by what is not equally true and valid conduct cannot receive its design from what lacks the same legitimacy, self-determination provides precisely what is self-grounded, furnishing the identity of what confers and what enjoys validity that ever eludes all foundationalist strategies. Hence, because autonomous reason is a reason free of foundations, it provides the very logic of truth. Instead of proceeding with a given method and subject matter, for which it can thus provide no account, a self-determining reason generates its own form and content as the result of its labors, achieving a thoroughgoing systematicity where no term gets introduced until all its preconditions and constituents have already been established. As a consequence, the order in which topics are addressed is tied to their content, reflecting their constitutive position in the subject matter under way determining itself. The same freedom from the given is practiced by autonomous action in animating a domain of conduct owing its design wholly to itself, wherein agents exercise modes of self-determination that can only be performed within the self-ordered system of institutions that their own activities constitute. Thereby eliminating the abiding distinction between freedom and normative institutions that persists in liberal theory's treatment of autonomy as a foundation of ethical construction, the system of self-determination provides a self-grounded conduct in which givens play no juridical role. In both theory and practice, the identification of normativity with self-determination thus achieves a positive alternative to appeals to privileged givens or privileged determiners.[3]

Nevertheless, it might be objected that freedom only figures as a new foundation when metaphysics and foundational epistemology are supplanted with the presuppositionless, conceptual self-development of an autonomous reason and when teleological and procedural ethics are replaced with a theory of the self-ordered system of the institutions of freedom. However, because self-determination in theory and practice is only what it has determined itself to be, it has no given character prior to its own development. This original indeterminacy is precisely what allows self-determination to be self-grounding, rather than being a first principle from which derivative terms are legitimated or being something owing its character to some antecedent foundation.

Insofar as the appeals to privileged givens, privileged determiners, and self-determination exhaust the options for justification, aesthetic theory is subject to a completely parallel differentiation of metaphysical, transcendental, and systematic approaches, with fateful implications for the legitimacy of each alternative.

Metaphysical aesthetics locates the standard of beauty in privileged givens comprising antecedent forms of independently discovered reality. On this basis, the work of art gets construed as an imitative artifact whose ultimate reason for being must lie in its edifying effects. Artistic creation thereby gets rendered an edifying imitative craft, and the criticism of art revolves around knowing of what the work is an imitation, comprehending what edifying effect is to be sought, and judging how well the work succeeds in its twofold mission. As examples from Plato to Mao can attest, the antecedent content privileged for artistic construal may be variously interpreted, but the basic logic of any such aesthetic enterprise remains the same.

Transcendental aesthetics, by contrast, repudiates the metaphysical assumption that the standard of beauty is something to be found in reality. Instead, it turns to the structure of reception by which beauty is apprehended, rooting the determination of beauty not in any objective features but in the subjective or intersubjective processes by which objects of beauty are appreciated. In virtue of this turn away from given reality to the determining process of aesthetic judgment, aesthetics becomes transformed into a critique of taste. Only after establishing what occurs in the reception by which beauty is recognized does transcendental aesthetics turn to determining indirectly the features of works of beauty and the character of the activity by which they are created. Once more, the history of aesthetic theory from Hume to Dickie readily testifies to how the privileged structure of reception may be characterized in various ways, be it psychologically, linguistically, culturally, or institutionally, without altering the fundamental logic of the transcendental turn in aesthetics. For whether reception be defined as an a priori structure of consciousness or as a historically embedded discourse of art appreciation serving wills to power rooted in gender, race, class, or some other factor of difference and domination, aesthetic phenomena remain determined by a privileged process constituting their appearance. Hence, as in the case of any transcendental epistemology or procedural ethics, the description and authority of the privileged determiner of normativity remains open to question, for what can possibly legitimate the standpoint that offers it as the Archimedean arbiter of what counts as aesthetic worth? Either that standpoint describes the conditions of aesthetic reception with the same dogmatic direct reference characterizing the metaphysical appeal to the given or it falls into the vicious circularity of psychologism, treating them as constructs whose conditions still need to be ascertained.

This problem subverts the most fashionable postmodern proposals for precluding any philosophical account of art. These positions have by now a familiar and common ring. Followers of Foucault, on the one hand, deny the unqualified objectivity of any conception of art on the ground that the very boundaries of what counts as aesthetic phenomena are defined by historically given conceptual schemes, whose sheer arbitrariness renders their assertion a play for domination. Derrideans claim that the very assumption of a unitary concept of art reflects a logocentric bias, blind to how meanings are constituted in the ever elusive, ever corrigible play of linguistic interpretation. And Wittgensteinians, such as Wollheim, assert that aesthetics must abandon its search for a conceptual determination of art and recognize that all aesthetic categories are merely family resemblances rooted in empirical linguistic practice. Indeed, if we follow Rorty's resignation to the unavoidability of arbitrary privileged vocabularies in discourse, we end up being urged to turn to art itself for enlightenment, forsaking the vain aspirations of a conceptual determination of aesthetic phenomena.[4] But then, Rorty's own all-too-prosaic theorizing forfeits its own message, for not only does he make his case without creating literary art, but he employs philosophical argument to impugn the claims of reason with universal abandon, as if he could somehow transcend the particular limits of privileged vocabularies, whose hold he so readily absolutizes. The avatars of Foucault, Derrida, and Wittgenstein fall prey to the same self-defeating incoherence, for they must repudiate their own global claims about aesthetic phenomena and the conditions of aesthetic discourse if they are to practice what they preach.[5] After all, if, following Foucault, art, like theory and all other cultural productions, is ruled by historical conceptual schemes serving particular interests, how can anyone achieve a neutral, universally applicable insight into this predicament? Or if, as Derrida would venture, the meaning of art, like every other semiotic phenomenon, disseminates in the endless, indeterminate flux of reference, leaving deconstruction of its significance an arbitrary play, how can reflection about this result command any fixed, privileged significance of its own? Or finally, if, in a Wittgensteinian vein, the making and appreciation of art owes its meaning to contingent conventions of linguistic usage, how can this general situation be validated, given how discourse about art could never escape being relative to purely arbitrary language games, whose own character would only be construable through the blinders of some further linguistic practice?

To avoid such dilemmas, systematic aesthetics seeks the standard of beauty neither in antecedently given objects nor in function of structures of aesthetic reception. Instead, it recognizes the autonomy of art, making possible an account of the special individuality distinguishing works of aesthetic worth, an individuality always eluding the grasp of metaphysical and transcendental theories. They perennially fail in conceiving this key individuality precisely because they root the aesthetic character of an object not in its unique appearance, but in something antecedent and thereby common to other entities determined by the same privileged factor. By abandoning the foundational appeal to privileged givens and privileged structures of reception, systematic aesthetics overcomes this limit of its competitors and finally allows reason to lay hold of art.

Toward the Rehabilitation of Systematic Aesthetics

The following work aims at rehabilitating systematic aesthetics. To this end, it attempts to show how metaphysical, transcendental, and systematic aesthetics comprise the fundamental options for the philosophy of art, how metaphysical and transcendental aesthetics internally undermine themselves, and, finally, how their dilemmas are overcome by systematic aesthetics.

Part 1 begins by analyzing the essential features of metaphysical aesthetics, devoting chapter 1 to an immanent critique revealing how the metaphysical conception of art as an edifying imitative craft drives itself toward collapse, no matter what particular contents get privileged. Chapter 2 examines how the failure of metaphysical aesthetics gives rise to transcendental aesthetics and shows how the transcendental strategy of construing the philosophy of art as a theory of aesthetic reception is internally flawed, however the structure of reception itself be construed.

Part 2 introduces the project of systematic aesthetics as a remedy to the problems afflicting the other two approaches. The basic elements of the systematic theory of art are then developed, establishing the features universal to art that set the stage for addressing the particular forms of art and the individual arts. To begin, chapter 3 outlines the emergent rationale for systematic aesthetics, sketches the nonmetaphysical, nontranscendental method that should be followed, and indicates how aesthetics must start with the minimal determination of beauty, presupposed and incorporated in all further dimensions of aesthetic phenomena. In order to identify the special individuality that pervades everything aesthetic, chapter 4 examines the different logical relations between universal and individual, thereby establishing that the individuality of beauty must be formulated as a concrete universality. Chapter 5 next explores whether the forms of nature can embody concrete universality so as to decide the issue of whether beauty proper can reside in natural things as well as in works of art. Insofar as the investigation shows that the concrete universality generic to beauty is not given in nature but only in rational agency and its products, beauty is here demonstrated to be artistic beauty and aesthetics is shown to be the philosophy of art. Chapter 6 proceeds to examine how artistic beauty involves not just the sensuous display of concrete universality, but an exemplary meaning revealing fundamental truths of humanity that can invest an individual configuration. Chapter 7 then investigates what contents are susceptible of artistic construal, showing how the divine and ethical conduct provide privileged themes for beauty. Whereas chapter 7 explores how the divine can figure in the content of art, chapter 8 conceives how the encompassing world, the precipitating situation, and the agency of conduct must all be transfigured in being artistically construed. Turning from the meaning of art to the external reality of its configuration, chapter 9 examines how the artwork is determined in function of being a sensuous thing and of being in relation to an audience. With the nature of meaning and shape in artistic beauty established, chapter 10 advances to conceive the constitutive features of artistic creation. Chapter 11 examines the resulting character of the reception of art, recovering the abiding truths of catharsis and aesthetic judgment, and analyzing the role of interpretation and the relation between aesthetic theory and art criticism. In conclusion, the Postscript certifies the closure of the preceding account of art in general and indicates how, far from signaling a dead end, it provides the necessary prerequisites for conceiving the particular art forms and the individual arts.

Throughout, the discussion aspires to be systematic rather than interpretive in character. Nevertheless, at each juncture the thought of historical thinkers is drawn on, not to be interpreted in its own right but rather to illustrate the basic theoretical option under examination. In this regard, part 1 focuses on Plato and Aristotle as paradigmatic advocates of the metaphysical approach to art and takes Hume and Kant as foils for examining transcendental aesthetics. Following these critical analyses, part 2 reconstructs the basic features of the systematic theory of art by engaging in a critical dialogue with Hegel, whose *Lectures on Aesthetics* still represent the most significant contribution toward systematic aesthetics. No pretense is ever made of providing an adequate interpretation of the aesthetic theory of any of these thinkers or of the more contemporary figures who are also brought into play. Rather, their arguments are introduced only as exemplars of paths of inquiry among which we must choose.

***

A portion of this work was written with the support of the Humanities Center of the University of Georgia. My essay "The Individuality of Art and The Collapse of Metaphysical Aesthetics," which appeared in the *American Philosophical Quarterly* 31, no. 1 (January 1993): 39–51, is incorporated with some changes in chapter 1. Material published separately as my article "Natural Beauty and the Philosophy of Art" in the *Journal of Speculative Philosophy* 9, no. 1 (February 1995) (copyright 1995 by The Pennsylvania State University; reproduced by permission of The Pennsylvania State University Press), is contained in slightly altered form in chapter 5.

Part 1

The Dilemmas of Metaphysical and Transcendental Aesthetics

Chapter 1

The Immanent Critique of Metaphysical Aesthetics

Aesthetics originates when our ordinary acquaintance with objects of beauty becomes torn with controversy over what defines the nature and limits of aesthetic worth. This generates not merely an urge to advance from uncertain opinion to knowledge about the particulars at hand, but a deeper compulsion to conceive beauty in its universality, determining what it is that makes something an object of aesthetic worth in distinction from any other kind of thing. Such a striving to determine beauty per se is not inherently metaphysical, even though metaphysical thought always begins by asking, What is? How this question is tackled is rather what differentiates the fundamental modes of aesthetics.

The Rationale for Metaphysical Aesthetics

The metaphysical approach characteristically answers the question of what a topic is by turning directly to given reality as its standard of truth. This makes perfect sense, provided the universal character being sought is an intelligible nature, independent of our thought but inherently conceivable by a passive exercise of contemplative reason. Such an assumption appears natural, for if some subject matter has no independent, intelligible nature, it is difficult to see how inquiry into what it is can be rescued from the strife-torn relativism of conventional or purely personal identifications.

Yet when applied to beauty, metaphysical reasoning might appear of little use. For whereas metaphysical thought seeks the measure of what is in what exists by nature, as something found in passive reception of intelligible form, art, so central to the existence of beauty, is expressly artificial, issuing from the conscious activity of individuals, the very source of everything arbitrary, perspectival, and conventional. As it turns out, however, the dimension of art by which it is an artifact is perfectly suited to metaphysical construal.

To be an artifact is to be a product of craft, of purposive formative action that imposes an antecedently conceived form on a given material.[1] The formative activity of craft creates neither the form it imposes nor the material on which it operates. Both are independent givens. By being conceivable apart from its realization, the form imposed on the material is something general in character. As such, it can inform many different materials, resulting in a plurality of artifacts of the same kind. What the artifact is is thus identifiable in virtue of the form it embodies, which determines it as one of a certain type. The material in which its form is realized may individuate it from other exemplars of the same form but in no way contributes to its perfection, which depends instead on the presence of its form.

Consequently, if one confronts an artifact and inquires into what it is, surveying its sensible qualities will be of no aid unless it leads one to think the form providing the purpose of the craft activity producing it. This is why an archeologist examining presumed artifacts can only understand what they are by discovering their function, which requires thinking the form they embody in common with any other artifacts of that type.

What makes the appeal to the paradigm of the artifact a characteristically metaphysical route is that it renders reality, be it of nature or art, something whose knowable character is rooted in an antecedent given, which, being intelligible to thought, amounts to an intelligible form. Although the artifact conception treats existence as if it were the product of artisans divine or mortal, the measure of reality remains something to be discovered rather than constructed. The correlation between the artifact conception and the appeal to a discovered measure of aesthetic value may not be fully recognized by many an aesthetic theorist who construes art as the embodiment of independently given intelligible content, but the logic of the connection has irremovable implications for the outcome of any such venture.

Employing the paradigm of the artifact to art has an immediate plausibility. Not only does it allow the produced work to retain a rational nature, susceptible of philosophical investigation, but it reflects a dimension of art that is ubiquitously acknowledged. Whatever else art may be, it always comprises an artifact arising from an exercise of craft. Works of art are not simply natural things. They either issue as products of some sort of making, which, as in the case of "found" art, may even be so formal as merely taking a natural object and presenting it for display, or consist, as in the case of performance art, in an activity that is itself the work of art. Moreover, the artist, however original, cannot create ex nihilo but must always work on a given material, be it stone, canvas, film, the artist's own body, or language. For this reason, every artist must have a technique for mastering the given material and imprinting it with artistic form.

Nonetheless, that the work of art is unavoidably an artifact issuing from an exercise of technique by no means signifies that the nature of the artwork can be reduced to this one dimension. The metaphysical approach characteristically attempts to conceive the *whole* of art in terms of the categories appropriate to artifacts and their production and evaluation. The success or failure of metaphysical aesthetics will thus largely rest on whether such categories are sufficient for grasping what is unique to art.

Art as Artifact

What then, are the basic implications of conceiving art as artifact? First, with the artwork conceived as a product of craft, where an antecedently conceived form is imposed on a given material, what the work of art is is defined by this antecedent form. It stamps the artwork with an identity residing in an intelligible essence. Since this form is given prior to its particular embodiment, the material on which it is impressed contributes nothing essential to that form, but entails only indifferent accidents of its realization. The meaning of the work of art thus lies wholly in the antecedent form, which can be understood and defined apart from the artistic product that is its embodiment. This holds true not just when the work is created as an imitation of an antecedently existent embodiment of a form, as in the Platonic scheme of art, but more generally whenever the work figures as a representation of some prior factor, where, as Nelson Goodman observes, representation is not reducible to resemblance, and the work denotes what it represents without simply imitating it.[2] In every case, by being held to embody something antecedent, the work of art obtains a meaning that is inherently reproducible in other embodiments without detriment to its significance. The meaning of the artwork is therefore rendered something of a general type.

Artistic creation, for its part, here becomes a formative activity, guided by the prior apprehension of the form to be embodied in the given material of the work of art. Hence, the artist should know beforehand what he or she will make. Further, since this theme is defined by a form inherently susceptible of multiple embodiments, it can be known and communicated to others apart from its particular realization. Accordingly, the act of the artist, which consists of imposing this form on a given matter, is limited to the execution of an idea previously conceived by the intellect. Producing neither the idea nor the material of the artwork, the artist's act is confined to informing preexisting material. Artistic production thereby comprises a skill that can be taught like any other. All that is required to become an artist is learning the technique of how to embody a preconceived idea in a given material.

As for art appreciation, it now revolves around comprehending the antecedent form that gives the artwork its meaning. Since the artist produces the work by following the guide of this preconceived form, he or she should know the meaning of the work. Art criticism, be it engaged in by artist or audience, will consist in evaluating how well the given form has been embodied in the given material. The work of art thereby is always to be judged by reference to an independently given end, which is conceivable in distinction from the sensuous apprehension of the work itself. In other words, art criticism becomes a matter of interpretation, uncovering through a labor of translation how the artwork embodies a content that has a separate realization elsewhere.[3]

From the outset, these implications of the metaphysical construal of art as artifact appear fraught with problems. On the one hand, they seemingly fail to characterize art with sufficient specificity. If art is defined as a product of artisanal activity, how can any distinction be drawn between works worthy of presentation in a museum and tools produced for any mundane use? What might otherwise be distinguished as the fine and useful arts seem to be placed on a par, leaving artistic creativity indistinguishable from artisanal skill and rendering aesthetic judgment no different from technical evaluation of a tool's functionality. On the other hand, the application of categories of technique to art seems to contradict some of the key features that are commonly acknowledged to be generic to art.[4]

First of all, the work of fine art, unlike the product of craft, has an individuality whose unique originality is not an indifferent accident but a crucial contribution to the work's aesthetic value. For this reason, a copy of an artwork, which may well exhibit completely comparable technique, lacks the imaginative originality by which it could command comparable aesthetic worth.

Second, fine art is marked by a unity of meaning and configuration, where the meaning of a work cannot be separated from its sensuous form. This unity is tied to the individuality of fine art, which ensures that the significance of a work is not something shared by others and thereby distinguishable from them all as the common meaning they instantiate. Were the artwork a mere artifact, with a nature common to other embodiments of the same form, its meaning would not only be devoid of originality but would be something inherently separable from its particular realizations. In this connection, manifold manifest particulars of the artwork are essential to its significance,[5] unlike a tool, whose reproducible function need not be impeded by the alteration of any of its sensuous features unrelated to its common use.

Third, given the unity of meaning and configuration of the work of art, the artist does not, indeed cannot, have a preconceived idea of what the work will be prior to the act of artistic creation. An idea that is not already joined to a sensuous configuration is not yet an artistic one. Hence there is no blueprint or formula that the prospective artist need only embody to create a work of art. On the contrary, when the artist produces something reducible to a formula that can be apprehended apart from the configuration of the individual work of art, the product may be a good example of craft, but it is a sorry failure as an example of artistic creativity. What makes artistic creativity worthy of the name is that the essence of the work of art is not given prior to its production, but rather arises within its realization, as it must to be in unity with the relevant particulars of its configuration.

Fourth, since the artist creates without a preconceived idea exhaustively dictating the aesthetic features of what will be created, he or she need not be aware of what the finished work artistically signifies or how it should be aesthetically interpreted. Nor is it any artistic defect that the artist, as often lamented, understands not what he or she creates. An artisan, by contrast, would be poorly skilled if the function of his or her product remained a mystery to its maker.

Fifth, although artistic technique can be taught like any other craft, artistic creativity is a matter of genius, whose unique originality defies transmission through teaching. To be teachable, artistic creativity would have to be governed by general rules or common patterns. Yet given the individuality and unity of meaning and configuration of fine art, the creative act that produces it cannot be reducible to any rule-governed skill.

Sixth, art criticism properly judges a work of art in regard to its significant originality and internal unity of meaning and configuration. As we shall see, this does not entail excluding all connections with our world, but it does preclude centering the evaluation of art on its accord with an independently given standard, like the governing purpose of an artisanal production.

If the project of metaphysical aesthetics is not to be abandoned, these distinctive aspects of art must somehow be captured without transcending the nature of artifacts and artisanal production. To this there can be but one solution: art must be distinguished from artifacts lacking aesthetic character by differentia identifying it as a particular species of artifact. What can this species be, this brand of artifact that defines art, whose artisanal production distinguishes artistic creation and whose technical evaluation can comprise aesthetic judgment?

Art as Imitative Artifact

Plato provides the plausible answer: that the required species is none other than the imitative artifact, whose production is an activity of imitative craft and whose appreciation revolves around judging the fidelity of the imitation.[6] *Mimesis* or imitation hereby becomes a central category of metaphysical aesthetics, introduced to redeem *techné* (craft) as a suitable framework for determining what art is.

Imitation in its aesthetic employment is not confined to the copying of another work of art, be the latter an artifact issuing from mortal artisanship or the craft of a divine demiurge who imposes form on the chaos of matter. It rather extends to representation in general, to the extent that the representative function of mimetic craft involves the imposition of an antecedently given form on some given material, where that form resides in the perceived appearance of something existing in nature or in another given artifact. The work that results "represents" the original not as a sign standing for it, but rather as an artifact reflecting the appearance of the original.[7]

Since the "original" that is imitated need not be an actually existing thing, but may well be another representation, whose own embodiment of intelligible form is given in a separate product of imagination, the imitation of mimetic art can be considered, as Danto puts it, nonextensional.[8] However, whether imitative art is about something real or merely imaginary, the key factor is that it always represents an independently given theme, thereby getting structured in terms of the craft categories of embodied form.

If the application to art of categories of craft entails such further appeal to imitation, the subordination of art under the category of imitation involves its own imposition of the categories of craft. To define art as an imitative object, produced by an activity of mimetic image making, is automatically an embrace of the craft framework. Because the production of an imitative image must proceed from a given form that is then imposed on the given material of the particular art, the mimetic artist produces art as an artisan. This can be true even if the likeness making involves not only the imitation of real things but an imaginative, fantastic image making, as Plato adds in the *Sophist*.[9] Indeed, if imitative art is to appear to its audience as a copy rather than as the original, there must be something about its appearance that distinguishes it from what is given in reality, something that stamps it, broadly speaking, as a work of fiction. No matter how fictional it may be, the work of art can still be produced as a copy of an antecedent form, provided the resulting image realizes a preconceivable idea, be it through the combination or transposition of forms given in nature or convention. Moreover, imitation can equally apply to works that express inward states of character of the artist or other individuals, rather than describe external phenomena. Here again, artistry exhibits a mimetic craft to the degree that the produced image mimics the given reality of the soul.

Yet even if the concept of imitative artifact can accommodate the fictional and expressive dimensions of art, it seems to render problematic the whole rationale of artistic production. Robbing the work of art of a unique, independent significance, mimetic theory casts the value of art in doubt.[10] For the moment one grants that the work of art be an imitation of a given original, the questions arise, For what end? Why copy what already exists?

Could it be for pleasure? This seems a suspect reason on two accounts. First, would not the furnishing of the imitated object be a more worthy satisfaction of desire than providing a mere copy? Second, the art object is characteristically not consumed like ordinary objects of desire. Instead, it is left untouched, as something simply to be allowed to appear and, if need be, to be protected from personal use by the guarding conventions of a public museum or performance hall. Moreover, as Plato points out in the *Laws,* pleasure serves as a legitimating standard only for what furnishes neither utility nor truth of likeness, but only accompanying charm and amusement.[11] Yet art as imitative artifact must in some respect be judged according to how well it copies its original.

If not for pleasure, is art, qua mimetic, then for the sake of knowledge? Here we must contend with Plato's classic critique of whatever educational pretensions imitative artistry might entertain. Since the imitative artwork, as itself either a sensuous object or words conveying sensuous phenomena, copies other sensuous things as they appear to the artist, it is automatically inferior as a source of knowledge to what it imitates. Not only is it at one remove from the original, and thereby something different, but it results from an attempt to copy the original not as it truly is, but merely as the artist perceives its sensible appearance.[12] And if the artist imitates not nature but creations of other artists, the work is at a triple remove from the truth, comprising an imperfect replica of an imperfect replica of an appearance. Hence, if artists did aim at knowledge and really knew both what they were imitating and the character of their imitative artistry, they would be interested in the realities themselves rather than in making copies.[13] Makers of imitative images thus reveal through their persistent practice of their own craft that they know appearances only. Whereas the users of objects must have true knowledge of them and their function to employ them properly, and the makers of useful objects must have correct belief about them gained from the user who knows, imitators can imitate without knowing anything of the true character of the objects they copy.[14] Furthermore, since what the imitative artist produces is not merely conceptual and objective to thought but something imagined and appealing to sense and feeling, it encourages those irrational elements of mind that are at furthest remove from the intelligible forms by which artifacts are knowable.[15] Creating works with an inferior degree of truth and appealing to parts of the mind that are cognitively inferior, imitative artistry is thus doubly unsuited for serving the pursuit of knowledge.

Edification as the Rationale for Imitative Art

What then remains as a reason for pursuing mimetic craft? Although imitative art may be inferior to observation or thought as a vehicle of knowledge, the appeal of its sensuous replica to sense and feeling makes it a useful instrument for cultivating those not yet ready and willing to undertake rational study of the true and the good.[16] By employing the suggestive powers of art, imitative artists can bring the young and others to take displeasure at ugly depictions of the false and base, and pleasure at beautiful portrayals of the true and right, while they are still unable to apprehend the reason for their respective repulsion and admiration.[17] In this way, imitative art can help mold the character of individuals by cultivating the proper emotive responses sanctioned independently by reason.

Although Plato and Aristotle both emphasize this edifying role of art in relation to the education of the young, it hardly follows that art should be a matter for youth alone. Imitative art can have the same salutary effect on mature citizens who are capable of using their reason to differentiate illusion and truth and vice and virtue, because the wellsprings of good living do not lie in reason alone but require the consonant contribution of will. Since the training of desires to produce dispositions to take pleasure and displeasure in the right objects already inclines the individual to choose the proper course of action, art's appeal to sense and feeling gives it a power to influence character in a way reason cannot.[18] This influence may be of paramount importance in youth when character formation reaches a certain fixed plateau, but it retains a value that makes art of use throughout life. Through this edifying function, imitative art thus wins a very significant reason for being, placing artistic pursuit at the very core of individual cultivation.[19] Hence, it will be natural for Marxist-Leninists, to take one modern example, to employ art mimetically to bring the untutored masses to a proper class consciousness of the truths known to the political vanguard through the science of historical and dialectical materialism.

One is tempted to object that characterizing art as an edifying imitative artifact drastically restricts what creations can count as genuinely artistic. Readily representational media such as the visual arts and literature appear eminently suited to play their edifying roles, but what of such seemingly nonrepresentational "arts" as architecture or music? Music is perhaps the most extreme example, since "pure" music, devoid of lyrics or program, seems incapable of representing anything given externally. Yet, Plato and Aristotle both turn to music more than any other art when it comes to forming the character of the young. Musical education is most sovereign for them because melody, harmony, and rhythm reputedly take strongest hold on the soul and combine to form modes and rhythms representative of different characters.[20] Hence, even though music is devoid of the spatial externality allowing the visual arts and literary imagination to portray objective reality, the musical modulation of time can mimic the temporal flow of the inner life of individuals, in all its emotive variety. Similarly, architecture's frozen music of harmony and proportion can shape its masses of heavy material to provide an environment for action reflecting the character of those who will inhabit it. It can thus come as no surprise that Hitler will encourage Speer to make the Reich's public architecture the emblem of the Aryan spirit, that Stalin will demand fealty in symphonies from Prokofiev and Shostakovich, or that a newly arisen rock and roll will be lambasted for corrupting the youth of America.

Granted the wide range of media susceptible of edifying employment, once edification becomes recognized as the only legitimating purpose of imitative art, the subject matter of aesthetic imitation becomes restricted to what can be edifying. Broadly speaking, imitative art will properly portray what is ethical. Since the ethical consists of normatively significant action in which ethically relevant character is displayed, art, metaphysically construed, will imitate neither nature in general, nor human affairs in their totality, but, as Aristotle maintains in his *Poetics*, *praxis*—understood as the sphere of ethical conduct and its institutions.

Moreover, since the edifying function of imitative art is essentially a public concern, centering on forming the right sort of character of citizens, Plato is perfectly consistent in calling for public scrutiny and censoring of artistic production. Given how a correspondingly metaphysical vision of the good life can take different teleological versions,[21] one might quarrel with Plato's edict that the only poetry worth admitting to the good state are hymns to the gods and praises of famous men,[22] just as one could object to Zhdanov's and Mao's decree that art embrace a socialist realism serving the masses. Nevertheless, art mimetically construed is just as appropriate a matter of political regulation as public education.

If art is of value for its edifying imitation, then it follows that art criticism must consider whether the subject to be represented has the proper ethical character, as well as whether it has been imitated sufficiently accurately and with the skill adequate to have the desired edifying effect. To this end, art criticism will focus on a meaning that can be formulated apart from the work. The aesthetic value of the work will depend on the ethical significance of this independently given meaning as well as on an evaluation of how well the work embodies this meaning in a salutary way. Hence, to paraphrase Plato, the competent art critic requires three types of knowledge: knowledge of what the artwork imitates, knowledge of the ethical truth of this original, and knowledge of how well it has been executed.[23] Significantly, since the work should influence the sensibility and feeling of its audience in a salutary way, what counts is not simply an accuracy providing epistemic satisfaction, but rather the sort of depiction that will produce the appropriate cathartic effect on the emotions. When Plato prescribes how art should truly imitate the divine[24] and what stories and narrative modes are appropriate for educating the guardians of the state,[25] he tends to emphasize the importance of correct depiction, as if this merely involves mirroring the given nature of the subject matter. However, if the edifying role of art is duly acknowledged, imitation can no longer be taken quite so literally.

Nevertheless, so long as the edifying role of art relies on imitation, artistic creation should be predicated on the artist's prior apprehension of what is to be depicted, with particular regard to its ethical significance, as well as on the technical skill and knowledge of how to mimic it in a particular material. Then, however, artists should know the meaning of their works and be able to teach others to produce equally beautiful objects. Yet, as Plato himself admits, artists characteristically do not know beforehand what they will create, nor, unlike other artisans, can they afterwards always explain their work, let alone be most knowledgeable about its significance, nor can their artistry be taught like other crafts. How can these features of artistic creation be squared with the imitative edification ascribed to art?

Plato offers a solution indicative of what can be done within the limits of the categories of edifying mimesis. Artistic activity can retain its character as imitative craft while allowing the artist to create in ignorance if the artist creates in a divine trance, where, without consciously knowing what is being imitated, he or she still executes a predetermined idea, working as the possessed instrument of divine inspiration.[26] If the appeal to divine artifice offends, one could just as easily follow Kant and substitute Nature, having it work through the unknowing artist, embodying preconceived form in some given material.[27] Either way, the work of art remains an artifact, whose significance can neither be foretold nor best interpreted by the artist, and whose production can hardly be taught to others by one who creates in a blind frenzy.

The Self-Transcendence of Imitative Craft

In proceeding from craft to edifying imitation, metaphysical aesthetics seems to have met success, constructing a coherent account of the work of art, art criticism, and artistic production. Yet, on closer examination, the metaphysics of art is rent by a troubling tension that threatens to explode the conceptual framework it has erected. Aristotle's *Poetics* brings this internal rift to a head by grappling with the problems left unresolved in Plato's seminal development of metaphysical aesthetics.

Like his mentor, Aristotle accepts the basic metaphysical notion that fine art is an imitative craft whose value lies in its edifying consequences.[28] He accordingly explains aesthetic value in terms of a natural propensity to imitate and take pleasure in viewing imitations, where the pleasure received is rooted in the satisfaction of learning something ennobling.[29] Further, Aristotle limits the subject matter of fine art to ethical conduct (*praxis*), where the characters of agents are revealed in action in respect of their virtue and vice. What marks Aristotle's development of metaphysical aesthetics beyond its initial statement by Plato is Aristotle's recognition that imitative art can only fulfill its function if it transfigures, rather than merely mirrors, the given content of its artistry.

On the one hand, Aristotle keenly recognizes the implications of how art's edifying effect on its audience is not purely intellectual but involves its sensuous impact on emotion. In the paradigmatic case of drama, the effect is achieved through the catharsis of incidents arousing pity and fear.[30] To achieve such catharsis, drama must not mimic simply any ethical conduct but carefully choose its plot to produce the requisite reaction. Generally, drama must depict a certain type of ethical conflict and its resolution, involving a clash of ethical principles rather than merely natural calamities.[31] Moreover, Aristotle maintains, it will not do to portray a good man passing from happiness to misery nor a bad man passing from misery to happiness nor an extremely vicious man falling into misery, since none of these cases inspire the proper fear or pity. An edifying plot must instead involve an individual who is not preeminently virtuous and whose misfortune is brought about not by any depravity but by some great error that reveals a moral purpose.[32] Then the drama can move its audience to identify with the protagonist and emotively respond to the moral conflict portrayed.

Yet, even here, plot construction is not simply a matter of copying appropriate actions. To achieve its artistic ends, dramatic art, like any other, must alter what it represents to give it a distinctly aesthetic form. To obtain the properly edifying catharsis, drama must incorporate elements of explicit dramatic convention, making clear to the audience that what they are witnessing is neither real action nor a natural object, but rather an artistic representation with its own fictional arena. Imitative art may indeed mimic appropriate subject matter, but artistic mimicry must be markedly different from its original simply to be recognizable as an imitation. Brecht's polemic against Aristotelian poetics thus fails to comprehend how *Entfremdung,* or aesthetic distancing, is already recognized by Aristotle to be basic to artistic mimesis.[33]

The difference between artistic representation and its object, however, is not limited to strutting on a stage with all the external machinery of dramatic illusion. It equally involves a transformation of the action portrayed, whereby it becomes distilled into specifically dramatic action. This involves more than conforming to the formal unities of place, time, and persona, and restricting the length of the performance in accord with the limits of audience retention.[34] Rather, plot must be infused with a special unity where all that occurs is necessary, yet not predictable. To achieve this distinctly aesthetic necessity, plot cannot simply imitate individuals in all the contingent and irrelevant detail of their existence. Instead, characters must be depicted for the sake of the action, leaving aside all features that are not pertinent to it.[35] Further, incidents should not be copied in the order in which they actually occur, subject to all the chance occurrences and intervening events that have little to do with the ethical conflict at stake. Each incident should rather arise as the probable consequence of antecedent incidents, with each revelation of character rooted in this connection.[36] Otherwise, artistic representation wanders from its edifying function, losing itself in an aimless diffusion.

The unifying thread underlying these transfigurations of the content of imitative art is set in relief by Aristotle's telling comparison of poetry to philosophy and history. History, not art, describes what has happened in all its particular detail. Because historical narrative is committed to representing what has been in its immediate givenness, the particulars it portrays are immersed in disconnected series of events, full of accidental and meaningless aspects.[37] Consequently, the particular content of history is not necessarily expressive of anything of universal, substantial interest. Philosophy, by contrast, conceives what is necessary and universal, leaving aside the particular as something incidental to the realization of the universal. Art occupies an intermediary position, for what art describes, Aristotle maintains, is not what has happened, but a kind of thing that might happen, a particular of a certain type whose possibility is probable or necessary.[38] Granted that a universal statement concerns what will probably or necessarily transpire to a kind of thing, the particular represented by art is therefore conjoined with what is universal. Unlike philosophy, however, art does not dispense with the particular. The work of art constitutively involves a sensuous content, be it realized in sensuous material, such as the stuff of buildings, sculpture, painting or music, or in sensuous images produced in the imagination through literature. Accordingly, art affects its audience in an emotive and not merely intellectual way. Nevertheless, unlike history, art represents particulars that are wholly infused with universality. In contrast to the prosaic reality described in historical narrative, art portrays particulars that in all respects exhibit what is universal and necessary. For this reason, although the work of art will affect its audience in an emotive way, this affect will consist in not mere feeling, but in a catharsis involving an intelligent grasp of what is universal in the sensuous configuration before it.

Owing to this key unification of universal and particular, art cannot be imitative in the sense of simply mirroring reality as it immediately exists in all its contingency. Instead, the imitation specific to art mirrors in sensuous form what is universal and necessary. This requires more than copying what is given to sense. To achieve its unique marriage of universal and particular, art must employ the imagination to produce sensuous images in which each detail is imbued with abiding significance. Since art can only accomplish its edifying function by representing ethical affairs, art's imaginative unification of universal and particular entails portraying interactions of particular individuals that convey universal, necessary conflicts of moral significance. To this end, dramatic plot must submit to just those sorts of constraints that Aristotle propounds to ensure that each incident arises as the necessary or probable consequence of antecedent action.[39] Taken in earnest, the requisite unity entails that plot exhibit a heightened meaningfulness, where all details contribute to the action's central problem without ever becoming predictable or formulaic. In this sense, the necessity of plot development is not mechanical in character, exhibiting a form that can equally order a different particular content. The particular content would then be a matter of indifference to the significance of the work, destroying its unity of sensuous configuration and meaning. Instead, plot and, indeed, artistic form in general must exhibit an autonomous development, combining necessity and freedom such that every stage is both unexpected yet unavoidable the moment it occurs.

What allows art to fulfill its edifying role is precisely this imaginative melding of the particulars of action with what is universal and necessary. By uniting universal and particular in sensuous configuration, artistic imagination is able to convey truth more directly than history, yet without rising to the pure abstractions of philosophical thought. On the other hand, by retaining the particularity of the sensuous image, which has direct influence on emotion and desire, art can influence action more directly than mere philosophical argument.

Yet if artistic imitation must transfigure what it represents so as to achieve a unity of particular and universal, artistic creation must undergo its own transformation. Instead of falling within the confines of rote craft, artistry must now combine two capacities. On the one hand, the artist must comprehend what is universal and necessary in ethical life and no longer what is just the given form of existing particulars. On the other hand, the artist must possess a power of imagination to construct sensuous particulars in thoroughgoing unity with the universal.

By the same token, the art critic can no longer determine aesthetic value by judging how well the work of art mirrors what is immediately given. The art critic must instead judge whether the artist has captured in sensuous form what is universal and necessary in the reality of ethical life, creating particulars that convey the pure possibilities of their type without ever appearing to be ordered by an external, separable formula.

Aristotle leads the metaphysics of art to this threshold, where the inherent requirements of aesthetic inquiry begin to transgress the confines of the categories of imitative craft. On all sides, the reality of art has come to entail a unity of particular and universal that seems fundamentally incongruent with the framework of edifying imitative art. The root of the problem is that art seems to require a melding of sensuous configuration and universal significance where, on the one hand, the particular can no longer be incidental to the realization of the universal, and on the other hand, the universal is such that it cannot be expressed apart from the particular sensuous content of the work of art.

This new unity not only challenges the scheme of embodied form underlying craft production, but it equally eliminates the problem of seeking an instrumental justification for the practice of art. Conjoining universal and particular, the work of art takes on an independent value because what it conveys cannot be expressed through other means. If the work of art's essence were merely universal, comprising a form both antecedently conceivable and realizable in other embodiments, then it would be dispensable.

The characteristic uniqueness of the work of art exhibits precisely this interpenetration of particular and universal, where any noticeable change of detail would detract from the work's meaning. Although any object is individual, the work of art hereby has an *essential* individuality, where what is unique about it is fundamental to its value. By contrast, a mere artifact can be variously altered without impugning its perfection, since the reproducible form giving it its identity and function has no trouble surviving changes in the incidental details of its execution.

The categories of imitative craft are similarly challenged by how the work of art transfigures what it represents. What distinguishes artistic representation from any corresponding reality is not something on the order of the difference between the embodiment of form and the form itself. It rather involves an imaginative creation separating the world of aesthetic representation from the givenness of particular existence.

These aspects of the unity of particular and universal, individuality, and imaginative transfiguration all go together and all underlie a further feature to which metaphysical aesthetics has inadvertently led: that the meaning of the work of art can no longer be conceived independently from the sensuous apprehension of it.[40] If art was imitative in the mechanical manner of craft production, then the work of art would be like a tool, becoming comprehensible only when its purpose is discovered, where this purpose is conceivable apart from the sensuous apprehension of any particular example fulfilling it. However, because art infuses the detail of its sensuous configuration with meaning, creates something unique, and transfigures, rather than rotely copies, whatever it portrays, what a work of art signifies cannot be detached from its particular appearance.

To do justice to these features, features that metaphysical aesthetics is compelled to admit, the philosophy of art must break from the categories of craft by drawing a radical distinction between the useful, mechanical arts and the fine, creative arts.[41] The course of metaphysical aesthetics has itself revealed just how the teleological conception germane to craft production is applicable only to the useful, but not to the fine arts.[42] The conceptual framework of embodied form does have its place in construing the useful arts, where the artisan produces a functional object in virtue of antecedently apprehending the purpose that gives it its identity and form. In such craft, the entire formative activity of the artisan is governed by the understanding of this purpose, which is why the exercise of craft is eminently teachable and repeatable without detracting from its excellence. Further, the purpose, providing the form of the artifact, gives it an intelligible essence, definable in distinction from the accidental qualities that attend its realization in a particular material by a particular artisan. This intelligible essence, in which the meaning of the artifact resides, is particular in the sense of being distinguishable from the form of an object having a different function. However, it is not individual, since every other artifact that is or may be produced according to the same purpose exhibits the identical form. Accordingly, when it comes to judging the useful artifact, the critic has an independently given, common standard by which to measure its success: the function dictating its form.

With fine art, by contrast, the categories of technique can only capture a very partial and subordinate aspect of the work, its creation and its criticism. What eludes the craft conception is the pervasive unity of universal and particular that resists the drawing of any distinction between an intelligible essence of the work of art and the sensuous accidents of its embodiment. If a putative artistic creation is still governed by the remnants of such a differentiation, it is a mark of aesthetic failure, signifying either an inability to rise above the trite, predictable formulae of handicraft or a surrender to allegory, where the meaning of the work is given independently of its sensuous configuration, which then forfeits its own value. A true work of fine art, however, exhibits a unique originality, where neither the meaning nor its embodiment can be detached. Owing to this unity of form and content, neither can be given prior to the artistic activity from which the work arises. Hence, the fine artist does not simply execute a preconceived plan in the manner of an artisan, but rather engages in a creative activity for which no antecedent given can provide the measure of the finished work.

Nonetheless, the imaginative originality of the fine artist does not operate ex nihilo. The fine artist still employs a given material as an artistic medium on which the ideas of imagination must be imprinted. This is true even in literature, which might well be the most creative of arts.[43] Even something as artificial as language can never be a total creation of an author, as private language arguments underline by showing how no meaning can be certified unless some intersubjective content be available to contrast with subjective assurances. Fine art therefore always involves an element of technique that artists must master to be able to use a particular medium as a vehicle of creative imagination. Like any other technique, this can be taught, and such skill, whether in the crafts of architectural drafting, stone carving, drawing perspective, color composition and paint mixture, harmony and counterpoint, or rhythm and meter, is what schools for the fine arts can reasonably aim to teach.

However, if technique is not totally supplanted by artistic creativity, it is subordinated as an instrument of aesthetic imagination. Technical mastery may be needed for an artist to give full vent to creativity, but brilliant technique cannot independently confer aesthetic value on a creation or make its author a great artist. Although technique remains an indispensable vehicle, only through the original activity of creative imagination can the artist rise above being a virtuoso artisan. This creative facility, the genius of the artist, simply cannot be captured by the categories of craft, because it consists not in embodying given form but in creating the aesthetic form in the first place. The artist as creator eludes the metaphysical conception and calls for a revolution in aesthetics.

Finally, the demands of art criticism break the mold for evaluating edifying artifacts. If fine art is imbued with a creative originality in which universal and particular are inextricably joined, then art criticism must abandon the procedures suitable for judging functional products. Above all, the art critic must avoid evaluating the work of art in terms of any independently given criterion. No longer can art be judged according to its edifying effects or its success in conveying some antecedently given knowledge. Nor can the artwork be deciphered as if it were an allegory, in search of a meaning whose essence can be detached from the accidents of its presentation. Instead, art criticism must grapple with a sense of aesthetic value that somehow resides in the unity of universal and particular specific to fine art.

This unity of aesthetic form is the fatal stumbling block at which metaphysical aesthetics arrives, exploding the limits of its own theoretical paradigm. What art as edifying artifact cannot suppress, yet cannot comprehend, is the dimension of individuality, comprising the unity of universal and particular at the heart of the originality and freedom of artistic creation. In light of the breakdown of metaphysical aesthetics, the ultimate success of the philosophy of art will now depend on developing the conceptual resources for conceiving individuality in the form in which it underlies the reality of art.

Chapter 2

The Impasse of Transcendental Aesthetics

The collapse of metaphysical aesthetics reveals that what characterizes fine art cannot be grasped by appealing to intelligible antecedent givens and the corresponding paradigm of edifying imitative craft. Neither the work of art, nor artistic creation, nor art criticism can be made to fit the mold of embodied form on which metaphysical thought relies in seeking a given nature for art. Again and again the dilemma surfaces that the individuality permeating art is simply incommensurable with the abstractions of embodied form.

The Rationale for Transcendental Aesthetics

Aesthetics is left at a crossroads. On the one hand, new categories must be found to comprehend the individuality of art that escape reduction to an intelligible essence. On the other hand, aesthetics must abandon the metaphysical strategy of turning to some given reality as the natural measure of art. Where then can aesthetics turn? The breakdown of metaphysical aesthetics suggests that what art is cannot be answered by contemplating its putative objective reality and finding some general properties that define its nature. The experience of the metaphysical approach indicates that no set of objective qualities can unambiguously identify an entity as a work of art.[1] Yet, if the nature of art cannot be discovered by direct appeal to any given objective features, aesthetics has nowhere else to turn, it appears, than to the audience that confronts art. Instead of asking what art is and seeking its objective form, aesthetics has the option of asking how the audience of art is able to judge something to have aesthetic value, that is, to be beautiful, broadly speaking. Since the answer must be obtained independently of any objective description of art, the reception of beauty must somehow be the source for determining what counts as art. Little else seems possible, for if what makes an entity a work of art is not rooted in any objective features, it must instead by sought indirectly in terms of the subjective or intersubjective features of aesthetic experience. In this way, the collapse of metaphysical aesthetics gives rise to a transcendental turn, transforming the philosophy of art into a critique of aesthetic reception. Here aesthetics becomes a theory of taste, where the only viable path for grasping art consists in focusing on the type of experience that can have beauty for its object.

This move from conceiving art as an edifying imitative artifact to examining the structure of aesthetic reception reflects the same shift that underlies the move from precritical metaphysics to transcendental philosophy. Following the skeptical challenge to the metaphysical strategy of construing objectivity directly by immediate contemplation of what is, transcendental philosophy substitutes construction for discovery, conceiving objectivity as determined by the structure of knowing. Applied to aesthetics, the transcendental turn signifies conceiving art not as something given independently of the awareness for which it can be an object, but regarding it as determinable only as it is given in the experience for which aesthetic judgments are possible.

Transcendental aesthetics thus arises primarily in reaction to the dogmatic character of metaphysical aesthetics, exemplified in the misbegotten strategy of conceiving art by stipulating putatively objective concepts based on direct reference to what is taken to be given. The failure of the metaphysical paradigm of the edifying imitative artifact to capture salient features of aesthetic phenomena recedes in significance, for what motivates the transcendental turn is not so much the content of the categories employed to conceive art, but whether they are immediately "discovered" or mediately "constructed" in terms of the structure of aesthetic reception.

On this basis, the central problem of aesthetics is conceiving the generic features of any awareness of beauty, or, to put the matter in linguistic terms, of any reference to beauty, where these features are determined in indifference to the particular object being judged to have aesthetic value. Given the prohibition against seeking any independently given nature of art, aesthetics here becomes, in the first instance, reduced to a theory of taste, whose focal point is the subjective or intersubjective process whereby judgments are made about beauty. Thereby aesthetic theory gets transformed, broadly speaking, into a theory of reception, where the effect of appearances on their audience assumes priority in determining the bounds of aesthetic worth. Moreover, since rhetoric addresses how representations influence rational agents, the transcendental turn in aesthetics might be said to subsume aesthetic theory under rhetoric, *provided* that the reception of beauty can be tied to some pragmatic end.[2]

Now beauty in general, rather than artistic beauty, becomes the central theme, for two complementary reasons. First, granted that aesthetic reception pertains to beautiful objects whether they are natural or artificial, the conditions for experiencing beauty are not specially linked to artistic beauty. Second, since the objective features of the object, including those that identify it as a product of nature or as an artistic creation, do not enter into determining what makes it possible to judge the object to be beautiful; all that is at issue is how one becomes aware of beauty per se. If there is to be any universal element in such judgments, allowing taste to rise above personal preference, it will have to be accounted for in the relation between the appearance of the judged object, whatever it may be, and the structure of awareness by which it is aesthetically appreciated. In the absence of any given nature to which legitimate reference can be made, beauty, the general object of aesthetic judgment, will have to be characterized exclusively in terms of the subjective or intersubjective elements of aesthetic experience.

Such an approach comprises a complete reversal of the metaphysical conception of art as edifying imitative artifact. From the transcendental perspective, the latter is dogmatically objective in two respects. By conceiving art as imitative, the metaphysical conception appeals to an objective concept of the original that is imitated. By conceiving art as edifying, the metaphysical conception locates aesthetic value in moral effects that are given equally independently of aesthetic awareness. Characterizing the work of art in terms of such objective features, metaphysical aesthetics subordinates the identity of art to cognitive or practical interests, thereby losing sight of what is specific to the work of art.

Significantly, in making these critiques, transcendental aesthetics precludes certain characterizations of the work of art, as if aesthetics were still in a position to determine what objective features an object must possess to be beautiful. This need not come as a surprise, for transcendental aesthetics does have something to say about the character and production of the object of beauty. Expressly rejecting any direct reference to the given reality of art, transcendental aesthetics may well focus on the structure of aesthetic judgment as it transpires in the audience of beauty, be that audience construed subjectively or intersubjectively. Nevertheless, transcendental aesthetics will still arrive at correlative features that the object of a possible aesthetic judgment must have in order to sustain the acts of reference constitutive of such an awareness. These features, constructed in function of the subjective or intersubjective nature of judgments of taste, will, for their part, dictate how objects of beauty will have to be made to have the appropriate appearance ingredient in aesthetic appreciation. The reality of the work of art and, by extension, the process of its creation will thereby be determined, albeit indirectly, in view of the requirements of aesthetic judgment.

This reintroduction of a characterization of the object of beauty parallels the treatment of objectivity in transcendental philosophy in general. Although the turn to investigate the conditions of knowledge or reference is made in order to refrain from making direct claims about what is given, objectivity still ends up being characterized within the investigation of knowing. This is unavoidable to the extent that knowing constitutively refers to an object of awareness, and objects of knowledge have certain features simply in order to be given to cognition, whether cognition is construed in terms of acts of consciousness or linguistic usage. Consequently, even though transcendental philosophy introduces its inquiry as a necessary preliminary to establish the competency of knowing and so allow for subsequently conceiving those objects falling within the limits of knowledge, the transcendental critique of knowing ends up containing its own doctrine of objectivity, comprising an internal realism exhausting what can be known a priori about reality.[3] In the same way, transcendental aesthetics may first turn to examine how judgments of beauty are possible in express avoidance of directly addressing the question, What is an object of aesthetic worth? Nevertheless, the critique of taste will end up constructing its object, so far as it can be characterized in any universal way.

Therefore, the problem of grasping the individuality of art reappears. It already provided a basic impetus to the transcendental turn in aesthetics. If art is fundamentally individual, where the meaning of a work cannot be separated from its sensuous detail, then no merely universal concept can capture the nature of the work of art. Accordingly, transcendental aesthetics has good grounds for maintaining that the beauty of an object cannot be derived from any universal form it may have. Yet, does this guarantee that no objective categorization can be made of art or beauty in general and that aesthetics must turn to the structure of aesthetic experience to find the source of the unity of universal and particular underlying aesthetic phenomena? Although the metaphysical paradigm of the imitative edifying artifact may fail to capture this ubiquitous individuality, might beauty still be found in objective features that are conceivable, yet individual?

The denial of any objective categorization of things of beauty rests on two key assumptions: first, that concepts of objects capture universals given independently of the particulars to which they relate, leaving the particular external to the universal; and second, that any categorization of the beautiful not issuing from the structure of aesthetic experience relies on the dogmatic reference to the given that fatally typifies metaphysical discourse. Provided these assumptions can be upheld, transcendental thinkers have the right to regard their critique of metaphysical doctrine as a mandate to transform aesthetics into a theory of aesthetic reception. Yet, even then, transcendental aesthetics must still conceive the individuality of beauty, which remains a key challenge whether it be sought in the art object or in the subject of aesthetic experience.

Given these basic features with which the rationale for transcendental aesthetics stamps its origin, how does the theory of aesthetic reception work itself out? The turn to the reception of art can be made in two primary ways: the conditions for judging an object to be beautiful can be determined empirically or can be located in an a priori structure. In either case, the conditions of aesthetic reception can be construed in terms of the awareness of the single subject or in terms of intersubjective structures, characterized linguistically, hermeneutically, as institutions of domination, or in some other way. Hume's "Of the Standard of Taste" provides the classic statement of the empirical approach, whereas Kant's *Critique of Judgment* introduces the a priori strategy that seeks to redeem transcendental aesthetics from the dilemmas afflicting the former. Although both characterize reception in terms of the structure of consciousness, the internal logic of their positions applies equally to intersubjective construals of aesthetic reception, be these advanced as empirical phenomena such as historical linguistic practices, cultural conceptual schemes, and institutions of the "art world," or, on the other hand, as a priori structures of communicative competence and ideal speech situations. In every case, the same dilemma recurs, deciding the fate of transcendental aesthetics.

Aesthetics as an Empirical Theory of Taste

In light of the difficulties of discovering the nature of art in any immediately given objective qualities, it is natural to turn to the experience of appreciating an object as a thing of beauty and allow the workings of taste to decide what counts as aesthetic reality. Whether this experience be understood as the private awareness of the individual or as the public conventions of a linguistic community or cultural tradition, it appears closest at hand as a fact to be observed and studied like any other empirical phenomenon. On this basis, aesthetics becomes an empirical theory of taste concerned with observing what transpires in an audience appreciating beauty, how this process determines the object of beauty, and how it can be produced and evaluated.

Although the turn from discovering the nature of art to constructing beauty out of an empirical study of aesthetic experience leaves undecided how that experience be described, Hume's appeal to the consciousness of beauty brings out the dilemmas that afflict any empirical theory of taste.

Hume's starting point seems reasonable enough. If no objective description can be given to sanctify the beauty of a thing, then all principles of beauty would seem to be matters of subjective taste. Accordingly, when an individual judges something to be beautiful, this judgment is not cognitive, providing knowledge about the object, but rather aesthetic, signaling how the individual reacts to the sensuous appearance conveyed by the work. As such, beauty is not a quality in things themselves, but something residing merely in the mind that perceives those things.[4] What, however, is the noncognitive reaction in the individual that is specific to the appreciation of beauty? For Hume it is nothing but the immediate, empirical givenness of pleasure at the appearance of the object. To judge something to be beautiful is simply to be aware that its manifestation gives one pleasure. What the object may be and how it was produced are of no direct consequence to this determination. For this reason, what is judged is beauty per se, without further concern with whether it is natural or artistic.

Yet if the awareness of beauty is merely an awareness of pleasure, how is this to be distinguished from the satisfaction attending the consciousness of any object of desire? The empiricist theorist of taste has a ready answer: the pleasure constitutive of beauty is a satisfaction obtained by the mere appearance of the object. Unlike other satisfactions of desire, aesthetic pleasure is felt without consuming or otherwise using the appreciated object. It is simply left alone to show itself, as in a gallery, stage, or concert hall. So long as the viewer recognizes that the pleasure obtained from the object's appearance is disinterested in these respects, that individual knows that the pleasure is distinctly aesthetic. Hence, in declaring that an object is beautiful, an individual is maintaining that its appearance has produced a pleasure free of the need for consumption and use applying to other gratifications.

However, if, as Hume maintains, this judgment is an empirical one, consisting in the single, immediate experience of the individual, the perceived beauty seems to reflect a purely subjective response with no necessary connection either to the responses of other individuals confronted with the same appearance or to any features of the object itself that appears. The aesthetic value of something then becomes a merely private matter, with no more descriptive or prescriptive authority than any confession of personal preference. In that case, aesthetic judgment is fundamentally arbitrary and solipsist, displaying a sentiment referring to nothing beyond itself,[5] condemning art criticism to expressions of idiosyncratic reactions of no inherent interest to others. Indeed, why anyone should take pleasure at the mere appearance of something becomes an indecipherable mystery.

The empirical theory of taste has but one remedy to this impasse. If judgments of beauty are to have any communicable ground, permitting discursive evaluation of aesthetic objects, and if such a ground can no longer be discovered in any objective features of beautiful things, then it can only be sought in some observable common dimension of aesthetic experience. Given Hume's psychological construal of aesthetic experience, he must seek the wanted common ground in some shared pattern of psychological response to the appearance of objects of beauty. If some conformity can be observed in the feelings of pleasure that individuals take upon the appearance of the same object, then beauty becomes communicable, conveying the same effect to all who have a like psychological nature.[6]

Moreover, it then becomes possible to discover by further observation what common qualities appearances must have in order to elicit the shared pleasure of beauty. In this indirect manner, the beauty of objects can be associated with empirical features of their appearances. Then, it becomes possible to predict how an object must appear in order to give an audience aesthetic satisfaction. By extension, these same empirical rules that govern what appearances must be like to be judged beautiful provide lessons to artists who are concerned with producing beautiful objects. Given that rules can be discovered according to which certain types of appearances can be produced, empirical observation of which types give aesthetic pleasure furnishes a body of empirical rules for artists to follow in creating beauty.[7] Here, what will decide the aesthetic value of a work of art is the empirical fact of what psychological response it stimulates among its observers. Art criticism must take these facts as the basis for aesthetic evaluation, distill what general associations can be found between the production of aesthetic pleasure and different sorts of appearances, and thereby arrive at empirical standards of taste. These standards may take the form of objective patterns to which appearances must conform, but they remain subjectively determined, insofar as they derive from prior observation of common psychological reactions.

In this way, the empirical theory of taste seems to have reached its goal, providing a coherent account of aesthetic value, the character of beautiful things given by nature or art, the process of artistic creation, and art criticism. Yet, Hume himself is aware that certain problems remain. If success in differentiating the appreciation of beauty from personal fancy requires an empirically discoverable identity in human psychology, or in some other basis for a common taste, there should be no controversy in aesthetic judgments. How, then, can one account for the undeniable occurrences of aesthetic disagreements and lack of taste among individuals who are members of the same culture, as well as between those of different cultures?[8]

An easy answer might lie in divergences in the apprehension of the object's appearance due to all those internal and external variances that can afflict the conditions of individuals and their relation to the object. Once every individual is brought to a state of "normal" psychological and cognitive functioning and placed into a common relation to the object, then taste would retain its universal unanimity.[9] Indeed, art criticism could here play a guiding role, directing the attention of the audience to the salient features of the object of beauty and providing whatever knowledge will help make commonly comprehensible the iconography, allusions, and other discursive factors that might influence how the appearance of the object will affect the feeling of those regarding it.[10]

Yet what determines the standards of "normal" appreciation of beauty? If the unity of psychological nature is itself an empirical given derived from observations of how individuals react to putatively beautiful things, how can one determine when divergences in taste reflect differences in psychological nature rather than deviations in the condition of individuals and/or their relation to the object? Observing whether the reactions of suspect individuals alter is of no avail. Changes could just as well reflect deviating conditions of common as of uncommon natures, whereas shared constancy could just as well reflect deviations of uncommon natures as constancy among like psychologies. For this reason, the mere fact of durable admiration for works recognized to have abiding artistic greatness cannot settle the issue as Hume would pretend.[11] No matter how prevalent be uniformity of sentiment, this cannot unambiguously identify the sound, as opposed to the defective, state of the individuals involved. Since such uniformity may itself be a product of diverse external and internal conditions, the appeal to a privileged psychological state cannot supply any determinable standard of taste and sentiment. Moreover, unless one makes the nonempirical assumption of the spatiotemporal uniformity of both human psychology and nature in general, observations of current reactions will have no applicability to adjudicating the beauty of objects at any time in the future, nor any trustworthy application to the reactions of any unobserved individuals to any unobserved objects whatsoever.

Compounding these dilemmas is the abiding problem of retaining the specificity of taste. If the measure of beauty lies in shared pleasure in some appearance, how is aesthetic enjoyment to be distinguished from the gratification arising from sexual voyeurism or the mere entertainment of spectator sports and similar diversions? The only psychological resources for drawing a distinction would lie in either the intensity of the feeling or the extent to which it is shared by others. Yet again the question arises as to how the line should be drawn to distinguish feelings that are intense or common enough to qualify as aesthetic. Interpreting any observed data will once more be bedeviled with the problem of determining when deviations of common natures are at play.

None of these difficulties is peculiar to Hume's choice of human psychology as the empirical factor on which judgments of taste are founded. The same questions would arise if observed linguistic practices, cultural traditions, or any other empirical structure of aesthetic experience were selected as the arbiter of beauty. In each case, the necessity of the chosen structure would remain in doubt, leaving the boundaries of beauty beyond reach. An institutional theory of art, for instance, can provide no basis for identifying what institutions qualify as taste-dictating bastions of the art world without taking for granted what defines art and its aesthetic worth. Consequently, if aesthetics is not to abandon the form of a critique of taste, a nonempirical grounding for aesthetic experience must be uncovered to uphold the normative element of aesthetic judgment and the specificity of beauty. Kant's *Critique of Judgment* provides the paradigm of such an undertaking, on whose success hangs the promise of transcendental aesthetics.

The A Priori Critique of Taste

Abandoning the limited horizon of the empirical critique of taste, Kant sets out the fundamental strategy for enabling the turn to aesthetic experience to provide a universally binding account of beauty, capable of distinguishing the aesthetic from the nonaesthetic and making possible criticism of the comparative aesthetic value of natural things and artistic creations. Instead of generalizing about particular observations of aesthetic awareness, transcendental aesthetics must now determine the features that are constitutive of any possible judgment of beauty. In disregard for all particular factors that differentiate individuals and cultures, what must be established are the universal requirements for experiencing an object as beautiful, requirements to be sought not in independently given properties of the object but in the structure of its reception.

To this end, judgments of beauty remain just as "aesthetic" as they did for the empirical critique of taste. They still determine not the object of the judgment, but rather the relation between the representation individuals have of the object and its effect on their experience. However, although this leaves aesthetic judgment "subjective," in the broad sense of construing beauty as determined by the structure of aesthetic experience, be it construed in terms of consciousness or the intersubjectivity of language and cultural tradition, the a priori critique of taste aims at uncovering how aesthetic judgment can still be universal. Given the repudiation of metaphysical aesthetics, aesthetic judgment cannot be objective, determining the object of beauty by ascribing conceptual features to it, either in respect of obtaining knowledge of its nature or in deciding its moral value, as something that ought to be willed. In this respect, being aware of beauty will not entail thinking a concept of the object that appears. Aesthetic experience must instead involve becoming aware of a subjective modification, that is, a feeling, in response to the appearance that is then judged to be beautiful. To maintain the universality of aesthetic judgment, this response can be neither merely subjective, like pleasures that vary from individual to individual, nor merely objective, like the moral approval attending the awareness of something judged good in virtue of its own character. Somehow, the response to beauty must be grounded in a feature necessarily ingredient in aesthetic experience, given independently of any aspects of the object of beauty as well as independently of any empirical factors, such as facts of human psychology, linguistic practice, or historical tradition, pertaining to the reception of beauty.

Due to Kant's retention of Hume's appeal to consciousness as the locus of aesthetic experience, he formulates the task at hand as a matter of determining the subjectively universal grounding of aesthetic judgment. Since an a priori critique of taste can equally lay hold of an intersubjectively construed structure of aesthetic reception, for which intersubjectively, rather than subjectively, universal factors are at issue, what lies generically at stake is establishing the universal structure of aesthetic reception constitutive of judgments of beauty, however that structure be described. As it turns out, the basic thrust of what Kant argues regarding how consciousness is aware of beauty applies equally to any attempt to conceive how linguistic practice or culture provides an a priori grounding of aesthetic experience.

Given its turn away from an ontology of beauty to aesthetic judgment, the a priori critique of taste must distinguish the beautiful from what has no aesthetic value by differentiating aesthetic judgment from other forms of awareness or reference. Instead of arriving at the universal features of beauty by contrasting beauty with the true or the good, transcendental aesthetics must proceed indirectly, distinguishing the type of judgment apprehending beauty from those that refer to other kinds of objects as their generic subject matter. Through this process of elimination, transcendental aesthetics can attempt to lay hold of the determining apprehension in whose process beauty is constituted as a possible object of reference. Then, with the beautiful marked out descriptively through the eye of aesthetic judgment, transcendental aesthetics can proceed to determine the normative standards by which the relative beauty of objects, natural or artificial, can be assessed.

The Transcendental Search for the Defining Features of Aesthetic Judgment

To demarcate the domain of aesthetic judgment on the basis of principles, rather than corrigible generalizations of contingent psychological, linguistic, or sociological observation, it makes sense to follow Kant's strategy of first identifying the types of judgment that cannot ascribe beauty to their objects.[12] By this process of elimination, the remaining form of judgment applicable to aesthetic questions might be identified, albeit negatively.

Granted that the dilemmas afflicting the metaphysical approach are emblematic of any attempt to conceive beauty directly *in res,* aesthetic judgment cannot be objective in the sense of ascribing features to an object that pertain to its own independent nature. This applies, as Kant rightly suggests, equally to objective judgments that are theoretical and practical. Theoretical objective judgments are cognitive, determining the truth by assigning concepts to objects that specify what they are. Practical objective judgments are ethical, determining the good by bringing ends under concepts that specify whether agents are obligated to bring such states of affairs into being. Given that beauty cannot be identified by means of any given qualities of things or by their ethical ramifications, aesthetic judgment must be of some other kind than objective.

Yet, nonobjective judgments, that is, judgments determining the state of the subject in relation to the appearance of an object, do not automatically address beauty. If the ground of such a subjective judgment is something empirical in the subject, such as contingent feelings or sensations, all that is ascribed to the appearance of the object is an effect on the subject of a wholly particular and private character. This may suffice in judging whether something pleases or displeases an individual, which is a practical judgment specifying how an object is connected to the desire of that person. However, it offers no guide for distinguishing whether an appearance has aesthetic value, inherently communicable to others and subject to critique.

Accordingly, if aesthetic judgment is to be subjective, it must be pure in the Kantian sense of referring the appearance of an object to a modification of the subject that, on the one hand, should be common to anyone apprehending that appearance, yet on the other hand, not consist in cognizance of either what the object is or whether it ought to be willed into being. Then, the judgment will enjoy a subjective universality extending to all potential members of the audience of beauty, provided, of course, that exercising this sort of judgment is sufficient to make one aware of beauty.

Yet even if the foregoing comparison of forms of judgment eliminates objective and empirical subjective judgments as vehicles of aesthetic experience, the possibility of a nonempirical subjective judgment providing for the awareness of beauty depends on the resolution of two further questions. First, what kind of noncognitive, nonedifying response could it be that the appearance of an object would elicit in all prospective subjects? Unless some such response can be uncovered, the possibility of pure subjective judgments remains in doubt. Second, even if such a response could be assured, would it provide not just a necessary, but also a sufficient condition for judging the beauty of an appearance? Unless this question can be answered affirmatively, the possibility of pure subjective judgments would represent too formal a condition for accounting for aesthetic experience.

Kant's efforts to resolve these issues are emblematic for any undertaking of transcendental aesthetics. If aesthetic discourse is not to revert to direct description of the nature of beauty as a criterion for aesthetic judgments, the basis for judgments of taste must be located in some feature of reception that enjoys universality without involving objective knowledge claims or moral judgments. Moreover, given that no particular thing can be assumed to give pleasure to every rational agent at all times, no fact of desire can provide the universal ground that must be found. In other words, becoming aware of what an appearance is or what moral value it possesses no more establishes its beauty than does being aware that it gives one pleasure. To the degree that cognitive and moral judgments lack aesthetic character, all judgments of taste will have to be singular, ascribing beauty not in virtue of a general concept to which the appearance corresponds ("all roses are beautiful"), but in virtue of a special subjective response accompanying the individual empirical representation comprising that appearance ("this rose is beautiful"). Accordingly, there will be no rule pertaining to the features of an appearance compelling acknowledgment of its beauty.[13] Yet, on the other hand, a judgment of beauty cannot consist in connecting personal satisfaction to an appearance, since that provides no basis for attributing satisfaction to everyone.[14]

What then can comprise the standard on which judgments of taste can be made? What element in one's experience of an appearance can possibly provide the basis for a subjective yet universally binding judgment? Given Kant's recourse to consciousness as the locus for construing aesthetic experience, this question takes the following form: How can one judge the beauty of an appearance independently of any concept applying to it, on the sole basis of some internal modification of one's awareness that allows one to presume that all other subjects will undergo the same response when confronted with that representation?[15] The same question can equally be formulated in terms of linguistic practice or a universal hermeneutics, with intersubjective factors substituting for modifications of consciousness.

Having established by a process of elimination that judgments of taste must be individual and enjoy subjective universality, Kant must now locate a source of universality in the subject. The faculties of desire and feeling cannot qualify, insofar as what individuals desire or feel is contingent and particular. This leaves the faculty of knowledge, whose universality is a precondition of its own validity. Yet, aesthetic judgments are not simply cognitive. Hence, if the cognitive powers are to supply the subjective universality required, they must enter into a relation with the representation of the putative object of beauty that somehow provides universality without knowledge.

This can be achieved if the cognitive powers relate to the given representation such that the ensuing state of mind is universally communicable independently of assigning any concept to the appearing object. But how can the cognitive powers deal with an appearance so that, without affording knowledge of it, they engage it in the same way as they would any other subject? Kant's answer is that so long as the cognitive powers refer the appearance to cognition in general, they engage in a subjective activity that is universal. Since cognition in general must be universal, the activity of relating an appearance to it would amount to the same thing in any subject performing that mental act, unlike any referral of a representation to feelings or desires, which vary from time to time and from individual to individual.

But what is it, then, that transpires in the occupation of the cognitive powers with a putatively beautiful appearance? Because this occupation does not consist in a cognitive judgment, where definite concepts are ascribed to the representation according to some rule, the cognitive powers must operate without rule or conceptual limitation. In positive terms, the cognitive powers can be said to be in free play with the representation. Accordingly, when the mind is aware of this free play of the cognitive powers with the appearance of some object, its awareness consists not in any objective knowledge but in a feeling of its own inner state. Moreover, because what it feels concerns the one universal resource within itself, consciousness here entertains a feeling that it can presume any other subject will also experience when occupying its cognitive faculties with the same representation. Thereby experiencing an inner modification that is subjective, yet universal, the individual, Kant would have us maintain, judges that the representation is beautiful.

In what, however, does this "free play of the cognitive faculties" consist? It must be sufficiently determinate that any individual can recognize it and realize that feeling it is something different from simply feeling pleasure. Otherwise, it will fail to play the role of an identifiable standard for subjectively universal judgments. Moreover, some connection should be determinable between the engagement of free play and the features of the appearance. Although the connection cannot be cognitive and consist in some judgment about the objective character of the object perceived, this does not mean that no connection can be allowed. It still should be possible to identify what it is about the representation that makes it appropriate for the free play of cognitive faculties, so long as all that matters is the form of its appearance rather than a concept of its nature. For if no relation can be specified, how can the appearance in question be counted on to elicit the same response in other rational beings?

In the face of these demands, Kant is at pains to elucidate the free play of cognitive faculties and the features a representation must possess to occasion it. Owing to the nature of the argument, there is very little that can be said. Granting that the faculties of cognition consist in the understanding and the imagination, where the former supplies concepts and the latter reproduces and combines intuitions so as to be conceptually determinable, the free play will consist in an occupation of the understanding and imagination with an appearance. For this occupation to be universal, yet noncognitive, it must permit the understanding and imagination to harmonize to the degree required for cognition in general, yet avoid imposing any concepts or rules on the appearance that might yield knowledge. What, however, does such harmony signify, and how is it to be recognized? Given the transcendental turn from contemplating the given nature of art to analyzing aesthetic judgment, this question must be answered before addressing what features the appearance need have. Only afterward, in function of this harmony, will it be possible to consider the character that the appearance must possess to be an object of aesthetic judgment.

The problem besetting Kant is that the only way he can sustain the noncognitive character of the harmonious activity of imagination and understanding is to render it indeterminate.[16] To express this, Kant employs a succession of paradoxical formulations. The free play of understanding and imagination is said to involve a purposiveness without a purpose, a lawfulness without a law, a free and indeterminately purposive entertainment, and a free lawfulness of the imagination.[17] Kant is searching for some positive organizing principle determining the free play at issue, yet the only resources he has at hand, purposiveness and lawfulness, are woefully inappropriate. Any attempt to make beauty depend on the applicability of categories of purpose and law to an appearance reinstates the difficulties of the mimetic conception of metaphysical aesthetics, where given universal forms proved incapable of grasping the individuality constitutive of fine art.

Kant is aware of this difficulty. Yet, being unable to supply any other concepts that can unite understanding and imagination, he must deny what he affirms in one and the same breath, retreating to the tortured locutions of "purposiveness without purpose" and "lawfulness without law." Whatever is judged beautiful may well be recognized to have the "formal purposiveness" of setting in play the subject's cognitive powers independently of any cognition of what the appearance is or any moral interest in its existence.[18] Even so, what that play is and why that particular appearance should elicit it in everyone remains as mysterious as before. Similarly, the imagination, in freely conforming to law in judgments of taste, may be productive and spontaneous, toying with the appearance in conformity with the law of the understanding without referring it to the concept of any object.[19] Yet this still leaves unclarified what the imagination must be doing with the appearance to make it freely conform to the understanding without cognitively reproducing representations under laws of association. Nor does it explain why this activity should be a common response to the same appearance.

If this abiding indeterminacy leaves in doubt the possibility of recognizing when one feels the free play of cognitive faculties supportive of a subjectively universal judgment, it equally makes questionable whether any features of an appearance can be identified that make it occasion a judgment of beauty. This is a key problem for an a priori transcendental aesthetics, even though any immediate objective determination of beauty must be eschewed. Unless the structure of aesthetic reception can constitutively determine the object of aesthetic judgment, the subjective universality of taste has nothing to which it can refer. Hence, just as a transcendental epistemology must determine those features of objectivity that are ingredient in knowledge, so transcendental aesthetics must succeed in indirectly determining what character an appearance must have to be judged beautiful.

The Quest for a Transcendental Constitution of the Object of Beauty

If nothing else, Kant's negative criteria of what the harmony of understanding and imagination cannot involve mandate several features that must be excluded from beautiful appearances. On the one hand, the appearance cannot be entirely bereft of conceptual significance. If all it displays is pure sensation, as in formless color or sound, the appearance gives the understanding nothing with which it can occupy itself. The imagination may reproduce or modify the representation, but if this elicits any feeling, it will be no more than pleasure at a contingent charm, conditioned by the particular sensibility of the observer. On the other hand, the appearance cannot be entirely conceptual or lawful. If everything about the representation can be reduced to some abstraction or formula, once this conceptual form is understood the understanding has nothing left with which to occupy itself.

In other words, instead of fitting any particular design, the representation should be amenable to all kinds of possible designs, where the imagination can relate it to an endless array of forms produced by the understanding, none of which exhaust its meaning. Conversely, the appearance should not be so unsymmetrical as to make it incommensurate with any possible design.[20]

Kant reasons that these complementary edicts mandate that the form, rather than the sensible content of the appearance, must be the bearer of beauty. Since the quality of sensations cannot be assumed to be uniform in all observers, the matter of the representation, such as its colors or tones, can only please in a purely personal, contingent manner. Their delineation, on the other hand, can please in a subjectively universal way because it appeals to both understanding and imagination.[21] Yet what kind of delineation marks an appearance as beautiful? Stiff regularity[22] or studied, calculated composition[23] will not do, since once again the play of the understanding will cease the moment the governing form is conceived. But again, how can the positive character of beautiful delineation be captured?

Significantly, Kant appeals to nature as a remedy. Although beautiful art must exhibit purposiveness, as something designed to elicit the free play of the cognitive faculties, it must equally be free of all arbitrary rules and constraints that aim at pleasing by producing mere sensible feelings or a definite object conforming to a certain concept. Beautiful art must accordingly look like a product of nature while equally showing itself to be art. In this way it can at one and the same time be designed, yet not seem to be designed. Conversely, nature will appear beautiful by looking like art, seeming to manifest purposiveness without being produced in function of any particular aim.[24] Kant may hope that this appeal to nature concretely fulfills the formal edict of purposiveness without purpose, yet it does so at the risk of reintroducing the metaphysical concept of mimesis, where art retains aesthetic value by imitating independently given things. This is evident in Kant's troubling conclusion that judging art requires comprehending the concept of what the artwork is supposed to be, leaving artificial beauty dependent on the work's agreement with this purpose.[25]

To avoid this all too cognitive implication, one might attempt to reinterpret the appeal to nature so as to exclude the imitation of particular things. Instead, one might venture some abstract idea of natural form as that which artificial beauty resembles. In that case, however, the appeal to nature yields a wholly indeterminate result of no help in distinguishing objects of beauty.[26] It should come as no surprise that when Kant attempts to conceive the internal purposiveness of natural systems in his *Critique of Teleological Judgment,* he similarly can find no other specific idea than that of the external purposiveness of products of craft, a concept as incongruent with life as it is with beauty.[27]

As if cognizant of the tentative quality of his appeal to nature, Kant makes a further ploy to bring definiteness to the object of beauty, a ploy that again echoes an inability to escape the categories of metaphysical aesthetics. Here he maintains that beauty comprises a symbol of the moral good and that taste is ultimately a faculty for judging the sensible illustration of moral ideas. Only by symbolizing morality can an appearance give pleasure warranting the agreement of everyone.[28] If this is so, beauty can no longer be equally natural and artificial, unless beautiful nature is restricted to the given appearances of rational agents. More importantly, this appeal to an analogy between beauty and the good reintroduces an imitative element and the cognitive dimension mimesis retains. After all, if judging an appearance to be beautiful requires recognizing its symbolization of morality, then aesthetic judgment entails subsuming the appearance under the concept of the good. In that event, however, the transcendental turn away from objective determinations of beauty is all but abandoned in a reversion to the metaphysical approach.

Does transcendental aesthetics have any nonmetaphysical resource for characterizing what an appearance must be like to set in motion the mental (or, alternately, linguistic or interpretative) free play constitutive of aesthetic judgment? To escape the utter singularity of an orderless content while retaining an order that cannot be reduced to a separable form—this might well seem to be a recipe for the individuality toward which metaphysical aesthetics groped in exploding its own mimetic conception of art. Why not follow this avenue?

Kant seems to point in this direction when he elsewhere qualifies beauty as something exemplary. Yet, when he seeks to explain beauty's exemplary character, he can do so only by negatively employing the categories of rule and form, categories appropriate for conceiving artifacts but hardly sufficient for construing fine art. A beautiful appearance is reputed to be exemplary to the degree that it is recognized to comprise an example of a universal rule we cannot state.[29] Our inability to state a rule that an appearance exemplifies, however, hardly gives that appearance any special standing. On the contrary, so long as the appearance remains an instance of a rule, it shares the particularity of an artifact, which, in its capacity as an example of an antecedent form, stands undistinguished from every other instance, devoid of an affirmative individuality. Here again, Kant lacks the conceptual means for giving any positive supplement to his negative proscriptions.[30]

The Perplexity of Aesthetic Ideas and Genius

This shortcoming comes to a final head in Kant's characterization of aesthetic ideas, which allegedly comprise the particular representation that the artist imaginatively creates and then realizes in producing a work of art. Insofar as the aesthetic idea defines what an appearance must exhibit to count as created beauty, it ought to provide the positive principle enabling the possibility of subjective universal judgments to be a sufficient condition for judgments of beauty. Not only should the aesthetic idea provide a rule for the derivative features rendering an appearance subject to aesthetic evaluation, but it should allow for defining artistic activity, whose constitutive genius might now be identified as a talent for producing aesthetic ideas.

What then is an aesthetic idea? It is a representation of the imagination that occasions an unlimited train of thought without conforming to any definite concept. Consequently, it cannot be completely encompassed by the conceptual means of language, but carries with it an element irreducible to discursive analysis.[31] An aesthetic idea can thus be called an unexpoundable representation of the imagination, insofar as it cannot be exhaustively expounded in concepts.[32] Such a representation warrants the title of idea insofar as its presentation of an imagined content to which no concept is adequate makes it a counterpart of an idea of reason, which, in the Kantian scheme, is a concept to which no corresponding intuition or representation of the imagination can be found.[33] Both sorts of ideas are incapable of providing knowledge, but for inverse reasons. Whereas a rational idea has no cognitive value because it involves a concept to which no intuition can be given, an aesthetic idea has no knowledge to offer because it is an imagined intuition to which no concept can correspond. Granted that objects must correspond to concepts in order to be known and experienced, it follows that the imagination must be creative, rather than imitative, in producing an aesthetic idea.[34] For the imagination must go beyond the given in generating aesthetic ideas if they cannot be tied to any specific concept and if everything appearing in nature must be conceptually determined.

So far, the aesthetic idea remains true to the requirements of subjective universality without retreating to metaphysical categories of edifying mimesis. Yet, has it contributed anything to make the object of beauty or artistic activity any more determinate than before? To begin with, how can an aesthetic idea elicit a bounty of thought while remaining elusive to each and every concept? An aesthetic idea achieves this feat, Kant maintains, by being an imagined representation associated with a given concept to which it connects an indeterminate multiplicity of partial representations. In adding such ineffable thought to that concept, the aesthetic idea is supposed to set the cognitive faculties in free play, producing the feeling attendant on the contemplation of beauty.[35] Yet again, what is it about the imagined representation that allows it to occasion more thought than can ever be expressed by words?

This becomes a problem in characterizing artistic genius, which now gets construed as a faculty for creating aesthetic ideas. In engendering an aesthetic idea, genius must somehow unite imagination and understanding, not to provide cognition, but to produce a representation eliciting the free play of these cognitive powers comprising the subjective state of mind communicable to others. Yet since an aesthetic idea cannot be reduced to any rule or design, there can be no formula for producing it according to a premeditated purpose that could give art its measure. Accordingly, the capacity to create aesthetic ideas cannot be taught or be acquired by following any given pattern of behavior. What, then, can the genius be that the artist must set in play? For Kant, there is nothing left but the nature of the artist, a nature that cannot be characterized by any rules or concepts, both because it represents a formal capacity irreducible to the causal behavior of empirical agency and because it represents an ability to do what cannot be comprehended under any laws of the understanding.[36]

This threatens to leave genius in the same paradoxical position as the *sensus communis*. Like that capacity for appreciating beauty, genius, the capacity to produce beauty, seems beyond the pale of knowledge, as one more noumenal entity about which nothing determinate can be established. Moreover, again an appeal must be made to nature, this time to nature in the subject, as the foundation for the purposiveness without purpose that has been so hard to pin down. Just as metaphysical thought invoked a transcendent demiurge to implant artistic form in the artisan making imitative artifacts, so Kant appeals to a supersensible nature giving a law to art that neither the artist nor the audience can expound. Although artistic genius should exhibit an exemplary originality, producing an aesthetic idea that no prior concept can adequately foreshadow, genius's basis in nature sustains the anomaly of a critique of taste that reverts to metaphysical notions from which all content is withdrawn.

With aesthetic judgment, the object of beauty, and genius all victim of an inscrutable formality, it would be vain to expect any more determinate lessons for art criticism. Since the evaluation of art must, on transcendental terms, proceed from a reflection of the subject on what is communicable in its own apprehension of beauty,[37] the ineffability of the "free play of the cognitive faculties" and the derivative vagueness of aesthetic delineation and of genius leave the critic little to do but register the experience accompanying particular appearances.

The Fundamental Dilemmas of Transcendental Aesthetics

Are the difficulties afflicting Kant's critique of taste avoidable blunders that a consistent transcendental aesthetics can overcome, or fatal ailments inherent in any privileging of aesthetic experience? The answer to this question revolves around two complementary problems. The first consists in a deficient formalism reflecting an inability to determine the specificity of aesthetic judgment, the work of art, or artistic creation. At each juncture, Kantian aesthetics exhibits this shortcoming, failing to supply categories necessary and sufficient to characterize aesthetic phenomena and falling back on metaphysical conceptions that ill fit the task at hand. But is such formalism the fate of any transcendental aesthetics? The second problem involves the reduction of aesthetic reality to what is given in the apprehension of the beauty of an individual object. Art may not be conceivable as imitative craft, but does it follow that the predicament of the art critic in judging the aesthetic merit of a given object can define the limits of the philosophy of art?

The first problem of formalism is fundamentally rooted in the whole approach of transcendental aesthetics. It does not depend on whether aesthetic experience is construed in Kantian terms of consciousness or in terms of intersubjective structures of language or tradition. So long as beauty is determined in function of the structure of aesthetic apprehension, all aspects of beauty owe their character to a factor that provides their aesthetic worth not in virtue of being a privileged content to which they conform, but by being the privileged determiner that constitutes what can count as an object of beauty. Because beauty is thereby determined by the prior principle of the structure of aesthetic experience, aesthetic categories are rendered functional and derivative in character. Instead of comprising concepts characterizing what is independent and self-determined, they consist in terms describing what is grounded in a structure of apprehension with its own antecedently defined nature. For this reason, it is no accident that Kant ends up reinstating the metaphysical categories of purpose and law despite his awareness that metaphysical aesthetics cannot establish the beauty of any object in virtue of its correspondence with such concepts. Although no particular form here stamps an appearance with beauty, the dependence of aesthetic worth on the lawfulness and purposiveness of an externally given determiner entails the same appeal to privileged givenness that is so incommensurate with anything individual and autonomous. In view of this logical problem, the transcendental turn in aesthetics is simply incapable of overcoming the conceptual incongruity that already subverts the metaphysical approach to art. Because functional categories cannot grasp the individuality of art, transcendental aesthetics is unable to identify the terms that are necessary and sufficient for characterizing the beauty it seeks.

Whereas the critique of taste is thereby left fatally formal, its whole turn to aesthetic judgment suffers from a limited vision as one-sided as the metaphysical reduction of artistry to technique. Just as metaphysical aesthetics took art's component artifact dimension and made it sovereign over all aspects of beauty, so transcendental aesthetics takes the relation of audience to an individual object of beauty as if all aesthetic reality were exhaustively determined by it. The formalism and ineffability at which the critique of taste exhausts itself may well define the predicament facing the art critic whose discourse is limited by all the interpretive and pragmatic problems afflicting any judgment of an independently given appearance. Yet judging the aesthetic value of an individual object is constitutively embroiled with the problem of subsuming an individual under universal determinations of beauty. It is not concerned, and indeed, cannot be concerned, with the fundamentally different enterprise of conceiving the universal character of art, which alone can supply art criticism with a conceptual standard to apply to particular works. If the standpoint of the art critic is elevated to the position of privileged determiner for aesthetics, in exclusion of all other vantage points on art, aesthetics is automatically robbed of the ability to provide determinate principles to guide the evaluation of individual works of art. Caught in the representational opposition of given object and structure of experience, aesthetics can only offer formal pronouncements of arguable authority. In this respect, the outcome of transcendental aesthetics accurately reflects where we would stand if reason were powerless to determine art in general.

Of course, the turn to aesthetic judgment proceeds from the assumption that no independent determination of art is possible. However, if aesthetic theory can free itself from the particular categories of metaphysical aesthetics, it is far from self-evident that all aesthetic issues must be treated in function of how an audience apprehends an individual work of art.

For these reasons, transcendental aesthetics must forfeit its hegemonic claims. Like metaphysical aesthetics, it has seized on an irrefutable aspect of art and given it an unsustainable sovereignty in determining aesthetic reality. Yet because the critique of aesthetic judgment has had to make sense of the factor it has absolutized, it has contributed to the understanding of the relation of audience to the individual work of art in a way that can be fully appreciated when its own one-sided standpoint has been overcome.

Part 2

Systematic Aesthetics

Chapter 3

The Mandate of Systematic Aesthetics

The failures of metaphysical and transcendental aesthetics offer a twofold lesson. On the one hand, the categories of mimesis, of art as edifying imitative artifact, cannot be employed to capture the special unity of particular and universal, of sensuous configuration and meaning, underlying the nature, creation, and appreciation of art. On the other hand, aesthetics cannot be reduced to a theory of taste, where the subjective or intersubjective process of aesthetic reception is privileged to the exclusion of any independent, objective determination of art. Although the turn to a critique of aesthetic reception issues from due recognition of the failure of metaphysical aesthetics, it operates with too narrow a view of how an objective conception of art can be constructed. Identifying the metaphysical appeal to the given of mimetic theory with all possible objective approaches, transcendental aesthetics assumes that any attempt to determine objective concepts of beauty must employ discovered abstract forms, with no indwelling individuality. Moreover, by deriving aesthetic phenomena from the structure of reception, transcendental aesthetics treats that determining structure just as much as a privileged ground as the given forms to which metaphysical aesthetics makes appeal. Hence, despite its antimetaphysical motivations, transcendental aesthetics only reintroduces the appeal to given foundations that condemns its categories to an empty formality.

The Rationale for Systematic Aesthetics

Yet if the transcendental turn to aesthetic reception does not preclude a rational conception of art that avoids recourse to given forms emblematic of the categories of imitative craft, how should aesthetics proceed? To begin with, aesthetics need not dismiss out of hand the contributions of mimetic theory and the critique of taste. The categories of craft do have an application in construing the technical element in art, just as the analysis of aesthetic reception does have a role in determining how objects of aesthetic worth are perceived as such. However, if both these conceptions can be integrated within aesthetics, they can no longer comprise privileged starting points that ground beauty in something other than itself, while mandating how every other feature of art is to be derived. Instead, aesthetics must turn away from conceiving beauty in the metaphysical terms of the embodiment of privileged givens or in the transcendental terms of issuing from privileged determiners. Negatively speaking, this signifies that beauty must be conceived without foundations. Positively speaking, this signifies that beauty must be determined autonomously, deriving all its constitutive features from factors that are themselves aesthetic in character.[1]

This mandate for a foundation-free, autonomous aesthetics has a paradoxical ring. To begin with, it seems to contradict the broadly acknowledged fact that aesthetic inquiry is not where philosophy must begin. On the contrary, to the degree that aesthetics involves categories, sensible appearances, creative agents, an intelligent audience, and matters of ethical significance, the philosophy of art must be prefaced by at least philosophical logic, the philosophy of nature, the philosophy of mind, and ethics if it is not to incorporate themes of which no account by reason has been given. Yet, even if all these fields of philosophical inquiry are prerequisites for an undogmatic conception of aesthetics, this does not mean that any of them independently mandate the character of aesthetic value. The topics they address may be enabling conditions for the being and conception of aesthetic phenomena, but that hardly signifies that what they are provides any standard for selecting between the competing aesthetic conceptions that they may well make possible.

However, if the dependence of aesthetics on prior branches of philosophy does not make beauty juridically founded on nonaesthetic factors that are incorporated in the theory and practice of art, how can arbitrariness be avoided in determining the starting point of aesthetics and the course of its argument? The absence of prior standards, be they given in reality or in function of structures of judgment, seems to leave aesthetic theory in a state of anarchy. Aesthetics may have won autonomy by default through the collapse of the complementary strategies for determining beauty in terms of a distinct foundation, yet this appears to leave aesthetics with no ground to stand on, ushering in the fluidity of boundaries plaguing contemporary artists and critics alike. Arbitrariness, however, is not equivalent to freedom. If the frontiers of aesthetics are simply at the beck and call of individual license, then aesthetics is not autonomous, but subordinate to an extraneous will whose deciding activity falls outside the domain of aesthetic phenomena, as an antecedent principle dictating the shape of beauty.

The Rational Reconstruction of Aesthetics

What then can possibly allow aesthetics to steer clear of arbitrariness, yet still free itself of foundations and supply an autonomous determination of beauty? Two resources are available: immanent categorial development and rational reconstruction. Immanent categorial development consists in a conceptual self-determination wherein a subject matter presents itself in its theoretical self-constitution, independently of the application of any external principles or introductions of extraneous content. To develop immanently, categories must follow one another in terms of their respective content, beginning with a term incorporating no others in the series and proceeding to whichever comes next in an order of constitution where the prior terms provide sufficient conceptual prerequisites for those that subsequently incorporate them. What brings the development to a close is the arrival at a content incorporating all prior terms, a content comprising the totality that has been under way determining itself by means of its own constitutive elements. In such a development, the order of categories is bound to their content in function of the methodological demand that nothing be introduced whose prerequisites have not been established.

This ordering is conceptual and not temporal in character. Hence, the necessity of the categorial advance does not translate into a historical genesis, where each succeeding category comes into existence prior to those that conceptually follow upon it. Not every category need be capable of an independent realization. Indeed, none of the universal and particular determinations of beauty can come into existence independently of the individual determinations marking the creations of the individual arts. However, since the conceptual order of categories does reflect how categories are incorporated by one another, the realization of a particular category in time will necessarily require the prior or simultaneous actualization of any other term contained in its own determination.

Significantly, since the final term in the development comprises a totality incorporating all prior categories, it represents a subject matter whose determination has been accomplished by its own resources, without reliance on any terms that are not contained within it. In virtue of this unity, immanent categorial development is not only free of foundations, but is self-grounding and self-determined.

How can aesthetics follow such a categorial development? Although categorial immanence might seem to represent the very form of truth, representing how a subject matter can be presented independently of any assumed principles, it equally appears to have a thoroughly hermetic character that divorces it from any relation to appearances. Since an immanent development of categories avoids appealing to any external givens as a resource for introducing new contents, the status of the self-determined subject matter it presents appears very much open to question. Not only does it seem indifferent to the problem of "saving the appearances," but it seems to have no determinable relation to any other competing theory.

This problem can be ameliorated when categorial immanence is complemented by rational reconstruction. Rational reconstruction takes up given representations from "appearances," past theories, tradition, or any other source and rethinks them by incorporating them within an immanent development of categories. In so doing, rational reconstruction determines both what other representations form their prerequisites and what representations incorporate them as constitutive elements. So organized, such given representations become elements within the self-constitution of a certain totality. This accomplishes two things. On the one hand, the introduction of given representations is now systematic, deriving not from any arbitrary appeal but from the internal necessity comprising the self-constitution of a specific subject matter. On the other hand, the subject matter in question can now be seen to display in systematic interconnection terms that otherwise have been arbitrarily and fragmentarily assumed in common experience and previous theory. This allows the totality in question to surmount its hermetic unity and have a "real" reference, bringing "appearances" into a coherent and nonarbitrary ordering, accomplishing what previous efforts at understanding have failed to do.

Rational reconstruction thereby supersedes the pragmatic assurances of reflective equilibrium, which consists in elaborating procedures of construction enabling a given set of intuitions to cohere. In contrast to reflective equilibrium, rational reconstruction not only establishes a coherent system of the given representations it incorporates but provides an ordering capable of accounting for every term it contains without relying on any prior assumptions.

For this same reason, rational reconstruction must not be confused with transcendental argument,[2] understood either as foundational epistemology or simply as the account of the presuppositions of something given to experience. Because rational reconstruction appropriates given terms only insofar as they can be reintegrated in a categorial self-determination, it cannot issue from a foundational epistemology, where the investigation of knowing or reference is taken to be the privileged inquiry in function of which all truth claims are to be adjudicated. In that case, the determination of any objective domain would depend on the putative transcendental conditions of knowing, rather than comprise a categorial self-constitution. Moreover, since those transcendental conditions cannot be themselves transcendentally constituted without subverting the constitutive distinction between conditions and objects of knowing, they remain metaphysical stipulations of the sort that transcendental inquiry sets out to overcome. Hence, whatever objectivity is determined through them turns out to rest on a dogmatic foundation—the transcendental conditions themselves, whose content and privileged status figure as irreducible givens.[3]

Similarly, rational reconstruction does not work back from some alleged fact of experience to uncover its presumed preconditions.[4] If rational reconstruction remained slavishly bound to any such assumed givens, such as representations of perceived artworks, of their origin in acts of creation, of discourse about them, or of their treatment by the "art world," any question of why such facts qualify as aesthetic would be ruled out. To escape such theoretical blindness, so rampant among Wittgensteinian and institutional theorists of art, rational reconstruction appropriates given appearances only at the expense of robbing them of their immediate presence and altering its content however needed to further the immanent categorial development to which it might contribute.

In the case of aesthetics, this can be achieved by identifying the minimal term incorporated by all further aesthetic factors and establishing its primitive role by following out how these order themselves in a continuous ascent of increasing concretization, exhaustively constituting the conceivable totality of art. Along the way, aesthetic terms can be freely appropriated from past theory and experience, provided their authority resides not in their prior givenness but in their integration into the immanent development of the resulting concept of art. If the categories ingredient in the minimal category of aesthetics can themselves be accounted for in a similar rational reconstruction, the entire development can unite into a systematic theory free of foundations.[5]

Awaiting such an achievement, the immanent development of aesthetic categories can still satisfy the fondest dreams of any effort at reflective equilibrium, for two complementary reasons. On the one hand, the domain of aesthetic appearance will have been accounted for on its own terms in the most thoroughgoing way. On the other hand, an autonomous determination of beauty will have been shown to be the only remaining path for aesthetics in the light of the collapse of the attempts to conceive beauty by appeal to independent givens or determining structures of reception.

Appropriating Hegel for the Rational Reconstruction of Aesthetics

The prime theoretical resource for appropriation into the rational reconstruction of aesthetics is Hegel's *Lectures on Aesthetics,* which still comprise the chief contribution to aesthetic theory that relies on an immanent categorial development in explicit departure from metaphysical appeals to the given or transcendental constitutions. Unfortunately, Hegel's *Lectures on Aesthetics* suffers from a failure to demarcate strictly two types of aesthetic discourse: that of systematic aesthetics proper and that of art criticism. Systematic aesthetics addresses aesthetic reality per se by means of an immanent categorial development, whereas art criticism evaluates particular works of art, optimally applying categories deriving from systematic aesthetics to empirical observations of given creations. Because art criticism engages in an act of judgment applying universal categories to empirically given individuals, it always involves an element of subjective discretion regarding the accuracy and representative authority of its empirical observations, as well as the correctness of its application of categories to them. Accordingly, art criticism always arrives at corrigible, questionable conclusions of an entirely different epistemic character from the universally valid determinations at which systematic aesthetics aims. If Hegel's only fault were his interspersal of innumerable critical interpretations of individual works of art within his systematic argument, this could be easily remedied by simply separating the two types of discourse so as to allow the categorial development to stand alone. However, at times Hegel conflates these two levels of analysis and permits empirical observations of a purely historical character to govern the putatively systematic development of aesthetic categories.

Hence, if the rational reconstruction of aesthetics is to draw on Hegel's abiding achievements, this must be done with care. The following discussion will therefore freely borrow from Hegel's arguments when they conform to the rigor of categorial immanence, but critique and amend them when they go astray.

By way of anticipation, it can be said that systematic aesthetics must operate at three successive levels of determination. It must begin with the most rudimentary level, which consists in the determination of the universal features of aesthetic phenomena, features that are generic to the existence, creation, and reception of any object of aesthetic worth. Once this is accomplished, systematic aesthetics is in the position to conceive the particular forms of art,[6] forms that all incorporate the universal features of art, but do so with further qualifications that differentiate the possible modes of artistic expression. This will involve a rational reconstruction of the sort of distinctions that Hegel draws in conceiving symbolic, classical, and romantic art. Upon completion of this task, systematic aesthetics can address the most concrete dimension of aesthetic phenomena: the individual arts, each of which incorporates not only the universal features of art but also the particular forms that artistic expression can take in all its different media.

Our first task then is to determine the minimal feature of art that is ingredient in all its other universal determinations and thereby incorporated in its particular and individual realizations as well.

With What Must Aesthetics Begin?

At the outset, the starting point of systematic aesthetics is unavoidably stipulative precisely because it comprises the primitive determination of aesthetic reality. As a starting point, it can only implicitly constitute the minimal term incorporated in all further aspects of art. Not until systematic aesthetics has advanced beyond it can this starting point explicitly prove itself to have been the primitive term ingredient in every aspect of aesthetic reality. Since such a vindication consists in nothing less than the completion of systematic aesthetics, the starting point progressively relinquishes its stipulated character in tandem with the development that proceeds from it in increasing confirmation of the beginning's necessity.

This does not signify, as Derrida charges, that systematic aesthetics begins under the illicit guidance of an assumed telos involving, on the one hand, the commonsense representation that there is art, and, on the other hand, conceptual presuppositions that art has an ahistorical unity, that art is to be conceived in terms of the form/matter, meaning/configuration, and nature/technique oppositions of ancient metaphysics, and that all artworks are to be accordingly thought of as "discursive," expressing an independently given inner meaning.[7]

First, even if one wanted to employ a representation of art or of artistic creation as a heuristic guide, it could not confirm the elementary character of the starting point or the validity of the ensuing development, for two reasons. To begin with, any given representations of artworks or of their creation are singular and thereby lacking in the universality of a principle. Moreover, the stipulation of a representation of art cannot of itself identify which determinations within it are constitutive, and not incidental, to its aesthetic worth. Even if the rational reconstruction of systematic aesthetics were to end up "saving the appearances," this would still not replicate the representation alleged to provide a heuristic guide. What systematic aesthetics arrives at remains a conceptual determination, which may capture what is endemic to individual genres of art in their realization of the properties of art in general and the particular modes of artistic construal, but not the singular features that identify a representation.

Second, as we have seen, the very enterprise of an autonomous determination of art already casts aside the conceptual framework of technique, which Derrida, following his mentor, Heidegger, tends to attach to all nonhistoricist speculative thought. What Derrida does not countenance is the prospect at hand, that categories can develop in terms of their own content without appeal to subject/object or form/matter dichotomies, or, for that matter, to any other governing principle, such as the hermeneutics of interpretation.

Third, although determinacy may lie in negation, where the categorization of something involves its opposition to an other, this does not leave the development of a subject matter always predicated on a given contrastive framework that sets its identifying boundaries. In advancing this claim, so basic to the hermeneutics of deconstruction, Derrida ignores how the opposition of something and other does not serve to individuate either.[8] Something, qualified in no further respect, may well have its constitutive boundary as *a* determinate being in virtue of comprising no more than what its other is not, but its other is equally *a* determinate being providing that boundary only by comprising the nonbeing of its other, which is the something to which it stands opposed. The other of something is thus a something in its own right in just the same way that something is, whereas something is an other in just the same way that its other stands in relation to it. Hence, something and other actually have the very same structure, each being a something as well as the other of something else. The opposition of negation is therefore an insufficient vehicle for establishing and sustaining the individuality of any term.[9] By itself, negation offers only a plurality of determinate beings, with no resource for distinguishing them from one another. Contra Saussure, the identification of meanings cannot be understood in terms of such an abstract opposition, even if negation may be incorporated in the further categories that first permit individuation to be achieved.

This is apparent in attempts to define beauty by contrasting it with the pleasant or the good. Certainly beauty does involve not being just pleasant or good, but these negations must be complemented by some positive determination to get at what distinguishes beauty from other factors neither pleasing nor ethical. By the same token, the pleasant and the good and any other term distinct from beauty must have some positive determination beyond negation to sustain their own identity as more than an abstract, undifferentiated something.

Consequently, meaning need not be haunted by the specter of an endless dissemination, where the identity of any term is vainly sought in the ceaseless alternation of negation and counternegation through which something and its other have their ever elusive difference. Since that movement cannot alone sustain any determinate distinction between its elements, its limitations are not those generic to individual entities, whose identity must rest on further categories. Moreover, its limitations are not those of discourse in general, which would become meaningless chatter if all it could do would be to reiterate how every term is the nonbeing of the rest. Unlike Hegel, from whom the deconstructionists borrow their understanding of determinacy, Derrida and his epigones make the mistake of absolutizing the relation of something and other, instead of realizing that it is just one of many categorial distinctions that are ingredient in individuality.

On all these grounds, when systematic aesthetics addresses the question of what art is by seeking the minimally determinate aesthetic factor, it takes the only route in which no positive criteria are granted any prior authority. Teleology and hierarchy are precisely what are excluded from the outset.

Nevertheless, a negative criterion is available from the start to eliminate pretenders to the role of what must come first in aesthetics. To qualify as the starting point, a candidate must contain no constituents that can stand on their own as specifically aesthetic factors. If a candidate does, it no longer represents what comes first in aesthetics, but rather something secondary to more primitive aesthetic factors.

In this light, no candidate seems more appropriate than the basic idea of beauty, understood as simply the most general idea of aesthetic worth. It commands first place insofar as neither the particular existence of a beautiful object, nor the activity bringing it into being, nor the object's appreciation and critique, nor particular modes of artistic expression, nor any individual art can be determined without already incorporating some reference to beauty.[10]

Yet what is this most abstract determination of beauty, presupposing no other aesthetic factor, yet ingredient in everything aesthetic? The very identity of aesthetics hangs on the answer. As the divergent positions of metaphysical and transcendental aesthetics already indicate, whether aesthetic theory addresses beauty in nature as well as art is a matter of controversy. Because metaphysical aesthetics rooted beauty in edifying mimesis, it had to construe aesthetics as the philosophy of art. By contrast, because transcendental aesthetics left the objective character of appearances secondary to the structure of aesthetic reception, its doctrine of taste had to apply equally to art and natural beauty. In wake of the complementary failures of the metaphysical and transcendental approaches, what decides the issue is whether the minimal determination of aesthetic worth is something of which natural and artistic beauty are species, or something specifically tied to artistic beauty, leaving natural beauty a derivative, secondary phenomenon. In the former case, aesthetics will address beauty in general, without any privileged concern for art, whereas in the latter case, aesthetics will be the philosophy of art, relegating beauty in nature to a merely adjunct position.[11]

Truth, Individuality, and the Minimal Determination of Beauty

Of key importance in resolving the identity of aesthetics are the complementary issues of the role of individuality in the minimal determination of beauty and the ability of thought to conceive the individual. The difficulties plaguing metaphysical and transcendental aesthetics have proved largely to revolve around the incommensurability of their conceptual resources with the union of universal and particular ubiquitously displayed by aesthetic phenomena. Because both theories limit conceptual truth to abstract universals, externally informing independently given particulars, the categories they employ can never grasp the union of meaning and configuration confronting them. Correspondence with their given models and laws of thought always requires excluding the particular detail of individuals, just as aesthetic form always escapes reduction to such formulae.

If, however, thought is not alien to individuality and universals can be conceived that are not indifferent to the individuation of the particulars to which they apply, then aesthetics is in a very different position. On the one hand, aesthetics will be enabled to think the unity of meaning and configuration seemingly basic to aesthetic worth. On the other hand, aesthetics will be in a position to consider truth as something pertinent to the form as well as the content of beauty, or, more precisely, to the relation of form and content. No longer need truth figure as an external standard, determined as a separable idea to which art must conform to be worthy. Nor need truth be banished from aesthetic consideration as something hopelessly alien owing to the irreducibility of beauty to any abstract form. For if the sensuous appearance of beauty unites the universal and the individual in a way that thought can grasp, then it will exhibit the conformity of concept and objective existence in which truth resides.[12] This conformity will dwell within the object of beauty—not in any merely physical sense, but rather in the ingredient relation of meaning and configuration where what the object's appearance is about is a significance to which it uniquely conforms. That relation may depend on a recognizable context of interpretation belonging to the constitutive relation of beauty to its audience. Yet, given that enabling condition, the adequation of meaning and shape still resides within the appearance of beauty, as a form of truth without which aesthetic worth vanishes.

For this reason, it is hardly aesthetically irrelevant to pose the question of whether a work of art is true or false. However, this is not because art relates to reality in the same way in which descriptive language does, as Danto suggests.[13] Although art, qua beautiful, involves an imaginative configuration "about" something, this meaning is not an independently given term that the configuration must "correctly" denote. Beauty is no more a matter of denotative excellence, where successful representation does not depend on resemblance between signifier and signified, than a matter of mimetic perfection, where the denoting term resembles what it represents. The truth in beauty breaks the mold of either variant of the representational model of knowledge insofar as the beautiful object consists *in itself* in an adequation of shape and what that shape is about. Consequently, the truth of a work of art is not independent of its beauty, but rather lies in the very same concretely universal relation of meaning and configuration that gives the work its aesthetic value.

Confirming these implications cannot consist in simply associating beauty with individuality and truth. By themselves, individuality and truth are not specifically aesthetic categories. Both have logical determinations, as well as applications within real domains in which beauty need not be a factor. As a purely logical category, individuality is explicable in terms of universality and particularity without any reference to aesthetic factors, just as truth is logically determinable in regard to concept and objectivity independently of beauty. Similarly, if every knowable reality is individual, then individuality and truth cannot fail to be at hand in natural and human phenomena in which nothing of aesthetic worth is at stake. Consequently, even if individuality and truth are ingredient in aesthetic worth, establishing their aesthetic role depends on identifying the further qualification they must receive in order to become elements in something specifically basic to beauty.[14]

However, if individuality and truth can be qualified in a way that helps define aesthetic worth, their own relation must be such as to permit a common place in beauty. If truth and individuality are both to figure in the constitution of beauty, whatever relation of concept and objectivity is ingredient in truth must involve individuality on both sides of the equation. Only in that case can the aesthetic unity of meaning and configuration exhibit the form of truth, since if the significance of a beautiful object is tied to its unique appearance, that significance must be individual as well. By the same token, only when concept and objectivity both involve individuality can truths themselves be offered by beauty that might not be available anywhere else. If instead the conceptual element of truth lacks all connection to the individuality ingredient in objectivity, then beauty's conjuncture of universal and individual exhibits something other than truth, whereas any truth in beauty would be something universal that could have multiple embodiments whose differences contribute nothing to the truth they express.

Hegel, for one, does implicate individuality and truth in the minimal determination of beauty by construing what is basic to aesthetic worth as what he calls the "Idea" as it is given in sensuous manifestation.[15] His notion of the Idea brings in both individuality and truth at once. For Hegel, the Idea consists in the unity of concept and objectivity, where the concept in question is a universal that actively determines every individuating feature of its particularization. This permits the Idea to represent the logical structure of truth because its unification of concept and objectivity both takes hold of the individuality marking objective existence and does so without appeal to an external connecting term, such as a reflective subject or a linguistic practice. If such extraneous factors had to be introduced, truth would be made dependent on an unaccounted-for foundation, whose real structure (qua knowing self or language) transcends the domain of logic while all the time incorporating logical relations.

Avoiding this dilemma, the Idea comprises a truth that is far removed from the familiar model of truth as correctness.[16] According to the latter model, truth consists in the correspondence of a concept with an independently given object. The concept in question is an abstract universal, abstract in the sense of specifying only certain general features of the object to which it is correlated, while failing to grasp the remaining individuality of that object's actual existence. Owing to this externality of concept and object, their connection lies outside both in a third term, comprising the proposition or judgment setting them in relation. As such, truth as correctness cannot help but fall into contradiction, for the concept it equates with its object can never make a proper fit. As much as the object may be identified with its characterizing concept, it is irrepressibly different from it, owing to its other individuating features. Effectively locating truth in the proposition or judgment connecting concept and object, the correctness model perennially falls prey to the old dilemma of the differentia, where every attempt to determine an entity fails owing to the abiding incommensurability of the entity and its determining factors. Just as substance can never be adequately characterized by qualities or predicates, since substance is that which has qualities or predicates but can never be a quality or predicate of something else, so the given object of the correctness model can never be uniquely identified by any concept, since externally applied concepts are merely universal, whereas objects are always individual.

Moreover, by taking the object as an independent given, against which the validity of the concept must be measured, the doctrine of truth as correctness falls into the foundationalist trap of the representational model of knowing. The representational model construes knowing as an instrument that approaches an independently given object and attempts to know it by interposing representations between it and the knower. However, because knowing has access only to its own representations, it can never do what is required to certify their truth, namely, compare them with what is not a representation, but the object in itself, as it lies outside its relation to the knower. Consequently, the doctrine of truth as correctness, endemic to the propositional or representational model of truth, must always take for granted the unconcealed manifestation of the fact, of the object in itself, to which true concepts and propositions putatively conform, a manifestation for which the correctness model of truth can never provide any account.[17]

By instead conceiving truth as the Idea, as the unity of the active universal and its objectivity, Hegel aims to overcome both sides of these interrelated dilemmas: the independent givenness of concept and objectivity and the discrepancy between the universality of concepts and the individuality of their objects.[18] For if the universal is active, in the sense of being able to specify the individuating aspect of the objectivity to which it applies, their correlation ceases to be an external correspondence of independently determined entities that are condemned to be incommensurate. However such a solution can work itself out,[19] what counts for aesthetics is that when Hegel construes beauty as the Idea manifest in sensuous form, he enables both truth and individuality to be ingredient in beauty, tying them to beauty's sensuous appearance in virtue of their interconnection.

Hegel's proposal, taken at face value by interpreting the Idea as truth, is deficient, however, in two inverse ways. On the one hand, it is too broad to provide a sufficient as well as necessary determination of what is minimally aesthetic. For if there are any sensuous entities existing in accord with their concept, that is, any sensuous objects that can be truly known, every one, on Hegel's terms, would seem to meet the requirements of beauty. In that case, the distinction between sensible truth and aesthetic value would vanish and beauty would forfeit its specificity.

On the other hand, Hegel's proposal is seemingly too narrow to incorporate all aesthetic phenomena. Most objects of beauty may well combine some sort of truth and individuality with a sensuous appearance. However, the creations of the literary arts possess their aesthetic worth not in the sensuous appearance of their expression in language, but rather in the ideal images produced in the imagination of the audience hearing or seeing the signs of their words. The same can be said of works of the performing arts, whose reality as unperformed music, dance notation, plays, and the like presents in an ideal form what obtains first an imagined appearance in the mind of the composer, choreographer, dramatist, and so forth, and then an external sensuous configuration through the imaginative artistry of performance.

If these objections do not completely disqualify Hegel's candidate for the minimal determination of beauty, they at least indicate that the terms employed must be further qualified to capture our prey. At first glance, the needed emendations appear easy enough.

To remedy the deficient narrowness of Hegel's proposal, the minimal determination of beauty must take into account the existence of arts whose sensuous creations are not simply directly intuited, but rather represented through the imagination of their audience. This can be accomplished by offering the revised view that beauty is truth manifest in sensuous form, be it intuited or imagined.[20]

To remedy the deficient broadness of the proposal, some means must be found for excluding nonaesthetic sensuous objects that might also be thought to be bearers of truth. This seems readily achievable by making explicit that beauty is not truth in its immediate sensuous existence but, more specifically, truth in its imagined or intuited sensuous *appearance*. Whereas given objects of sense may exhibit truth in conforming to their concepts, this conformity concerns their entire existence, rather than the dimension of pure appearance to which beauty pertains. By contrast, the exhibition of truth in a sensuous appearance, directly intuited or imaginatively construed, is something of which only a very special sort of object may be capable.[21] It requires that the bearer of beauty not only have a sensuous appearance that can conform to conceptual determination, but that it make such a comparison itself, by expressly meaning something of universal significance to whose expression its configuration is joined. To the degree that this relation of meaning requires the concomitant recognition of conventions of representation to allow the sensuous appearance to make its truth manifest, beauty's relation to a recognizing awareness is part and parcel of its appearance, rendering its relation to other basic to its own manifestation.[22] Although this relation to other need not leave the configuration of beauty otherwise undetermined, it does allow prosaic objects to be indiscernible from works of art, insofar as beauty depends at least in part on the specific contextualization that permits the sensuous appearance of the work to mean something and not just be itself. As Danto, for one, takes pains to point out,[23] an object can have the same sensuous appearance as a work of beauty, yet be deprived of aesthetic value by not being perceived in reference to a framework enabling it to mean something beyond its own physical being or beyond whatever magical or divine being it might be directly ascribed.[24]

Yet given all these emendations, it still remains unclear why the appearance of beauty deserves notice more than any other phenomena that express meanings, as well as why beauty need involve truth and what sort of truth it could constitutively concern.

To set the stage for resolving these issues, it is necessary to examine how beauty can be seen to incorporate that other dimension of the Idea, that of the individuality at one with its actively determining universal. As we have seen, whether or not we ascribe truth to beauty, we are ubiquitously confronted with that unity of configuration and meaning, of form and content, that defies formulation in terms of abstract universals whose unity cannot capture the individual.

For this reason, it is tempting to conceive the minimal determination of beauty in terms of this individuality. Beauty would then be identified as the sensuous appearance given to imagination or intuition in which meaning and configuration are indissolubly connected, just as are individuality and its actively determining universal. This characterization could have the advantage over one already introducing reference to truth of more easily accommodating natural beauty or, for that matter, "nonrepresentational" arts such as architecture, music, or abstract visual arts.

In what sense, however, is beauty to be defined in terms of individuality? Moreover, what light can this characterization shed on the place of truth in beauty and the type of truth that beauty might convey? Needless to say, the answer to these questions will bear on the relative status of natural and artistic beauty, as well as the very identity of aesthetics.

Chapter 4

The Individuality of Beauty

To claim individuality as a defining mark of a beautiful object might seem trivial and superfluous. Insofar as any existent thing is an individual, uniquely differentiated from all other members of whatever class or classes to which it belongs, the mere individuality of something of beauty in no way sets it apart from objects devoid of aesthetic value. Even an artifact is still an individual product, distinct from all its peers despite their common function and design.

Hence, if individuality is to differentiate objects of beauty from functional artifacts, what must count is the *type* of individuality involved. Already, the constitutive originality of a work of fine art has appeared to involve a unity of meaning and configuration, of form and content, where every appreciable detail of the work's sensuous appearance has an essential significance. The differences allowing artifacts of the same kind to be distinguished have no necessary bearing on their perfection, which consists in their capacity to fulfill their common function. By contrast, the alteration of any perceivable feature of a work of fine art can strike at its meaning and undermine its beauty. As a result, what distinguishes the individuality of a work of fine art from the individuality of a mundane thing seems to lie in the object of beauty having an individuality whose entire particularity is imbued with universal significance.

The Constitutive Connection of Universality, Particularity, and Individuality

Yet even this qualification appears insufficient, given the inherent connection of universality, particularity, and individuality that no individual can fail to exhibit. This connection, whose neglect has undermined traditional efforts to conceive the universal and the particular, is evident in such basic forms of universality as the class or a shared quality.

A class has its constitutive generality insofar as it has a plurality of members, be they actual or potential, just as a shared quality has its defining commonality by having a plurality of instances. As members of a class, entities are particular, just as are the instances of a common quality. Yet in belonging to a class, members are not distinguishable, for each belongs in just the same way as every other. The same is true of every instance of a common quality—in its capacity as an example of that quality it is undifferentiated from every other. In this respect, members and instances are undifferentiated particulars, contrastable to the universal to which they belong, but not to one another.

However, unless members and instances can be distinguished, their plurality collapses, and with it the general extension constitutive of class and shared quality. By themselves, the particularity of members and instances and the universality of class and quality are insufficient to maintain the differentiation on which they depend. There can be no members or classes and no instances or common qualities unless their particularity and universality are complemented by the individuality differentiating members and instances. In virtue of this each one is a unique member of a class and a unique instance of a shared quality, respectively. Owing to this crucial service, universality and particularity are thinkable and realizable only in conjunction with individuality.[1]

By the same token, the individual cannot be uniquely identified apart from universality and particularity. For if an individual is devoid of anything particular and universal, it may at best be distinguishable as something or other, or as something that determines or is determined by something else, as in the relational categories of essence and appearance, ground and grounded, cause and effect, and so forth. Yet by themselves, none of these distinctions single out the individual from other examples of "something," "other," "cause," "effect," and so forth. Only when particularity and universality are available to permit something to figure as one particular differentiated from others is the exclusive identity of the individual attainable.[2]

Consequently, the Platonic assertion of the independence of the universal from the particular is just as senseless as the complementary nominalist dogma that universals are inventions of subjective thought whereas individuals exist without any universality of their own.[3]

Individuality and the Forms of Universality

Yet, if universality and particularity must always be given in conjunction with individuality, this does not mean that the features by which particulars are individuated need stand in all cases in the same relation to the universal.

Individuality and the Abstract Universal

At one extreme is the universal determined as a class or as a quality or form where it comprises a single common feature of its particulars, existing indifferently alongside other properties in each member, instance, or embodiment. Here, the other factors individuating particulars are indeed prerequisites for the plurality on which universality depends, but they are otherwise undetermined by that one feature of class membership, universal characteristic, or form that unites them as particulars of the same universal. Owing to this independent givenness of the individuation of the particulars, the universal uniting them is abstract, failing to determine its own particularization. Consequently, abstract universals and their particulars are at farthest remove from the unity of universal and particular underlying beauty's melding of meaning and sensuous configuration.

Objects, to the extent that they are governed by efficient causality, paradigmatically exhibit abstract universality because their existence is determined from outside independently of what type of thing they are.[4] Consequently, beauty could be said to be at farthest remove from that dimension of physical reality comprising a sphere of causal necessity where objects are determined in regard to their mass and motion independently of their kind.

Individuality and the Generic Universal

By contrast, the universal determined as a genus plays an active role in determining its particularization. Unlike the abstract universal, the genus mandates the differentia of its species, rather than allowing the individuation of its particulars to be externally given.[5] For example, to paraphrase Aristotle, the genus number mandates its own species, since (whole) number must be either odd or even in kind. The differentia distinguishing odd and even numbers are not extraneous additions to the genus number but differentiations inherent in its generic character.

This determinate connection between the universal of the genus and the particularity of its species makes possible necessary judgments reflecting a system of knowledge contained in the descending relation of genus to its infima species. These judgments pertain to the particular, rather than the individual character of objects, for what can be inferred apodeictically from knowledge of the species of an object are those specific features mandated by the genus.

However, although the genus may be concrete in relation to its species, actively determining their differentia, the connection of each species to its individual instances replicates the extraneous, indifferent relation between abstract universals and their particulars. For although all members of a species share its differentia, the individuation distinguishing them from one another must rest on other features they uniquely bear. Hence, where generic determination ends and the differentiation of the infima species into its individuals begins, the species is tantamount to a class of given members. For example, a line must be straight or curved, but this generic necessity does not determine the length or curvature of any individual line. Each line will, in effect, belong to the class of straight or curved lines, where its class membership leaves completely undetermined every feature that makes it a unique member.[6] Consequently, individual judgments will still be purely *a posteriori,* reflecting how the generic universal fails to determine the individual character of the members of its species.

For this reason, the genus cannot supply beauty with the relation of universal and individual fusing aesthetic meaning to aesthetic form. Whereas beauty cannot be simply generic, the aesthetic value of an object must lie in something more than its species being.

Individuality and Type and Token

A solution cannot be obtained by appealing to the universality and particularity exhibited in type and token, to which Richard Wollheim has drawn attention in attempting to conceive the relation of a work of performance art to its particular performances.[7] As Wollheim maintains, types, such as the word "red" or the Stars and Stripes, exhibit a more intimate relation to their tokens (for example, a particular instance of the word "red" or a particular U.S. flag) than do classes to their members or shared qualities to their instances.[8] This is evident in how the type necessarily shares a far larger range of predicates with its token than do either class and class member or universal and instance. If a class shares a property with its members (such as when, to cite Wollheim, the class of big things is big) this occurs completely contingently, since class membership dictates nothing about the existence of its members other than that they possess the common factor grouping them together.[9] Analogously, no property possessed by a particular in virtue of being a universal's instance can necessarily apply to the universal. Redness, for example, is not itself red.[10] By contrast, all and only those properties that a token has in virtue of being of a certain type necessarily inhere in the type itself.[11] In this manner the number and position of stars, alternating bars, and colors that are necessarily possessed by every particular U.S. flag are equally possessed by the Stars and Stripes as such.

Significantly, the distinction of type and token seems most applicable to situations where some piece of human invention figures as the original exemplar to which further particular products get generated as copies, imitations, realizations, and the like.[12] Although this allows types to be just as much concrete, physical entities as their tokens, tokens will have properties that are neither necessarily nor contingently possessed by their type (such as, to take the case of a flag, size, number of stitches, and so forth).[13] Indeed, in addition to these "excess" features of tokens, there are certain properties that they uniquely possess, such as their location in space and time, whereas certain others are unique to types, such as being invented by a particular individual.[14]

Although these discrepancies between type and token are embraced by Wollheim to account for the role of interpretation in mediating between particular performance and the work performed,[15] they actually signal the inability of the type-token relation to grasp the unity of form and content in beauty. This failure is patent on two accounts. On the one hand, type and token leave the individuality of the type as well as of each particular token something given independently of their relation. Moreover, the independent existence of type and token makes their distinction inapplicable to the relation of form and content *within* each object of aesthetic value. Whether or not the performance of a work is logically its token, neither performance nor work exhibit the type-token relation in the union of meaning and sensuous configuration implicit in the imaginative ideality of the work to be performed or explicit in the intuitable actuality of its subsequent performance.

The type may actively determine much more in its tokens than do classes and abstract universals in their respective members and instances. But, like the generic universal, it fails to achieve the unity of universality and individuality required of beauty. An object can therefore have its beauty no more by being the token of an independently given type than by being the type of independently given tokens.

Individuality and the Concrete Universal

The logical unity of beauty must be sought beyond class and member, universal and instance, genus and species, and type and token in a universality that somehow actively determines every individuating aspect of its own particularization. This universal, whose counterpart is an individual that remains a paragon in every unique detail, is what thinkers since Hegel have sought under the rubric, "concrete universal."[16] It achieves the same melding of universal and individual that first Aristotle aimed at in the doctrine of entelechy, where the active form of the sensible object determines not just its kind, but its entire existence;[17] that later Kant would imagine issuing from an intuitive understanding or intellectual intuition surmounting the struggle of rationalism and empiricism by unifying thought and sense;[18] and that Lukács would locate in the proletarian subject-object of history, overcoming the surd of the given haunting modern rationalism.[19]

Beauty and the Concrete Universal

To understand how the logic of the "concrete universal" may be ingredient in beauty, we must first consider what more can be said about its special unity of universal, particular, and individual, leaving aside the question of its nonaesthetic embodiments. The basic desiderata are already manifest in a dual exigence. On the one hand, the universal, which remains self-identical in its differentiation, must obtain its identity not only in its common relation to its particulars but in the individuality distinguishing them. On the other hand, the individuality of its particularization must be so thoroughly penetrated by the self-identity of the universal that nothing extraneous is at hand.

Organic Unity and the Concrete Universal

Meeting these requirements might seem to involve an organic unity. The identity of an organism resides in the reciprocal functionality of its organs, where their particular differences are essential to the reproduction of the whole. Organs are not merely parts of a whole, whose unification resides in bearing a common feature, indifferent to their individuation. Rather, they unite into an organism in function of their differences, just as the unity of the organism consists in their differentiation as complementary organs whose distinct characters are necessary to their integration.

To the extent that the unity of an organism represents a form of universality, it comes close to the concrete universal. The organic unity is at one with itself in all its particular organs in a way that lays hold of their separate natures, whereas these unique characters of the different organs resolve themselves into an affirmation of the whole, sustaining and reproducing its order through their complementary working. It thereby seems that in organic unity the universal determines the individual existence of its particulars, whereas the individual existence of its particulars is thoroughly imbued with the universal that unites them.

If the concrete universal is organic unity and beauty exhibits this structure, then beautiful objects will display the logic of an organism. By extension, real organisms will share this element of aesthetic value, which, if not a sufficient condition, will at least be a necessary ingredient of beauty.

There is, however, a limitation inherent in organic unity reflected in the barrier separating nonintelligent life from the existence of rational agency or spirit. Although the complementary interrelation of organs posits anew the unity of the whole to which they belong from the outset, this unity has no distinct manifestation of its own. That is, the organism is immediately the working of its organs, and none of the organs distinguishes itself from the rest as the actual expression of the unity connecting them all. Consequently, although organic unity constitutively engages in its own reproduction, positing its differentiation and encompassing identity as the product of its working, it always does so from a given starting point where all its features are already at hand.[20] This signifies that the content of the organism has a perennial givenness over and against the active unification of it that the ensuing life of the organism represents.

What get continually posited as presupposition and result of the organic process are the different functions of the organs. However, each organ possesses further individual features that, like those accompanying any functional entity, in no way contribute to its perfection. In this respect, the interpenetration of universal and individual arrives at a limit, reflected in how an organism is subject to further orderings in terms of genus and species where it gets tied to others under universals that are indifferent to aspects of its differentiation.

Consequently, organic unity does not provide the concrete universal that can unite sensuous configuration and meaning as beauty demands. Beautiful objects are not merely organisms, and real organisms are not beautiful simply by being alive.

Self-Determination and the Concrete Universal

Although the logics of abstract universality, generic universality, and organic unity may have an important role to play in the mechanical, physical, and biological orderings of nature, they have all proven insufficient to capture the concrete universality with which beauty may be defined. Not surprisingly, a more appropriate logical resource is provided by self-determination, whose realization is so central to rational agents and those entities produced by and addressed to them.

Self-determination unites universality, particularity, and individuality in precisely the thoroughgoing way that allows for talk of a concrete universal. Self-determination is universal in the sense that the identity of the self that determines itself pervades all its particularizations. What is self-determined remains at one with itself throughout the development comprising its free existence. Yet to be at one with itself, that is, to be and sustain itself as self-determined, it must give itself determinacy and particularize itself. Because what is self-determined must owe its determinacy to itself and no other source, whatever particulars comprise the elements of its identity not only belong to the self undergoing determination, but do so uniquely. Moreover, since self-determination determines itself to be self-determined, the particular differentiation comprising the self under way determining itself is completely at one with the unity that arises as the result of the entire process.

Unlike organic unity, self-determination does not presuppose the given determinacy of the elements in which it consists. On the contrary, what is self-determined can have no given character, since what it is is what it has determined itself to be. In this respect, every unique feature is mediated by the unitary self that constitutes its own identity in and through the ensuing development in which it consists. Here the particular stages in which the self gives itself its self-determined character have all their differentiated features exhaustively incorporated into the identity of the unity that gives closure to the process. That is, the essence and existence of self-determination cannot be separated, for the activity by which self-determination gives itself its form is indistinguishable from that form's realization. Self-determined determinacy therefore can be said to exhibit, or better, to comprise, the concrete universal.[21]

If self-determination warrants this identification with concrete universality, then beauty's unity of sensuous configuration and meaning will display autonomy, permitting aesthetic value to reside in the object of beauty's own independent existence. This existence will have free independence to the extent that its ordering is self-contained and invests all elements of its content with a unique indwelling form. Given beauty's relation to rational agency, the existence in question is not simply equivalent to the physical being of the beautiful object. For, as we shall see, beauty's appearance for an audience is a constitutive element of its reality. Yet existence of the beautiful object can still be ascribed an independent authority to the extent that the reference to rational agency that enters aesthetic value is one lying within the domain of beauty's own constitution. That is, so long as the relation to others of the object of beauty involves a specifically aesthetic attitude, whose reason for being lies in the independent aesthetic worth of the beautiful appearance, the autonomy of aesthetic value remains preserved.

Conversely, phenomena exhibiting freedom may well have a privileged place either as bearers of beauty or as elements within beautiful representations. This will apply as much to the nature of the performers of works of art as to the sort of subject matter expressed or represented in objects of beauty.

The Historical Individual and the Concrete Universal

Although the characterization of the concrete universal and the individuality of beauty has so far been made in purely logical terms, it has become increasingly apparent that its logic transcends the various orderings of nature. Instead it has its most suitable application to the domain of rational agency, where self-informing activity, freedom, and individuality take center stage.[22]

In function of such freedom, rational agency erects its own second nature of convention, injecting history into its activities and productions. Yet does this mean, as Michael Foster suggests, that the concrete universal has its adequate realization in individual historical species such as "Ancient Greece," "Christianity," "the Industrial Revolution," and the like?[23]

Whereas the individual person has a given nature full of contingent features unrelated to the identity that the person gives itself, these historical species allegedly inform the whole existence of their component particulars. They do so in a way heralded by Darwin's conception of the real generation of natural species, which converts the activity of the generic universal in determining its own specific differentia into a historical process, where the development of the species consists in nothing but the succession of its actual generations.[24] Such historically developing species combine the generic concept's specification of particular features with the real causality that determines their individual existence in space and time.[25]

Indeed, since these particulars do not stand in relation to an abstract universal that leaves unaccounted for their differentiating identities, they ill fit their appellation as "particular." Properly speaking, they are themselves individuals, for whom the distinction between essential and accidental qualities loses significance.[26] This reflects how the historical species, such as "the Renaissance," determines not only the general features and spatial and temporal boundaries of its elements, but their exact place and time as well. Pace Foster, the historical species thus comprises the object par excellence of intellectual intuition, providing a unity that cannot be directly perceived by the senses, yet that all the same leaves no residue of extraneous contingencies.[27] Neither merely universal nor merely particular, the historical species comprises something overcoming their opposition. As such, it can be apprehended neither solely by thought nor solely by sense, but by the activity uniting both that alone has access to the concrete universal.[28]

If this were the case, and the historical species were the only adequate embodiment of concrete universality, it is hard to imagine how beauty could retain the unity of universal and individual. Historical epochs and institutions would now be the only qualifiers for that title, and neither can be adequately tied to any one sensuous configuration.

Moreover, it is far from clear why the unity of the historical species is not a nominalist tag, introduced by the external reflection of the historical thinker. In the case of Darwinian species, heredity and natural selection might perhaps qualify as the required objective link. But unless the identity of historical epochs and institutions can be rooted in an objective process of differentiation and unification, the universal they represent must forfeit its active relation to the given reality to which it is applied.

Even then, however, the exclusive application of concrete universality to historical species can be questioned. Qua product of rational agency addressed to rational agency, beauty may well have its reality as a historical individual, arising within a convention to which it contributes. Yet its unification of sensuous configuration and meaning may exhibit concrete universality in its own right, independently of the further relation between it and other objects of beauty belonging to a particular historical style and period.

Is Particularity the Central Category of Aesthetics?

Granted that concrete universality underlies the individuality of beauty and that the particularity of a beautiful object ties its universal significance to its individual configuration, does particularity become the key category in aesthetics? Georg Lukács upholds this conclusion in *Über die Besonderheit als Kategorie der Ästhetik* and *Die Eigenart des Ästhetischen,* privileging particularity over universality and individuality. Lukács ascribes primacy to particularity ostensibly because in its role of affording determination, it functions as the organizing mediation between universality and individuality, adding something concrete to the universal dimension of beauty and something typical to the individual.[29] In aesthetic experience, Lukács maintains, particularity thereby figures as the point of departure and of return, circumscribing a route from particular to universal and back again in which the individual gets transformed into a particular.[30] What allegedly allows the work of art to be an intensive totality, with a coherent unity of its own, is neither its being universal nor its being individual, but its being concretely determined, that is, particular.[31]

Yet, the determination germane to beauty is such that universality and individuality can hardly be relegated to a secondary position.[32] Unless the universal actively determines the particular, its determination cannot sustain the aesthetic unity of form and content, just as unless the individuality of the beautiful object is exemplary, its particular character cannot have universal significance.

Lukács's embrace of particularity reflects the residual commitment to mimesis that is central to his rehabilitation of Marxist aesthetics. Lukács looks on the primary question of aesthetics as a matter of determining what kind of reflection of human reality distinguishes fine art from the mimesis of science and of other prosaic functions of social life. The excellence of products of imitative craft resides not in what distinguishes them as unique individual creations but in their success in mirroring particular features that are antecedently given and multiply exemplifiable. Consequently, what has primacy in any mimetic scheme is producing something typical, something whose particularity or membership in a certain class counts more than its individuation from other class members. Thus, it can come as no surprise that Lukács ends up privileging particularity as a category of aesthetics, despite his Hegelian penchant to uphold the unity of form and content, of meaning and sensuous configuration in the work of fine art.

Although particularity cannot be excluded from aesthetics without forsaking the concrete character of beauty, privileging it over universality and individuality is equally pernicious. If the particular is given precedence over the individual, then the appearance in question risks expressing a typicality that is indifferent to its individual detail, leaving it something mechanical, predictable, and trite. Such has been the common stumbling block of so many "edifying" artworks, running the gamut from proletarian fiction to fascist monumentality to the unctuous Americana of Norman Rockwell. Conversely, if the particular is given precedence over the universal, then the appearance risks falling prey to mannerisms of form and idiosyncracies of content of no abiding significance. The annals of modernism are full of such adventures. Lukács is not ignorant of these dangers,[33] and his efforts to navigate around them suggest that, contrary to his attachment to the Marxist version of mimesis, his Hegelian predilections often lead him to honor the equiprimordiality of universal, particular, and individual conjoined in the sensuous display of aesthetic appearance.

The Individuality of Beauty as Real, Concrete Universality

The logic of concrete universality may be ingredient in beauty, but it remains an incomplete element unless it is qualified by a further logical relation. This relation consists in the logical idea of an objective reality that is in unity with concrete universality. Without this qualification, concrete universality represents a structure that could just as well be purely conceptual in form. Beauty, however, constitutively realizes its unity of universality and individuality in a sensuous configuration, be it immediately given to perception or, as in the literary arts, brought to shape through the imagination of its audience. Hence, beauty can be said to be structured as an objectivity in which concrete universality is realized. As we have seen, Hegel identifies the category of such a structure as the Idea, and when he characterizes beauty as the sensuous embodiment of the Idea he is appropriately taking account of this dimension.

Beauty as a Display of Objective, Concrete Universality

However, even this is not enough, for it fails to provide place for the reference to rational agency that constitutively informs beauty. Beauty does not merely give sensuous embodiment to the realization of concrete universality, but it provides a sensuous *appearance* or *show* of this Idea. To the extent that this manifestation is addressed to rational agency, leaving aside whether it is necessarily produced by rational agency for contemplation by others, the very reality of beauty incorporates its being for its audience. Beauty thereby involves reference to its apprehension by its audience, to the awareness by this audience of its own apprehending role, and to the ideal representations these apprehensions include. To the extent that beauty is for and, at least optionally, by rational agency, the concrete universal determining its unity of sensuous configuration and meaning must thus possess the logical resources for the correlative elements of cognition and ideality.

These resources can be hinted at by characterizing beauty as not just the sensuous realization of the Idea but as a show or display of the sensuous realization of the Idea. This largely underlies Hegel's further qualification of the logic of beauty, where he characterizes aesthetic value as the Ideal. However, when Hegel moves from his elementary conception of beauty as the sensuous appearance of the Idea to his concept of beauty as the Ideal, he immediately introduces a dimension that squarely places the Ideal within the domain of artistic beauty. This added dimension is the element of truth ingredient in beauty.

Does the minimal characterization of beauty fall short of the threshold of aesthetic value if it fails to incorporate truth? And does this addition of truth introduce a restriction that renders artistic beauty the fulfillment of the concept of beauty, relegating natural beauty to a derivative, deficient status? Alternately, does the beauty of nature challenge these implications and the introduction of truth on which they may rest? To resolve these questions, natural beauty must be examined to determine whether or not it can have any standing of its own.

Chapter 5

Beauty as Such and Natural Beauty

The logic of the individuality of beauty seems to tie aesthetic value to the domain of rational agency. None of the ordering principles commonly ascribed to nature—the abstract universality of efficient causality, the generic universality of species being, or the reciprocal functionality of organic unity—can adequately exhibit the concrete universality and correlative exemplary individuality ingredient in beauty. Only what has overcome bondage to natural givenness and achieved the autonomy of self-imposed determination can claim a unique existence of universal import.[1] In virtue of this formal requirement, beauty appears inextricably linked to rational agency and its products.

The tie to rational agency gathers further support from the proviso that beauty not only present a unity of sensuous configuration and meaning exhibiting concrete universality, but one conveying to a rational audience an appearance of inherent significance. Can anything but rational agency provide a source of appearances measuring up to this dual demand? Can anything other than an appearance providing exemplary insight into the fundamental concerns of rational agency qualify as a bearer of aesthetic value?

If these intimations are sustained, beauty becomes a sensuous display of rational agency to itself providing fundamental self-understanding. This could still allow for a domain of "natural beauty" consisting in the given appearances of rational agents in distinction from the appearances of their artistic creations. However, beauty will be one and the same as the beauty of art if it turns out, first, that the "natural," given appearance of rational agents and their prosaic activities lacks the concrete universality and significant meaning required of beauty, and, second, that only artificially produced portrayals and expressions of humanity can meet these requirements. Aesthetics will then become nothing other than the philosophy of fine art.

The Challenge of Natural Beauty

Yet if these conclusions are to be upheld, how can the beauty of nature be accommodated? A simple solution might seemingly lie in dismissing natural beauty altogether as an illusion, a category mistake, a misuse of language imputing aesthetic value to a domain incapable of possessing beauty proper. In that case, giving beauty its minimal specification with features peculiar to fine art would avoid the blunder of defining the universal character of beauty in terms of one of its particular varieties. Then the beauty of fine art would not be a particular type of beauty at all, for beauty could not fail to pertain to artistic creations. Nature would still enter into aesthetics both as an ingredient element in rational agency's creation and reception of works of art and as an element depicted to express the fundamental concerns of humanity. For rational agents make and appreciate artistic works as embodied selves living in a natural environment that they mold and perceive through their natural endowments of body and sense, even if in conjunction with their engagement in conventional roles within the "second nature" of a conventional world. Moreover, any sensuous presentation of exemplary truths must involve natural entities on two accounts. On the one hand, natural factors serve as an actual medium for artistic beauty's appearance and reception, and on the other hand, they figure as an imagined content entering into any aesthetic expression or portrayal of rational agency. Nonetheless, nature untouched by rational agency would still be stripped of any independent beauty of its own.

Yet if this dismissal is carried through, how can one make sense of the perennial "illusion" of natural beauty, so commonly recurring in mundane experience and aesthetic debate? Alternately, if natural beauty be granted an existence, how can beauty be characterized by concrete universality and freedom, let alone a self-understanding of rational agency? If nature can have a nonderivative beauty of its own, the possibility of identifying the beauty of art with beauty per se seems to be overturned.

To forestall this result, natural beauty might be absorbed into the beauty of art as a derivative poor cousin, aesthetically appreciated as if it were a projection of artistic intentions. In that case, however, how can nature exhibit the features specific to art that it must convey in order to possess aesthetic value?

Natural Beauty and the Philosophy of Nature

To resolve the issue, it is necessary to consider the modes of appearance that nature can offer on its own, bereft of the imprint of rational agency. Examination of these modes can help establish whether nature can have any independent beauty, as well as what kind of resource natural forms can provide for the projection of artistic beauty. For if beauty can reside in nature apart from art, then natural beauty will be a category of the theory of nature.[2]

Settling the aesthetic issue of the status of natural beauty prior to the conception of fine art therefore depends on the independent achievements of the philosophy of nature, which alone can provide necessary truths concerning the modes of natural existence. The provisional hypotheses of empirical natural sciences may serve as heuristic guides, but unless an a priori theory of nature can be developed, the question of natural beauty will remain a matter of pragmatic belief, sharing the fate of all issues that cannot be resolved independently of empirical observation.

This predicament underscores once more how aesthetics must be systematic, not only in the sense of developing its own categories immanently but in the broader sense of being part of a system of philosophy, whose various nonaesthetic inquiries can provide a prior account of those domains whose conceptualization is a prerequisite for aesthetics. Moreover, the question of natural beauty is hardly the only juncture at which the results of the philosophy of nature must be brought into play. The results of the philosophy of nature will have to be relied on many more times to resolve every other problem of aesthetics that hinges on the natural dimension of sensuous appearance and its apprehension, or on the role of nature in the life and artistry of rational agents. By the same token, every consideration of beauty in its relation to rational agency will presuppose the achievements of the philosophy of spirit (that is, of rational agency and its distinctive world). Any aesthetic theory that pretends to operate in

Beauty as Such and Natural Beauty   95

abstraction from these other philosophical inquiries cannot help but beg its questions.

If, however, we acknowledge this dependence of aesthetic inquiry and admit our own inability to provide here a full-fledged theory of logic, nature, and spirit, we have little choice but to employ certain plausible results from these other domains of systematic philosophy with the proviso that every argument based on them must remain provisional pending certification of these, its conceptual prerequisites. Given these limitations, what can be said about those aspects of the appearance of nature that might be vehicles of beauty?

The Limits of Natural Beauty

At first glance, it might appear that discriminating among the types of sensuous configurations in nature is unnecessary. Might not nature as such be pregnant with beauty, awaiting merely the appreciative audience?

Although Hegel ultimately ties beauty to fine art, he first suggests such a global adequacy. Maintaining that nature is the rudimentary, primary existence of the Idea, that is, of the unity of the concept's concrete universality and its reality, and that the beautiful displays the Idea in sensuous appearance, Hegel concludes that beauty begins as the beauty of nature.[3]

Significantly, the implied connection between nature and beauty does not involve an appeal to mimesis. Besides strapping beauty with the aesthetically deficient universality of embodied form, such an appeal would require treating nature as the artifact of a divine demiurge who imposes form on the chaos of matter. Plato, of course, embraces this option, which allows sensuous nature, as imitation of the forms, to possess a beauty akin to what products of mortal imitative craft allegedly enjoy. Indeed, in the Platonic scheme, the beauty of nature is superior to that of art, given how nature more closely approximates the original ideas than does imitative craft's copy of a copy.[4] Instead of embracing mimesis and the consequences of its Platonic formulation, Hegel confers beauty to nature in recognition of a structure common to natural and artistic appearance that renders nature in general a potential bearer, albeit an inferior one, of aesthetic value.[5]

Leaving aside the issue of whether nature can properly be construed as the first existence of the Idea,[6] there is a certain plausibility to the notion that nature is imbued with beauty and that beauty begins with natural beauty. After all, works of art must always incorporate natural sensuous configurations, either as a represented part of artistic portrayal or as the given medium of artistic expression. This is true even when the medium is itself a product of convention, such as language. Given that finite subjects do not create ex nihilo, even an author must rely on the sight, sound, or feel of words in conveying their fiction. But if nature is not already amenable to beauty, how can it ever be incorporated in artistic beauty?

Such a train of thought begs the question, for no matter how great a role natural configurations play in artistic creation, this does not confer on them any aesthetic worth of their own. Indeed, when Hegel speaks of beauty beginning with the beauty of nature, this might well signify that nature has at best an implicit beauty, merely foreshadowing what becomes explicit and actual when natural appearance figures as an incorporated element within a work of fine art. Alternately, even if beauty were inherently tied to fine art, nature could still comprise the starting point of beauty insofar as art's minimal realization could consist in simply taking natural things as they are given and placing them unaltered in the conventional context that marks them as "works" of aesthetic significance.

Moreover, even if it were the case that nature and beauty share the structure of the Idea, this does not guarantee that the *appearance* of nature exhibits the sensuous existence of concrete universality. The Idea in nature need not display itself as such in nature's sensuous configuration, but may remain hidden in processes unavailable to perception.

For these reasons, we must turn to examine the types of natural appearance and consider where beauty might therein be found. In doing so, we must recognize that if any mode of natural appearance proves independently worthy of beauty, *all* exemplars of that mode will have to be granted aesthetic value. If, however, only some members of a certain class of natural appearances have beauty, whereas others do not, then their beauty cannot reside in any natural principle. By the same token, unless one can differentiate in natural appearance what is beautiful from what is ugly, the concept of natural beauty remains empty.[7] This predicament cannot be avoided so long as beauty is sought as something given by the lawful constitution of nature.[8]

Beauty and Inorganic Nature

Granted the legitimacy of the conceptual revolution underlying modern natural science, inorganic nature presents a realm of efficient causality, whose laws apply to things independently of their kind. Whether figuring in the mechanism of moving bodies or subject to more qualitative physical and chemical processes, inorganic objects stand determined from without.[9] In their unique extension in space and time, they contain a manifold of physical qualities. Yet they possess these either in a uniform way throughout all their parts, as in a metal; in a variegated way reflecting the influence of external things, as in geological formations; or in terms of a pattern, which, as in crystals, may develop itself, but in doing so exhibits a form common to all minerals of the same type. Throughout, the connection between the individual detail of the inorganic thing and its ordering principle remains one of an external subsumption, where the law governing the thing is indifferent to what individuates it from other things bound to the same processes.

Consequently, the natural configurations of inorganic things can exhibit such forms as regularity, symmetry, lawfulness, and harmony, each of which can just as well apply to other things without regard for their individuality.[10] Similarly, nonliving things can display a purity of matter of no perceivable blemish, which, as sheer undifferentiated stuff, can have no particular relation to its configuration.[11] Yet can individual inorganic things exhibit beauty, either in their uniform subjugation to common physical laws, their dependency on the contingent influence of other things, or their display of homogeneity or of regular, symmetrical, lawful, or harmonious differentiation? In each case, the thing's form lacks any unique connection to its particular existence, leaving the unity of concrete universality sorely wanting.[12]

Is beauty any more at home in the different systems of inorganic nature, with their interrelated motions and processes where each member's movement and qualities depends on its situation in the whole? Weather systems, solar systems, galaxies, and the like might seem to offer an interpenetration of whole and part overcoming the discrepancy of form and content in those inorganic relations where bodies figure in their independent existence. Yet even here, each physical factor has some given character of its own that may figure in a network of reciprocal action and reaction, but still cannot have its individual existence fully accounted for by the system's unitary process.[13] Consequently, the appearance of such systems cannot be expected to exhibit the concrete universality allowing beauty to meld its variegated content to an encompassing form.

This applies to any such "celestial harmony" that could be exhibited, following Kepler, by the mathematical relations of solar systems, or, for that matter, by more terrestrial inorganic processes. The "music of the spheres" may well contain harmonic relations such as music employs as one of the acoustic materials of its invention. Yet since harmony consists in universal relations that have indefinitely multiple instances, harmony by itself cannot be beautiful.[14] In order to figure as an element of musical beauty, harmony must be complemented by the addition of individual melody and development.[15] Similarly, no acoustic phenomena of inorganic nature, be it the whistling of wind, the crash of waves, or the roar of thunder, can provide evidence that nature produces something of aesthetic value. Whatever unity it exhibits always stays grounded on the external laws of nature, by which the individuality of the appearance remains something extrinsic to its essence.

Beauty and the "New" Physics

Does, however, inorganic nature assume a face more amenable to beauty in virtue of salient features with which the "new" modern physics of quantum mechanics and relativity theory supplants the picture of the "old" modern physics of Newton? In certain respects, as Michael Foster has observed,[16] recent physical theory seems to ascribe to its object those very characteristics most central to rational agency: activity, self-determination, and individuality. Whereas classical and Newtonian physics left matter the passive recipient of form and the passive subject of external natural laws, respectively, the new modern physics makes energy fundamental, injecting matter with an active character formerly reserved for subjectivity. Similarly, whereas in the old modern physics matter was determined by the necessity of efficient causality while rational agency was left free, quantum mechanics injects an indeterminacy into the spatiotemporal position and spin of physical particles, emancipating matter from its former bondage to a law-governed mechanism. And relativity theory, for its part, imparts a uniqueness to every point in space-time, allowing every physical event to be exclusive of all others, conferring an individuality somewhat akin to the historically specific actions of rational agents. Do these developments give inorganic nature an appearance whose every detail exhibits an inner meaning for which no independent expression can be given? Do they, in other words, confer a concrete universality to the sensuous configuration of physical nature, as beauty would require?

As Foster suggests,[17] neither energy, nor the indeterminacy of position or spin of particles, nor the uniqueness of each physical event in its instant of space-time can come close to exhibiting the freedom and individuality emblematic of concrete universality. Energy may not be passive, but it hardly gives itself its own character. It remains subject to laws that it can neither enact nor evade. Similarly, the indeterminacy of quantum mechanics may signify a partial liberation from the hold of deterministic physical laws, but it hardly provides a positive principle of self-determination, where a unique character arises that entities impose on themselves. Finally, the relativity of space-time may render every event unique, but this exclusivity is formal, since each one exemplifies the same shared physical principles. Consequently, what makes it the unique event it is is simply that it is what the others are not.

Moreover, it may be doubted whether any one of these three features of the "new" physics is perceivable in anything but the artificial context of a confirming experiment, where the meaning at hand must be reproducible. As such, the significance of the observed event will not be tied to its individual sensuous configuration, but will instead represent a common principle, equally at hand in any other corroborating instance.

Beauty and Organic Nature

Life introduces something new in the sensuous configuration of nature, but is it enough to confer beauty on natural appearances? We have already seen how the logic of an organism comes close to the unity of concrete universality. In the living thing, the differentiations are no longer just parts of a whole subsumed under external principles of mechanism, regularity, symmetry, harmony, or homogeneity. In relation to its environment, a living thing may well exhibit such aspects, as in the bilateral symmetry so common in the external appendages of plants and animals. However, in respect to its own internal organization, an organism's differentiations go beyond these abstract forms.[18] Instead of being parts, they are organs, connected in terms of their complementary functions, sustaining one another in virtue of reproducing the living whole to which they belong.

Nevertheless, organic unity still fails to attain the thorough interpenetration of form and content, of inner and outer, of universal and individual, that concrete universality achieves. The complementary functions of organs are not directly perceivable, nor is their appearance *uniquely* appropriate to the function they perform. Moreover, the specific interdependence of a living thing's organs are common to all members of the same species, leaving the individuality of each creature something independent of its particular organic unity.[19]

Similar limitations apply to the spontaneity of movement that permits animal organisms to escape exclusive bondage to the fixed laws determining inorganic motion.[20] If this movement is a function of instinctual drives common to a species, its individuality falls asunder from its universal principle. If, on the other hand, it represents noninstinctual activity, can its individual detail be wedded to any unifying meaning, let alone one of inherent significance? So long as animal movement proceeds either purposefully in satisfaction of needs or simply accidentally, it fails to manifest any independent beauty.[21] Animal behavior may exhibit feeling and desire, such that its outer motions are tied to something inner. Yet without any perceivable basis for distinguishing this inner content from common instinct or singular accident, animal life cannot exhibit to itself or others an "ensouled" unity where bodily appearance and significant inwardness are one.[22]

Beauty and the Nature of Rational Agency

The manifestation of plant and animal life may not have sufficient resources to sustain a beauty of its own, but what of the immediate existence of rational agents? Might not the given sight of a person or the sound of a voice convey a beauty independent of art, exhibiting as it does the immediate intertwining of mind and body, underlying self-consciousness and the recognition of other individuals? Might not the prosaic activities of individuals have something beautiful in their given appearance, manifesting not just biological processes but significant affairs? Might not these possibilities give sense to the aspirations of the romantics to overcome the divide of life and art, to Kierkegaard's and Nietzsche's ironic program to invest existence with meaning by viewing it aesthetically, and to the parallel aestheticizations of politics that have haunted modern times?

Undoubtedly the given visual and auditory appearances of individuals can be attractive or unattractive in varying degrees. Yet can the pleasing character of the sight and sound of a person's natural facticity involve more than the attractiveness of an object of desire? Given the particularity of desire and love, the attractiveness of a person's appearance is relative to the particular features of that person and to the particular desires and affections of the appreciative audience.[23] Given, however, the universal dimension of beauty, the aesthetic value of personal appearance must involve a complete joining of the individual's sensuous configuration with an underlying meaning, corresponding to a reception whose pleasure is independent of the particular desires and emotional attachments of the audience.

Although individuals, in order to be recognized as such by others, must express their mind and will in their outer appearance, this does not mean that *all* aspects of their physical presence can manifest the unity of character and resolve, rendering it and its movements significant. There will always be manifold bodily features that either resist or remain indifferent to the humanity dwelling within, just as individuals will always find themselves subject to external exigencies of their environment of nature and convention, conflicting with one another and the aims they pursue.[24] Even such physical manifestations as facial expressions, hand gestures, posture, gait, and voice, where mind and will are most clearly evident, still retain details bearing no relation to what they signify.[25] These recalcitrant, irrelevant features may reside in contingent hereditary factors, shared differences of gender and race, or in personal idiosyncracies of temperament and physique.[26] As a consequence, the artistic depictions of individuals will need to resolve these discrepancies of meaning and configuration in their given appearance in order to create something of beauty.

The romantic notion that the intensity of inner experience renders it something of aesthetic value fares no better. The private emotional life of an individual not only makes itself manifest to a purely singular audience, namely the person engaged in self-observation, but remains caught in the singularity of personal feeling.[27] However intense such psychological episodes may be, they thereby lack the universality that could elevate their detail to something generally perceivable by and meaningful to others.

Similar limitations bar any direct ascription of aesthetic value to the manifestations of prosaic convention, no matter what normative value they may command. On all sides, individuals and institutions stand prey to external influences, contingently connected and devoid of meaning.[28] The ethical domain is no exception, despite its involvement with freedom and independence. Whereas the "essence" and "appearance" of objects of beauty are in thoroughgoing accord, so that neither can be manifest without the other, the "essence" and "appearance" of ethical affairs have no such bond. Indeed, one of the salient features of ethical affairs is that the normative significance of an act or institution need not be tied to its outer appearance.[29] This is true not only because inner intention plays a key role in moral and legal evaluation but because ethical activity is subject to all the contingencies of particular situations, leaving the realization of right always attended by extraneous factors and influences. Hence, the immediate appearance of conduct is never so joined to its significance as to exhibit the concrete universality of beauty. Prosaic life, however meaningful, is inveterately saddled with accidents whose sensuous nature is indifferent to the humanity at play.[30] Whereas the conformity of appearance and meaning is of primary importance to aesthetic value, it is only of secondary import in determining the ethical value of conduct. For these reasons, the immediate givenness of human affairs can never display an appearance whose entire individuality is pregnant with meaning.[31] As we shall see, only when the prosaic world undergoes the transfiguration of artistic imagination can individuals and their interaction sensuously manifest the concrete universality beauty commands.

The Reception of Natural Appearance and the Beauty of Nature

Given the limits inherent in the modes of natural appearance, can how nature is perceived and appreciated by rational agents have any bearing on the possibility of natural beauty?

Admittedly, the reception of natural beauty requires that its audience, at least during their aesthetic experience, relate to nature solely as an appearance, without regard for it as either an object of scientific investigation or as an object of need and material of production with which society reproduces itself.[32] For this reason, there is some plausibility to the observation that natural beauty is appreciated not by those whose livelihood is still bound to the land but only by those who have freed themselves from direct dependence on nature and can face it in a disinterested manner.[33] However, this requirement still leaves open whether natural appearance is such that it can be the object of an aesthetic experience when it is viewed with proper disinterest.

As we have seen, transcendental aesthetics is led to acknowledge beauty in nature if only because the formalism of its receptive account of aesthetic judgment leaves the object of beauty essentially indeterminate. Since beauty here still resides in the effect of a representation on subjective or intersubjective apprehension, the admission of natural beauty can lead a transcendental aesthetician like Kant to conclude that our concept of nature must be expanded beyond the efficient causality of a mere mechanism to allow for the teleological relation by which natural appearances can exhibit a purposiveness relative to our aesthetic experience.[34] Nevertheless, the failure of transcendental aesthetics to determine any objective features of beautiful things leaves it in no position to override the aesthetic deficiencies of natural appearance.

Conversely, the fate of natural beauty can no more be decided by the appeal to the social and historical mediation of the reception of nature with which a Marxist aesthetician like Lukács seeks to dismiss the possibility of any beauty in nature. Lukács maintains that how nature appears to rational agents is always conditioned by the dual relation of their economic metabolism with nature and their social relations with one another.[35] Although Lukács admits that nature always confronts individuals under two aspects, one portion standing in a regulated metabolism with them and another standing outside this interaction,[36] he still maintains that any beauty perceived in nature will be relative to the culture of its audience. In a similar vein, Adorno maintains that any attempt to fix natural beauty according to invariable concepts, independently of the historical context of its reception, only results in laughably arbitrary results.[37] Yet, even if this point be granted, it does not mandate that there is no beauty inherent in nature. Nature might yet possess a type or types of appearance that first allow for natural beauty to be experienced in different ways by different societies. Hence, the denial of natural beauty still requires an examination of the modes of natural appearance.

However, once this examination contributes to deciding whether beauty is the beauty of fine art, an interpretation of historical ascriptions of beauty to nature can be undertaken in view of the culturally specific modes of artistic beauty and the way in which natural configurations may or may not be congruent with their creative concerns.[38] Then what lies at stake is not natural beauty itself but rather an artistically shaped experience of nature, reflecting a particular cultural milieu and its self-understanding.[39]

Nature as a Vehicle of Beauty

Although the immediate appearances of neither inorganic and organic phenomena nor rational agents independently provide sufficient support for aesthetic value, this hardly precludes their incorporation within the imaginative creations of fine art. Systematically speaking, the role of nature in artistic productions can only be treated after artistic beauty has been determined in its own right. However, by way of anticipation, it warrants noting that natural appearances can be appropriated by fine art with varying degrees of transfiguration. Landscape, portraiture, film, and video can well produce images that remain relatively faithful to the given appearances they portray. Indeed, in the extreme case of "found" art, given things can be taken for artistic display without undergoing any transformation other than being placed within the context by which works of fine art are set apart from prosaic objects. Yet even here, where the transfiguration of nature into fine art is at its most formal, the given appearance of natural phenomena becomes infused with the nonnatural significance of being posited as fine art. This positing, which as such must be perceivable, makes the object present the view of the artist. By intention at least, all content of the given appearance is thereby rendered essential to its aesthetic form. Whether all natural phenomena are equally capable of bearing this external vocation and to what extent different degrees of transfiguration are aesthetically viable can only be decided in the course of determining the general features of the work of fine art, the forms of artistic beauty, and the individual fine arts.

In the meantime, it can be presumed that where nature is found to possess beauty, this, as Hegel rightly observes, neither arises out of nature itself nor appears for nature as beautiful. Rather, nature acquires aesthetic worth only for rational agents who perceive in natural configurations an analogue to artistic beauty.[40] Accordingly, contra

Danto, possessing a taste for beauty will not ultimately differ from having one for art.[41] Although an artwork may not be reducible to its perceptually indistinguishable material counterpart, as examples of "found" art testify, this does not mean that the material counterpart can possess its own beauty without projectively fulfilling the requirements of artistic beauty.[42]

Is natural beauty thereby rendered "found" art, meeting these demands with the arch play of a Duchamp, explicitly elevating something's mundane physicality into the framework of artistic creation? If so, the recognition of natural beauty cancels itself by collapsing into an act of creation by which a prosaic factor is transfigured into a work of "found" art. The connoisseurs of natural beauty can escape this outcome so long as they view their chosen prosaic appearance *as if* it provided an exemplary image bearing significant meaning for the human predicament, yet refrain from engaging in the imaginative pretense of identifying it as an actual artistic creation.

Chapter 6

Beauty as Artistic Beauty

The place of truth in beauty has already been intimated by two complementary factors: the logical form of beauty's unity of meaning and configuration and the correlative inadequacy of natural beauty. Beauty gives sensuous display to truth's inner logic to the degree that beauty presents an imagined or intuited sensuous appearance exhibiting concrete universality in relation to its meaning, that the conformity of concept and objectivity is the form of truth, and that by uniting in terms of concrete universality concept and objectivity can conform without succumbing to the complementary problems of the differentia and of the representational model of knowing.[1] Conversely, the limit of natural beauty consists in a failure to capture fully truth's form and to provide a configuration worthy of independent display.

Nonetheless, exhibiting the form of truth is one thing, displaying truth proper is another. Although the concrete universality of beauty may fit the formal structure of truth and thereby provide no obstacle to its inclusion, it is not clear that this provides any independent reason for incorporating truths of some specific sort into aesthetic value.

The Truth Ingredient in Beauty

However, there is another avenue that prepares the way for truth as well as for determining what kind of truth might be appropriate to beauty. This lies in the role of rational agency in beauty. As we have seen, rational agency is not simply that to which beauty constitutively appears. It is also that which most fully exhibits the logical structure exemplified in beauty's unity of sensible configuration and meaning.[2]

This suggests that the object of beauty will have to present rational agency in its sensuous appearance, either directly in rational agency's own facticity or indirectly in products of its activity. If this is so, then beauty would consist in a sensuous presentation of rational agency to itself. Beauty would then comprise a mode of self-awareness of rational agency, operating by means of its own sensuous display.

Although beauty thereby seems cast beyond the pale of mere nature, it does not immediately appear identical with artistic beauty. For even if beauty must employ the sensuous appearance of rational agency, this does not seem to require that it do so through its own creations. Apparently, the option still remains that beauty could reside in the nonproduced, natural givenness of the rational agent, whose bodily appearance might suffice as an emblem of beauty.

Can, however, the appearance of the natural facticity of the rational agent provide the unity of meaning and configuration, the concrete universality otherwise ingredient in the self-determination so central to rational agency? The problem is that for all the autonomy rational agency may command, its natural givenness is marked by internal and external factors that are by no means self-imposed characteristics of its freedom. Because finite rational agents create neither their own bodies nor the world they inhabit, rational agents, be they human or extraterrestrial, cannot fail to have bodily features that are not only given by nature independently of the will of the individual, but remain indifferent to the expression of the rationality and character that must take hold of other aspects of the body in order to be actual. By the same token, the individual agent cannot help but be immersed in a natural environment involving external relations that either resist or remain indifferent to the second nature of convention in which rational agents can erect an outer world embodying their autonomy. To the degree that all of these natural, externally given dimensions of inner and outer existence intrude into the immediate appearance of rational agents and the world they inhabit, the natural appearance of individuals is fraught with accidental, meaningless details that disrupt the unity of universality and individuality, of form and content, of inner and outer, on which beauty depends.

In order to overcome this discrepancy, the appearance of rational agency must be transfigured, superseding the contingency of natural givenness with a nonnatural, artificial configuration in accord with the concrete universality of beauty. This can involve the appropriation of the given appearances of agents in action as well as the given view that they have on different spheres of their surroundings.[3] Whatever degree of alteration such appearances may undergo, they can possess the unity of aesthetic worth only by becoming informed with a significance their own facticity lacks. Because the subject of the appearance does not lose its identity in this process, but rather retains what is shown to be essential to it, rational agency and its products undergo, as Danto aptly points out, a *transfiguration* rather than a *transformation* into something else.[4] This artificial configuration is none other than artistic beauty, an *ideal* in the sense that it replaces natural facticity with a significant sensuous form put forth by rational agency for itself as a vehicle of self-understanding.[5]

Since the posited images constitutive of artistic beauty have a meaning joined to their configuration, they are representations in the minimal sense of being about something. However, since the content they convey is transfigured in order to possess its aesthetically constitutive concrete individuality, the images of beauty are *expressions* of truths fundamental to humanity, rather than mimetic imitations of externally existing things or of emotions and feelings already dwelling within the artist.[6] This is true even if the images involve rote facsimiles of given appearances. If such images are to bear aesthetic worth, they must convey more than the immediate facticity of what they resemble. How they do this will depend on the context in which they are presented and appreciated, a context that must make its own appearance in conjunction with them in order to transfigure the images in an aesthetically significant way.

No matter what prosaic identity the appearance may have, if it is to count as an object of beauty the perceivable context of its presentation will show that it is the unique presentation of a view of something inherently significant to humanity. If the appearance counted instead simply as an entity with a meaning predicated on contingent, merely local and particular ends and interests, it would forfeit its aesthetic independence and universality and revert to an amusement or instrument of utility. To retain the free universality of its significance, the appearance of beauty must express a view about matters that are of value in themselves, unconditioned by the merely subjective, accidental concerns of audience or presenter. By so producing a transfigured, fictitious world of its own, the truth of art breaks the monopoly of given facticity to define what counts for humanity, exhibiting how, as Marcuse rightly observes, aesthetic form, autonomy, and truth are intertwined.[7]

However, in transcending the hold of given appearance so as to provide insight into what is fundamental to humanity, artistic beauty does not achieve an irreplaceable cognitive service only by contradicting the reality it transfigures, as Marcuse further insists.[8] In its thought-infused images sensuously displaying the universal in the individual, artistic beauty may just as well challenge as ratify the state of affairs it illuminates.

In any event, it is not enough to characterize artistic beauty, such as Pater suggests,[9] as a transcription of the artist's view of the world. Although this formulation does correctly acknowledge how artistic beauty conveys a self-understanding rather than an imitation of given facts, it leaves out of account art's concrete universality and unconditioned significance.[10] Unless the would-be artist's view of the world satisfies these additional requirements, its expression remains a prosaic confession.

Furthermore, the expression of the work of art will not consist in a metaphoric exemplification, as Danto maintains, following Goodman.[11] On this account exemplification signifies a member of a class standing for the class, whereas metaphor comprises a representation that presents a subject matter in light of the way in which it is conveyed.[12] Viewing the work of art as metaphoric exemplification would accordingly render it a representation conveying a member of a class that stands for the class, doing so through something distinct from that member. Although this permits the concept of expression to allow for a connection between how something is represented and what it is,[13] the connection is still not sufficiently strong to conform to the unity of beauty. As a metaphorical exemplification, the work of art would express a meaning that remains an independently given universal, namely, the class that is exemplified, which can just as readily be conveyed by any number of alternate samples and their metaphorical representations. The work of art must rather be understood to figure as an expression that not only transfigures the content it employs, but thereby conveys a meaning that is not so detachable from its individual configuration as to involve the abstract universality of a class.

To enjoy this nondetachable character, the meaning provided by beauty's transfigurative representations[14] must, as we have seen, specifically comprise a self-understanding of what is universal, yet sensuously expressible about rational agency. As a result, the object of beauty confronts artist and spectator alike with something that, however it differs in appearance from them, yet reveals something significant about them.[15]

Although the object of beauty will achieve this revelation in function of its appearance, the sensible features of the entity do not suffice of themselves for identifying its aesthetic worth. A purely physical identification of beauty is impossible given the essential roles of meaning and of contextualization, and of the beautiful object's concomitantly constitutive relations to its audience and to the agent responsible for presenting the object to aesthetic appreciation, whose presentation may or may not involve altering the physical being of that object.

If this seals the futility of any search for a definition of beauty in terms of exclusively sensible properties, it also indicates the dogmatism of the popular view that aesthetics' perennial attempt to determine beauty in general is a hopeless mistake.[16] The factors before us provide a minimal framework for bringing that attempt to fruition, a framework that also should make one beware of concluding that the possible indiscernibility of an object of beauty and a physical thing condemns aesthetics to silence about the sensible aspect of beauty. Even if the physical appearance of a work of art may be duplicated by an accident of nature or a craft exercise of forgery, or, conversely, a prosaic thing may be removed from its mundane surroundings to be exhibited as is for aesthetic appreciation, this does not mean that the requirements of beauty have no implications for what sensible properties appearances must have to command aesthetic worth. Such properties may not be sufficient conditions of beauty, but they still must play some necessary role at the level of art in general, as well as in reference to artistic style (the particular art forms) and artistic genre (the individual arts), if beauty unites meaning and configuration.

What must be avoided is any one-sided emphasis on either the form or the content of the object of beauty. Any aesthetic theory that invests beauty in the configuration of a work with disregard for its meaning, or, conversely, seeks aesthetic value in a meaning incidental to the shape of the work, ignores the unity of form and content basic to aesthetic phenomena.[17]

Beauty as Artistic Beauty 111

This multifaceted outcome is of fundamental importance. It signifies, first of all, that beauty is artistic beauty. Second, it implies that beauty presents a self-understanding of rational agency through an exemplary artificial[18] sensuous self-expression. Third, this means that the truth germane to beauty is not truth about logic, number, or nature, but truth about rational agency, the truth whereby rational agents achieve an essential self-awareness.[19] And finally, this mandates that aesthetics is the philosophy of fine art.

These ramifications cohere with the ordering that Hegel follows in determining the general features of beauty. Beginning with the concept of the beautiful as such and characterizing it as the sensuous show of the Idea, Hegel then proceeds to examine the beauty of nature as a way station for determining whether the concept of beauty entails further qualification. In the course of this investigation, deficiencies are uncovered that make manifest that beauty is necessarily artistic. As a result, Hegel brings his account of beauty in general to its conclusion by considering how beauty is realized in a work of art.[20]

In following this path, Hegel moves beyond reference to beauty's incorporation of the Idea as the form of truth in general to a more specific qualification. He ends up maintaining that the truth ingredient in beauty's individual configuration is not just any truth, but truth about the fundamental concerns of spirit, explicitly produced by and for spirit in an exemplary appearance.

Spirit, nonmetaphysically construed, signifies the reality of rational agency or what can be called humanity, understood broadly as encompassing all possible finite rational creatures without restriction to homo sapiens. Although we may have yet no evidence of nonhuman finite subjects in our galaxy or in any other, the relations of spirit pertain to any possible rational agents, without restriction to the natural contingencies of human species being. If beauty is determined in reference to finite rational agency, tying aesthetic reality in any necessary way to homo sapiens would thus be as illicit as limiting full citizenship rights to adult males. Given this species-independent determination of humanity, beauty would now consist in a created individual representation whose concretely universal appearance for sense and the imagination provides a self-understanding for rational agents, be they human or not.

If this provides the minimal threshold for aesthetic value, beauty can no longer be considered a genus with equiprimordial species of natural and artistic beauty. Because beauty will now preeminently lie in artistic creations and aesthetics will be the philosophy of fine art, natural beauty must be relegated to an ancillary position. Nature can now be ascribed beauty only derivatively to the extent that appearances given in nature fit projections of artistic concerns originating in rational agency's efforts at self-understanding. Moreover, due to the limited ability of natural configurations to display truths central to humanity, natural beauty would be doubly inferior to artistic beauty.[21]

Is this account specific enough to be constitutive of beauty, yet sufficiently general to be ingredient in all aesthetic phenomena? Of capital importance in this regard is the nature of the self-understanding to which the manifestation of beauty contributes. If all that lies at stake is providing an acquaintance with mundane features of humanity lacking any particular importance, beauty would only reiterate what is already familiar and fail to display something worthy of being regarded for the sake of its appearance.

Ethics, Religion, and Science as Domains for Beauty

To warrant independent display, beauty would have to provide a unique imaginative insight into those affairs of spirit, those humane affairs broadly considered, of inherent significance. Only then will beauty display something worthy of attention in a way possessing its own value. Three fields of activity seem provisionally appropriate: ethics, encompassing the entire domain of normative conduct, from property relations to morality to the different ethical associations of family, society, and state; religious worship and community, where matters of ultimate value are pursued in reference to belief in divinity; and science, understood as the self-validating endeavor where truth is sought through rational investigation.[22] Each sphere, according to its own self-understanding, addresses concerns of unconditioned value, which can first give meaning to instrumental pursuits.

However, science, despite its unconditioned character as self-justifying rational discourse, poses problems for incorporation in beauty because scientific truths are themselves wholly universal in character. Scientific dilemmas cannot be truthfully depicted by appeal to sensuous configurations, for the arguments at stake concern universal principles rather than particular applications.

By contrast, ethics always involves the application of universal principles of right and wrong to individual conduct and actual institutions. Hence, ethical conflicts are always realized in a form susceptible of imaginative construal.

Similarly, religious community perennially involves the element of representation in the narrative that forms the basis of religious dogma and worship. Unlike philosophical investigation of the infinite, which exclusively employs concepts, religion still relies on images in conveying its truths, even when the divine is believed to be beyond all sensuous representation. Consequently, religious truths are not incommensurate with beauty, even if worship itself focuses on the internal dimension of faith rather than on the external display of images.

If this leaves aesthetic construal free to address the spheres of ethics and religion, it also allows scientific activity to reenter as an adjunct theme. For even if scientific truths are too purely universal to be sensuously configured by themselves, the practice of rational inquiry can become entangled with ethical or religious affairs. In that connection, theoretical activity becomes enmeshed with particular circumstances that render it a potential factor in aesthetic depiction.

By producing individual representations whose configurations are united to meanings revelatory of these spheres, beauty would present something worthy of beholding for its own sake.

Can the Concept of Beauty Legitimately Refer to Religion and Science?

Beauty's reference to religious and scientific truths might appear problematic if ethics, art, religion, and science (philosophy) were to be systematically treated in succession, as in Hegel's system. It may make perfect sense for the determination of art to follow on that of logic, nature, mind, and ethics, given how beauty embodies categories (established in logic), consists in a sensuous configuration given in the world (whose physical and biological aspects are accounted for in the philosophy of nature), is produced by and addressed to rational agents (whose mental life is determined in the philosophy of mind), and provides an exemplary revelation of ethical truths (determined by ethics). Yet, if the art-religion-philosophy sequence of Hegel's doctrine of Absolute Spirit is correct, this should signify that religion and science follow art because the self-understanding of the forms of beauty is less determinate than and incorporated in religion and scientific thought. Granted that this is the case, how can art already refer to religious and scientific matters, when religion and science presuppose the relationships of beauty?

Perhaps beauty as such cannot involve reference to religious and scientific themes but can only address ethical problems. This focus is what Aristotle upheld in maintaining that art has *praxis* as its object. Even if this were true, it would still be possible for art to address religious and scientific themes, given the presence in theory and practice of religious community and scientific investigation. Although the theoretical conception of their presence might be subsequent to the independent conception of art, once religion and science are determined, the concept of art would be in a position to be redetermined to incorporate reference to these conceptually posterior spheres. Such redetermination would hardly be unique to art. In ethics, for instance, property rights get redetermined when they are legalized in civil society, just as political institutions get amended to provide for armed forces, government controls over foreign commerce, and foreign diplomacy once the plurality of states is determined in the concept of international relations.

Alternately, even if religion and rational inquiry can be conceived in their own right only after aesthetics, it still might be possible for religious and scientific problems to figure as themes for artistic representation. All that would be required is that the resources be available to depict imaginatively those religious and scientific problems susceptible of aesthetic construal. In this respect, art could provide exemplary, prescientific revelations of religious and scientific themes, even if the scientific account of religion and rational inquiry somehow presupposes the systematic conception of aesthetics.

Accordingly, beauty can provisionally be considered to incorporate ethical, religious, and scientific concerns as part of its substantial meaning. The scope of Goethe's *Faust*, for example, need not transgress the limits of aesthetic representation. It remains to be seen, however, whether the other dimensions of beauty's minimal determination differentially affect the aesthetic construal of these spheres.

The Exemplary Meaning of Beauty

Although the limitation of aesthetic meaning to truths of inherent value lends beauty a noncontingent worth, it seems to rob beauty of its independence at the very same time. For if beauty is held to comprise the sensuous presentation of a fundamental self-understanding of humanity produced by and for itself, the dilemma plaguing mimetic theory seems to reoccur. Again, the question arises as to what purpose is served by imaginatively presenting self-understandings that can be achieved either better or equally well in the prose of philosophical thought or the faith of religious worship. If beauty can offer nothing but the same self-understanding provided by religion and science, its display could only be justified on the terms adopted by mimetic theory: that beauty has a special edifying role owing to its imaginative construal of sacred or rational contents. Yet if its theme remains no other than what religion and science address, then beauty's aesthetic form stands in an external relation to an independently given content, destroying the unity of configuration and meaning, of form and content, of original individuality so ubiquitous in aesthetic phenomena.

It is therefore not enough for art to rise beyond the mimetic reproduction of a given particular entity to reproduce the general essence of the thing, or even to open up therewith a whole human world and the earth that shelters it, as Heidegger would have us believe.[23] Even then, the aesthetic unveiling of truth would add nothing to prosaic modes of philosophical speculation while relinquishing the special tie between meaning and configuration.

To maintain beauty's discrete integrity, the fundamental self-understanding revealed in a work's imaginative representation must be unique to art. Then, the meaning of beauty's sensuous configuration will not be independently given and beauty can retain the free unity endemic to the aesthetic dimension. The autonomy of art will be upheld in conjunction with its revelation of truth, and beauty will need no extrinsic justification for maintaining the worthiness of its appearance.

What fundamental self-understanding regarding ethics, religious worship, or the rational pursuit of truth can it be that beauty alone affords? The answer to this question revolves around the issue of what meanings can and cannot be joined to an individual sensuous configuration.

Three types of meaning must be excluded. A meaning that is inherently abstract, involving a universal that does not determine anything more about the particulars in which it inheres than that they bear a common quality, would not be susceptible of artistic representation. Beauty would be absent, since such a meaning could not be in any essential connection to the individual detail of the configuration in which it was embodied.

Conversely, a meaning that is wholly singular, conveying the immediate reference of a proper name, would equally be foreign to beauty. Devoid of any universal dimension, it could never be tied to a form of any wider significance.

Finally, a meaning that is systematic, comprising a concept that determines all factors of its realization without leaving the element of thought, would be inappropriate as well. Such a systematic meaning, to which philosophy aspires, be it under the rubric of synthetic a priori judgments or categorial determination, would not be fully presentable in any sensuous representation, for two complementary reasons. On the one hand, sensuous configuration introduces an element of detail transcending the limits of conceptual differentiation; on the other hand, conceptual differentiation retains a thoroughgoing universality that can never be fully retained by an image.

With these options eliminated, what meaning can there be that is unique to art? There seems to be little alternative other than a significance that is exemplary in character, involving a unity of universal and particular that only an individual sensuous configuration can convey. Although the exemplar bears a meaning that has universality, it differs from a mere example of an independently given universal in that the exemplar's universality is ingredient in its own individuality and cannot be otherwise defined.[24]

Leaving aside for the time being what more can be said about the internal structure of such exemplary meaning, its incorporation within beauty has important ramifications. Whereas scientific and philosophical truths are discursive, having a universal significance expressible in multiple formulations, beauty would present an exemplary truth of ethical and religious domains, uniquely representing norms and dogma in sensuous individuals.

Indeed, the differentiation of particular forms of art has its basis in the circumstance that not all ethics and religions can be equally susceptible of an exemplary imaging. Since abstract, singular, and systematic meanings are problematic themes for beauty, forms of ethics and religion that uphold such contents will provide specific difficulties for artistic representation, requiring different modes of treatment. Moreover, since the exemplary unity of universal and individual ties form and content together, the limits on meanings susceptible of aesthetic construal must entail correlative restrictions on what kinds of sensuous configurations are adequate to beauty.

The Freedom in Artistic Beauty

As we have seen, the concrete universality of beauty sets it in relation to the form of truth in general and, more particularly, to the autonomous reality specific to rational agency. If, as has been suggested, this renders beauty the beauty of art, affording rational agency with a self-understanding that only imaginatively determined appearances can provide, does this also entail a further value deriving from the autonomy that artistic beauty realizes?

Hegel, in distinguishing the ethical domain from culture under the rubric of the transition from Objective to Absolute Spirit, claims this additional worthiness for art, arguing that artistic beauty embodies a freedom that transcends the prosaic autonomy that individuals can enjoy through institutions of justice.[25] Existing structures of right may provide individuals objectively recognized freedoms of ownership, moral subjectivity, family membership, social civility, and self-government, but they always do so within the context of a state that is individual, limited in space and time, and subject to collapse from internal or external pressures. In the cultural spheres of art, religion, and philosophy, Hegel maintains, individuals give their freedom a realization that transcends the particularity and finitude of mundane existence. Artistic beauty confronts individuals with a realm of appearance produced by and for rational agency, unencumbered by the contingent, extraneous accoutrements of life in the state. Artistic beauty may still display itself in the medium of sensuous existence, subject to determination from without and situated in a particular time and place. Nonetheless, the beauty of the work of art surmounts these relations, detaching the art object from its mundane surroundings and their external exigencies, letting it show itself instead in terms of its own independent form and content to an audience transcending any particular period or community.[26] In this respect, art comprises a vehicle of autonomy in its own right, where rational agents stand in relation to their own productions in a way that surmounts the confines of prosaic reality.

Significantly, such autonomy does not confer value on artistic beauty in virtue of its embodiment or abetting of a freedom that is independently given outside of art, such as in the sphere of conduct and ethical institutions. The dilemma of affording art legitimacy in view of its edifying results is avoided, for the autonomy to which artistic beauty allegedly contributes exists nowhere else but in aesthetic reality—in the meeting of artist and audience mediated by the work of fine art. Far from giving beauty an instrumental worth, the freedom in art thus upholds the autonomy of aesthetic value.[27]

Indeed, art's integral freedom can be considered the key to aesthetic value. What is of value in general cannot derive its worth from anything lacking merit, on pain of having a worth conditioned by something valueless. Hence, normative validity must reside in what is self-determined: theoretical truth must consist in the activity of autonomous reason, which accepts nothing as true that is not grounded on the truths it has independently established, just as valid conduct must consist in the institutional reality of self-determined action.[28] In the same way, beauty must derive from nothing other than what is of aesthetic value, which is to say, beauty must be self-determined.

This can be seen as a mandate holding true on two conceptual levels. On a global scale, the development of categories from the most general to the most concrete determinations of the beautiful should amount to a self-constitution of the totality of aesthetic reality that proceeds without introductions of external privileged givens or outside interventions of privileged determiners. On the other hand, at each stage along the way the freedom inherent in beauty must be retained.

The specific character of this freedom stands in relief when one compares the relation of rational agency and objectivity in its theoretical, practical, and aesthetic engagements.

Taking ordinary theoretical consciousness as a starting point, we find the subject afflicted with dependency. To the extent that the knowing subject perceives objects that are presupposed to be independently given, its cognitive activity takes a passive posture, limiting its representations in function of the putative independence of their referent. This is true even if the form of objectivity is itself tied to categorial determinations of intuitions, for when knowledge of an individual object is at stake its empirical givenness must be paid heed. To obtain truth, the subject must here subordinate itself to its object or else fall prey to fantasy.[29]

By contrast, in the practical relation of an agent to things, it is the object that figures in a subordinate role. The agent has its own aims and wills to fulfill them through intervening on the given being of things. As a vehicle for the realization of the agent's aims, things figure as utilities, relinquishing their independence to undergo the annihilation, alteration, or manipulation that allows them to serve the subject. Here, the subject lords over the object.[30]

Yet the freedom of the agent in lording over things is just as limited and formal as is the freedom of the object in comprising the standard of truth for its observer. In both engagements the subject is determined from without and unfree. As a theoretical observer, the subject is bound and dependent because of the assumed independence of the things. As a practical doer, the subject is equally limited owing both to the dependency of its aims on externally aroused impulses and passions and to the persisting resistance of objects, whose natural givenness can never be totally absorbed into the functionality of utility. In both cases, what underlies the dependency of the subject is the separate independent givenness of subject and object.[31]

Similarly, the object is equally dependent and unfree as the focus of observation or of practical use. As the given object of perception, the thing is a particular individual immersed in a world of nature in which it is subject to the influence of countless other things and their relations. As the given object of use, the thing is explicitly stripped of its independence and made to yield at least some of itself in being impressed into the service of subjective aims.[32]

By contrast, when a beautiful thing is apprehended as such, the limitations on subject and object are removed. One the one hand, the bounds of theoretical engagement are overcome on both sides of the relation. The object, as beautiful, is no longer merely a thing determined by the contingencies of its external environment, so that its particular features have their unity torn asunder in every direction by the imprint of outside influence. Instead, the beautiful thing displays an appearance whose unique character, as aesthetic, is tied to its form, ready to be extracted from its contingent surroundings for show in its own right, as set free from interference by such sheltered contexts as museums, libraries, performance halls, and the like.

Simultaneously, observers of the beautiful object cease to subordinate their representations in passive conformity to the independent givenness of the thing. To the extent that the beautiful object exhibits concrete universality, its audience confronts in sensuous form the same structure that lies at the heart of rational autonomy. Individual and universal at once, the beautiful appearance does not demand of the audience that it conform its abstract concepts to an existent thing constitutively alien to them. Rather, the audience must apprehend the unity of meaning and sensuous configuration, calling on imagination and reason to recognize the interpenetration on display. Moreover, to the degree that beauty provides imaginative insight into fundamental truths of rational agency, the audience appreciating a beautiful thing communes with something in which it remains most at home, free from the extraneous pull of what lies outside humane concern.[33]

On the other hand, the limitations of practical engagement are equally overcome. In appreciating the object of beauty, individuals must bracket out their aims and interests and treat the thing as something whose value lies not in its utility, but in its independent appearance. This means that individuals free themselves of the external impulses and passions influencing their desires and relate to the object in a manner free of any such outer compulsion. No longer does the individual face an object whose very existence signals an unfulfilled desire of an agency caught in the subjectivity of unrealized aims. Now subjects can confront the object without that confrontation signifying the limit of their freedom. By the same token, the beautiful thing liberates itself from subordination to subjective aims, laying claim to an autonomy that can only be respected by leaving it free to show itself. No longer serving purposes imposed on it or resisting their imposition by means of its natural obduracy, nor subject any more to the power of other external things, the object of beauty stands as an end in itself, exhibiting a value intrinsic to the unity of meaning and sensuous configuration it displays. Existing for the sake of its own appearance and thereby transcending all transient needs and all historical conditions of functionality, the object of beauty can enjoy an independent value enduring through the ages.[34] Given its freedom from subjective interest, this value of beauty is inherently something deserving of public appreciation, liberated from the arbitrary confines of dynastic privilege, private ownership, and the like.[35] In all these respects, beauty leaves its object just as free and unperturbed as its audience.[36]

Two Tests for Confirming the Minimal Determinacy of Beauty

Two tests need to be executed to confirm that beauty has its minimal characterization in a sensuous configuration produced by and for finite rational agents, presenting an image exemplary of fundamental truths of ethical or religious activity.

One consists in demonstrating that all the elements in this characterization are devoid of independent aesthetic character. If any already possess aesthetic significance, then "beauty" is not the primitive term with which aesthetics must begin, but a derivative concept whose foundation lies somewhere behind. This test can already be undertaken by turning to the elements at hand and certifying that none, taken by themselves, have any specifically aesthetic character. A sensuous configuration need not be beautiful any more than need be any artifact produced by and for finite rational agents. Similarly, an exemplary image need not have aesthetic value any more than the presentation of ethical, religious, or scientific truths need have any beauty. Consequently, our characterization of beauty does not beg the question.

The second test, however, cannot be undertaken here at the outset. It consists in demonstrating that all further features of aesthetic reality incorporate beauty as a necessary ingredient. This confirmation of the elementary character of beauty can only be achieved by the completed unfolding of aesthetic discourse, whose conceptual development should amount to a progressive confirmation of the nonarbitrary character of its starting point.

Chapter 7

The Existence of Beauty in the Work of Art

The minimal determination of aesthetic value has issued in an identification of beauty with artistic beauty and of aesthetics with the philosophy of fine art. Consequently, systematic aesthetics must now determine the features ingredient in each and every realization of beauty in a work of art, no matter what form of artistic expression or what individual art is at stake. If, instead, aesthetics were to address particular artistic forms or separate arts without further ado, it would take for granted what qualifies these as realizations of artistic beauty, deserving of treatment in the first place.

Conceiving Aesthetic Value as Artistic Beauty

Where, then, must the account of artistic beauty begin? The realization of beauty in the work of fine art is ubiquitously acknowledged to have three constitutive dimensions: the creation of the work by the artist, the objective reality of the work itself, and its relation to its audience. All three seem inherently interconnected. The creation of the work of fine art can only count as such so far as its product conforms to what defines the actuality of beauty in art, which equally includes existing for its audience. By the same token, how the work of fine art exists reflects its genesis as well as its relation to the reception of rational agents. And similarly, the aesthetic reception of the work depends on the creative process that generates the object of fine art and on the objective features that mark its existence as something for aesthetic appreciation. Does this interconnection render the specific point of departure for theoretical analysis an arbitrary convenience?

It might seem that the only ground for starting with one aspect rather than another is the genetic ordering of these dimensions. Since the creation of the work of fine art precedes its actuality and the work's existence first makes possible its reception, is it not sensible to begin with artistic creation, proceed to the objective reality of the work, and conclude with an account of its relation to its audience?

This route may follow the temporal succession in which these dimensions of artistic beauty actually arise, but it founders on a dilemma that eliminates it as a viable path for conceptual determination. The problem is that unless the basic character of artistic beauty has already been established, the activity of the artist cannot be certified to have produced a work of fine art and count as an act of artistic creation. This applies not only to an external assessment of artistic activity but also to the self-understanding of the artist internal to artistic creation. To the degree that artists create works of art with a conscious awareness of the aesthetic character of their activity, an awareness that is itself predicated on an understanding of the aesthetic status of their product, artistic creation cannot even proceed without some prior notion of artistic beauty.

A like priority applies to the relation of the work to its audience. As the self-vitiating formality of transcendental aesthetics reveals, unless the art object can already qualify as an object of artistic beauty, the relation to its audience cannot be identified as aesthetic. For if, instead, the effect of the work on the audience comes first, as the locus for determining aesthetic value, beauty becomes a means to an external end, caught in the categories of technique that prove incapable of identifying what is specific to fine art. In these respects, artistic creation and art appreciation both incorporate and presuppose the determinacy of the work of fine art. Thus, if any of these three dimensions has any logical primacy, it is the actuality of beauty in the work of fine art.

Yet even this may be too concrete to be a proper starting point. Now that aesthetic value has been established to be artistic beauty, is there not something to be said about the beauty of fine art in general prior to an account of its realization in an actual work? The order of Hegel's treatment suggests such a course, for, although he addresses the work of fine art before conceiving artistic creativity, he deals first of all with the determination of artistic beauty in general, which he calls the Ideal.[1]

The basis for beginning with artistic beauty before addressing the work of fine art lies in a distinction that makes possible, and indeed necessary, a prior account of the beauty of art. This is the distinction between the content and the expression of artistic beauty. Admittedly, the unity of form and content, of universal and individual, or of meaning and configuration in beauty might seem to eliminate any distinction between content and expression. Yet these unities cannot be sustained unless some differentiation persists allowing for the constituent terms that are to be united. Otherwise, the work of art becomes reduced to a mere thing, whose essence resides in its physical attributes, completely ignoring the constitutive role of associated meaning, the contextualization underlying that association, and the relation to audience and artist that concomitantly enter into the transfiguration of appearance basic to the work of art. Hence, however interconnected content and expression may be, they retain a distinction that permits the "soul" of the work of art to be provisionally characterized in its own right. Needless to say, this does not prevent artistic beauty from becoming progressively further qualified in conjunction with its realization in the work of fine art in general, in particular modes of artistic expression, and in different individual arts.

As with the introduction of any new topic in a systematic account, what here provides legitimation are two complementary considerations. One is that the determinacy of the new relation incorporate no terms that have not already been established. The other is that subsequent argument confirm the introduction of the new topic by exhibiting how all further terms incorporate the one now at issue. In the present case, this signifies, first, that the beauty of art must contain no elements of independent aesthetic significance that have not already been determined in the minimal account of beauty; and second, that artistic beauty be incorporated within any further conception of the reality of the work of fine art, its reception, and its creation. Since the first desideratum can be addressed at once, whereas the second hangs on the course of subsequent argument, the justification of the advance can only be partly at hand and partly awaiting fulfillment.

Content and Expression in the Work of Fine Art

Provisionally speaking, beauty has two basic features that underlie its existence in the work of art: a content and the expression of that content. Although this distinction proves itself ingredient in any object of fine art, it is perhaps most plainly visible at the threshold of artistic creation. An account of artistic creation is not a prerequisite for identifying the content of artistic beauty in distinction from its expression, for all the reasons cited above that make the actuality of the work of art come first for investigation. Yet, to provide a provisional plausibility, it is worth noting the following by way of anticipation.

Given the intentional, purposive character of the production of the work of art by the artist, artistic beauty involves a content comprising a meaning that figures as an aim in contrast to its realization.[2] By contrast, the appearance that realizes this content is its expression. As an aim, the content might appear to function no differently than the purpose underlying the artisanal making of an artifact. If that were so, the putative work of fine art would lack the concrete universality of beauty and instead embody an antecedently given form indifferent to the sensuous detail of its individual realization. To escape this dilemma and qualify as an element in the realization of beauty, the content of the work of art must instead be uniquely tied to its expression so that the individual appearance expressing the content retains an essential relation to it.

This intrinsic connection between content and expression does not prevent their distinction from playing a constitutive role in the realization of beauty in fine art. To begin with, the content is *subjective* insofar as it comprises a provisionally represented meaning intended to be realized in a concrete expression by the artist.[3] Yet the content, in its subjective reality as a represented meaning that ought to be realized in an objective appearance, is not in the same position as the purpose antecedently conceived by the maker of an artifact. The latter purpose, being a common form given prior to its realization, dictates the complete essential character of the finished artifact without undergoing any alteration in its own content. By contrast, the content of the work of fine art cannot remain unaltered in its passage from its subjective reality as an aim of the artist to its objectification as the indwelling meaning of the completed creation. It can only achieve its unity with its expression through a process of transformation inherent in beauty's coming to determinate existence in the work of art. Thanks to this development, content and expression can be differentiated without violating the concrete universality of beauty.

The question raised by this distinction of meaning and sensuous configuration is whether there is anything that holds true of the content of artistic beauty, independently of how it gets expressed. When Hegel undertakes to determine the Ideal as such, he is addressing this very issue.

Beyond Mimesis to the Minimal Content of Artistic Beauty

The identification of aesthetic value with the beauty of art has minimally determined artistic beauty to be the display given in intuition or imagination of a sensuous appearance produced by rational agency, exhibiting concrete universality, and providing in its exemplary image a self-understanding for rational agents concerning those affairs of humanity of inherent significance.

The dilemmas of metaphysical aesthetics and the limitations of natural beauty together underscore how the beauty of art cannot offer rational agents this self-understanding by engaging in mimesis, be it of inanimate nature, animal life, the given physical appearance of rational agents, or the immediate reality of their ethical or religious practices. Any such direct imitation of given phenomena will fail to present the thoroughgoing unity of meaning and configuration characterizing beauty's concrete universality.[4] However faithful the mimetically produced image may be, it will have no value of its own, for it can neither surpass the original as an object of desire nor invest the appearance of its object with any more significance than its contingent singularity already commands.

What condemns naturalism as a bogus strategy for fine art is its inability to avoid this pitfall. By seeking to represent reality as it immediately appears, naturalism fails to comprehend that although beauty must convey truths of inherent significance for rational agents, its exemplary images can only do so in a way worthy of independent display if they transfigure the given, imaginatively reshaping the inner and outer life of humanity in created appearances whose detail is fraught with meaning. Achieving verisimilitude is artistically not enough, even if it involves retrieving for public view the lower depths of social life and the unacknowledged experiences of excluded minorities, castes, classes, genders, and sexual orientations. The unmasking of such concealed territories only attains aesthetic worth if it transfigures its find, infusing the banished appearances with the heightened significance required by the unity of form and content in art.

It is this transfiguration that makes art provide a truth that is irreducible to the mere correctness, the mere corresponding of representations to given phenomena, to which mimesis is limited.[5] The special unity of meaning and configuration in beauty requires that the conformity of content and expression be based on a content that is already concretely universal and thereby capable of fully manifesting its significance in a unique sensuous appearance.[6] Because given phenomena are always burdened by contingency and external influence, they cannot deliver such a content, except indirectly, when transfigured through the creativity of artistic imagination.

This is why it makes sense for Hegel to characterize the content of artistic beauty as the Ideal. Appearance as it is naturally or historically given is fundamentally inadequate for immediate appropriation as a vehicle of aesthetic value. To enter at all, it must undergo a purification by the imagination, stripping it of everything indifferent and extraneous to its meaning and injecting whatever content is necessary to make this meaning serve as a mode of self-understanding for rational agents.[7] The beauty of art is thereby inherently ideal, transcending natural and historical givenness and issuing as a product of imagination. Yet, though ideal, the beauty of art still has an external existence of its own, transcending the interiority of mind and the universality of thought. Remaining an appearance with a sensuous content, be it given to intuition or to literary imagination, the ideal of artistic beauty is neither abstract nor wholly intellectual. To paraphrase Hegel, in echo of Aristotle's famous dictum on poetry's relation to history and philosophy, the ideal of beauty in art falls between the extremes of the singularity of given existence and the universality of conceptual thought, coming to rest at that center where external and internal coincide.[8]

The transfiguration of given appearance into artistic beauty can, of course, take manifold forms, running the gamut from the formal contextual placement of "found" art to the more concrete modifications of realism to the imaginative play of abstract expressionism. Even when given appearances are artistically appropriated with the greatest verisimilitude, they are wrested from the space and time of their immediate existence and fixed within new boundaries that artistic imagination superimposes on nature and history.[9] Mundane objects whose given existence may be of paltry interest can be artistically employed to display an exalted creative vision,[10] just as epochal events may be completely made over in the artistic imagination in order to join their indwelling significance to a sensuous configuration.

In each case, the independence of artistic beauty from the given confines of phenomenal existence does not signify a flight away from reality. The opposition between mimetic art and art for art's sake represents a false dichotomy. It wrongly presupposes on either hand that a discrepancy in content between prosaic reality and artistic beauty deprives art of any inherent connection with objective truth. Quite to the contrary, artistic beauty's transfiguration of given phenomena is precisely what allows it to furnish exemplary configuration to the truths of humanity. For this reason, no external restraints must be put on art to compel it to address reality. The requirements of aesthetic value themselves mandate the sensuous construal of truth. Moreover, they mandate it in such a way that any attempt to subordinate art to independently given aims will reinstate the dilemmas of mimesis and undermine art's aesthetic integrity.

At this juncture, where the minimal determination of the beauty of art is at stake, what counts is identifying the common range of content underlying all realizations of artistic beauty. Granted the fundamental divide between given appearance and the beauty of fine art, is there anything more that necessarily pertains to the content of artistic beauty in distinction from its expression in the work of fine art?

The crux of the answer revolves around what else will have to be true about the created exemplary images of artistic beauty for them to provide self-understanding for rational agents about their fundamental concerns. In addressing this issue, it is impossible to escape a certain methodological limitation. Whatever pertains to artistic beauty per se must be so general as to be able to underlie every particular form of artistic creation and every individual art. However, to decide whether a candidate for the minimal content of artistic beauty satisfies this requirement of generality requires knowledge of the forms of art and the individual arts. Yet a systematic account of these depends on already determining artistic beauty, which figures as a structural component of them all. Consequently, when artistic beauty in general is at issue, any attempt to adjudicate a proposal by judging whether it can be incorporated in classical or romantic art or in architecture, music, painting, and the like can at best have an anticipatory value.

An entry into characterizing the beauty of art is provided by the two areas of fundamental concern that are susceptible of sensuous configuration. As we have seen, if beauty is to sensuously display truths of inherent significance to rational agents, the appropriate domains consist of the spheres of ethics and religious belief. Accordingly, artistic beauty can be said to incorporate in some respect truths about either ethical activity, broadly understood as the entire domain of normatively valid conduct and institutions, or the divine in its relation to rational agents. When Hegel proceeds to characterize the Ideal, that is, the beauty of art, by successively analyzing how religious and ethical truths must be construed in order to be sensuously configured, he points the way that should be followed.

The Divine as an Object of Fine Art

How can the divine figure as a content within the beauty of art? Although this question does not depend on whether the divine exists, it hangs on a general problem central to ontotheology: how the divine can be thought to appear in the element of sensuous reality. On the one hand, the divine seems to retain its infinitude and universal oneness only as a transcendent being to which no image can do justice. Yet, on the other hand, if the divine is above all sensuous individuality, it seems to forfeit its infinitude by failing to incorporate the finite, which thereby stands as a limit restricting divinity. This difficulty is compounded by how universality, particularity, and individuality are interdependent, such that the universal is determined by its particularization into a plurality of individuals and individuality depends on the differentiation of particulars falling under a common universal.[11] Applied to the mind-body problem, these considerations lead to the insight that the individuated identity of mind depends on it having a recognizable embodiment that is differentiated from the embodiment of other minds.[12] In function of these requirements, the divine cannot retain any individuality without relinquishing its exclusive oneness and transcendence.

Yet complementary dilemmas arise if the divine incorporates the finite to retain its infinitude or divides into a plurality of divinities to retain its individuality and spiritual unity. By encompassing the finite to eliminate it as an external limit, the divine runs the risk of succumbing to the pitfall of pantheism, where the identification of the divine with sensuous nature eliminates transcendence and renders divinity superfluous. By individuating itself through the differentiation of many divinities, the divine falls prey to the dilemma of polytheism, where the contrast of a plurality of gods renders each particular and limited, undermining the last vestige of infinitude. Whether or not these problems are resolvable, they set the parameters with which the artistic representation of the divine must cope.

If the divine is taken simply as unity, universality, and infinity, it is rendered an intangible idea available to thought but insusceptible of sensuous configuration by the imagination. Literature may be able to express such abstract content in words, but these words will have an aesthetic appeal only if they express something else particular in content, such as the feeling of devotion by which individuals may relate to their immaterial, undifferentiated deity.[13] Otherwise, the only option for giving sensuous shape to such divinity is by somehow presenting images that point beyond themselves, as emblems of a sublime deity that can only be perceived indirectly by means of symbolic representations.[14]

On the other hand, once the divine is taken to be a concrete unity, neither divorced from everything finite nor devoid of differentiation, it becomes a ready subject for sensuous configuration by the imagination. As concretely individuated, the divine is susceptible of imaging in two basic respects. First, in function of achieving identity by being distinguished into a realm of particular gods, divinity can appear as a polytheistic vision of a multitude of sensuously distinct gods. Second, in function of sustaining its infinitude by incorporating finite appearance, divinity can be represented in the sensuous form of finite beings, as well as come to perceivable shape in the activities of rational agents in their relation to the divine. In either case, this entanglement with mundane existence allows the sensuously construable content of the divine to involve the whole range of humane activities.[15] Needless to say, in all these configurations, the requirements of concrete universality must be met, so that every detail of the image be essential to the manifestation of the divine content at issue.

Hegel appropriately introduces these options as the three basic modes in which an essentially determinate divinity can figure as a content of artistic beauty.[16] In addition, he duly recognizes that the imaginable content of a concrete divinity must retain some means of holding together its manifold differentiation or else forfeit its own identity. To this end, the divine as an object of artistic beauty must exhibit some dimension of self-repose transcending the exigencies of the world. Even though the requirements of sensuous configuration mandate that the divine content involve mundane affairs and/or relations among particular gods, the divine will not be worthy of the name unless it equally rises above external influence and displays an inviolable, self-sufficient sanctity. This can be displayed as much by remaining impervious to the play of finite interests as by becoming their master, overpowering the particular passions of individuals and reconciling them with the divine in which their true essence putatively lies.[17]

The Transition to Ethical Action as an Object of Artistic Beauty

As we have seen, besides the divine, the other sensuously configurable content that can afford a worthwhile self-understanding to rational agents is the realm of ethical conduct and its institutions. Consequently, systematic aesthetics must address how the ethical domain must be determined to figure as an object of artistic beauty.

Hegel introduces this theme in a somewhat ambiguous manner, as if the move from the divine to ethical action were not simply a transition from one option to another but a reflection of how the particularization of spirit is bound up with development.[18] On this understanding, the systematic account of the beauty of art turns first to the divine as a matter of addressing how and why artistic beauty must adopt the form of the particular. Then it turns to action as a matter of accounting for how the content of artistic beauty must obtain its particularity by differentiating itself, that is, by its own activity.[19] Such an ordering poses several difficulties. First, the account of the divine as an object of artistic beauty already includes action, be it among particular deities or in the mundane world where rational agents relate to their gods. Indeed, the self-repose of the divine is constitutively tied to an immersion in the activity of worldly affairs. Second, the account of ethical activity involves determinations of the situation from which conduct unfolds that just as much precede the development of action as does the concretization of the divine. On both scores, it makes greater sense to make the move from the treatment of the divine to that of ethical action as a transition from one domain of artistic content to another. It must be recognized, however, that the two domains are not mutually exclusive. The imaginable relations among gods and between mortals and the divine can involve ethical affairs, just as conduct and normative institutions can have a religious dimension.

Preliminary Suspicions Regarding Ethical Action as an Object of Artistic Beauty

The turn to ethical action as an object of artistic beauty might seem to represent a regression to or perhaps a belated vindication of metaphysical aesthetics' affirmation of praxis as the privileged subject matter of imitative art's edifying labors. In one respect the parallel is valid, for systematic aesthetics is in a position to reappropriate that side of metaphysical aesthetics that groped with how the given appearances of praxis had to be transfigured in order to acquire aesthetic value. Yet whereas metaphysical aesthetics never freed its conception of this transfiguration from the external aim of edification and the categories of mimetic craft, systematic aesthetics must now carry through this liberation.

Before proceeding, it is important to note two related criticisms that have arisen in the face of Hegel's own attempt to accomplish this enterprise. Although the general content of artistic beauty should be sufficiently minimal that any form of art and any individual art can incorporate it, this requirement seems doubly violated by the account of how ethical action figures as an object of artistic beauty. For, to take Hegel's analysis as a guide, the way in which conduct gets sensuously configured (in respect to the general world condition of ethical action, the particular situation from which it ensues, and the individual action itself and the character it makes manifest) seems, first of all, to be applicable in its entirety only to literature, only partially to painting and sculpture, and not at all to music and architecture. Moreover, the state of the world, the kind of conflict, and the act and character that allegedly lend themselves to sensuous configuration seem to fit the classical form of art, but neither the symbolic nor the romantic forms. These discrepancies appear to reflect both a failure to attain a sufficient conceptual universality and a bias in favor of classicism. Such charges, which have been understandably raised by Adorno, Bloch, Lukács, and Szondi, among others,[20] need to be confronted in reference not just to Hegel's own particular writing but to the problem per se of determining ethical action as an object of artistic beauty. The resolution of the issue ultimately depends on also determining the forms of art and the individual arts themselves. At this point, however, it bears noting that although certain forms of art and individual arts may be best able to incorporate the full breadth of configurable conduct, this does not preclude the others from still being constitutively informed by its content. Symbolic and romantic art may yet address ethical themes in their particular way, just as character can be disclosed in the feeling expressed by lyric poetry or music, and just as the stature of action can be reflected by the environments in which architecture houses it and landscape and still life surround it.

Chapter 8

Conduct as an Object of Artistic Beauty

The central place of conduct as an object of artistic beauty hardly comes as a surprise, granted that aesthetic value resides in exemplary images providing significant self-understanding to rational agents. What else but the appearance of conduct can reveal affairs inherently important to humanity?[1] Not only does personal integrity lie in the actions in which character becomes manifest, but all normative institutions exist no place else than in the activities by which their members fulfill their institutional roles.

Yet because the immediate existence of conduct and institutions is unavoidably replete with external influences and contingencies of no ethical significance, the appearance of ethical activity must be transfigured in order to attain the unity of meaning and configuration required for aesthetic value. This transfiguration applies to all the fundamental dimensions of ethical action: the general state of the world in which conduct occurs, the particular type of situation from which a course of action arises, and the individual action itself together with the character of the agent it makes manifest.

To determine how this transfiguration occurs, two resources must properly be drawn on: the requirements of artistic beauty that have already been determined, and the character of valid conduct as established in ethics. Whereas the former requirements lie ready at hand within aesthetics, the anatomy of valid conduct lies determined outside in the systematically prior discourse of ethical philosophy. In addition to making aesthetics once more dependent on another philosophical inquiry, this predicament introduces another complication.

Ethics conceives valid conduct to consist in a system of different spheres, each with its own rights and duties, structure of interaction, and type of agency.[2] Consequently, a full account of how conduct figures in artistic beauty must consider these varied domains and whether or not different problems arise in their respective transfigurations as contents for art.

These different domains consist of the sphere of persons and property with its rights and duties of ownership, the sphere of moral agency with its rights and duties of moral responsibility, the sphere of the family with its rights and duties of spouses and of parents and children, the sphere of civil society with its economic and legal rights and duties, and the sphere of politics with its rights and duties of self-government. Granted that this differentiation is complete,[3] to what extent are these spheres susceptible of artistic treatment, and on what general terms?

To answer this question, some decision must first be made concerning which aspect of ethical action to begin with: the general world condition comprising the ultimate background of conduct, the particular situation from which an action arises, the course of the action itself, or the character displayed in it. Then, each aspect can be considered in due order in regard to the different spheres of ethics.

The General Background of Conduct as an Object of Artistic Beauty

Systematically speaking, the point of departure for determining ethical activity as an object of artistic beauty is the general condition in which action proceeds. Little else is feasible, for whatever particular situation gives rise to a certain action will already be predicated on this state of the world, as will, by extension, any individual action and any character that agents therein exhibit. Yet, in duly proceeding to identify what determination the general setting of conduct must possess in order to figure in a work of art, two sorts of answers are possible: one that applies equally to every form of ethical conduct, and one that differentiates between the common conditions of action in each ethical sphere. To provide either answer, it is necessary first to take into account the general state of affairs from which each mode of conduct unfolds and then to determine how the given appearance of such situations must be transfigured to bear aesthetic value.

Nature, Technology, and Convention: The Ubiquitous Environment of Conduct

Nature, technology, and convention present certain basic features that apply to the general predicament in which ethical activity proceeds.[4] Without their presence conduct cannot appear in any determinate manner, and for this reason aesthetics must comprehend how they are to be construed as a content for art.

In the first place, conduct is always situated within a world of nature. Action cannot fail to occur at a particular time and in a particular place with those necessary and contingent geographical features that are endemic to the environment of rational agents, whatever be their continent, ocean, or atmosphere, or their planet, solar system, or galaxy. In this respect, the artistic construal of action requires a certain fidelity to nature, for unless the background of conduct manifests enough natural features to provide a specific setting in the world, action and rational agency are cast adrift of any definite mooring that might allow them to have an individuated, sensuously determinable appearance. This minimal requirement does not dictate, however, that the environment in which conduct is depicted imitate nature as it appears in experience. It rather entails a fullness of detail imaginatively determined in function of allowing exemplary conduct to obtain a sensuous configuration. Artistically construable conduct must be situated in a world, but that world can just as well be a product of fantasy as a reconstruction of prosaic nature. In either case, the imagined natural environment should be one whose appearances are transfigured so as to be always relevant to the action under way. Direct imitation of all the contingent appearance of actual nature is just as aesthetically unsatisfactory as presenting a fictional world in unnecessarily extensive or arbitrary detail. As a content for art, the natural environment must appear in this implicit unity with the conduct it surrounds.[5]

Second, since rational agents can hardly act without working upon nature in service of their needs and purposes, technology and the satisfactions it sustains must equally be manifest. Once again, slavish imitation has no place, for the appearance of the metabolism of rational agents with nature must be tailored in conformity with the sensuous configuration of exemplary conduct. This conformity requires that the interaction of rational agents with nature not preclude any opportunity for action in pursuit of ethical aims. To figure as a content for art, the metabolism of individuals and nature cannot be so desperately demanding that all energies must be consumed in the struggle for survival, leaving no time for ethical conduct.[6] On the other hand, this metabolism cannot be so idyllically untaxing that natural necessity imposes no burdens on action. Then, the concrete conditions of finite agency would be obliterated, undercutting the sensuous configuration of conduct.[7] The place of technology must be an intermediate one, where the domination of nature remains a perennial but manageable challenge, leaving space for a sphere of action in which questions of the good life can be raised and contested, introducing needs whose satisfaction transcends any technological solution.[8] Moreover, the appearance of the metabolism between rational agency and nature must be configured to frame a collision within that accompanying ethical sphere, with all extraneous features left aside.

Third, since ethical conduct always involves individuals inhabiting specific cultural communities with customs and histories of their own, these conventional givens of mundane existence must also find their place.[9] For although exemplary conduct addresses problems of universal significance, the individuality of action automatically clothes any ethical encounter with usages and habits that are peculiar to a specific era and community. Once again, what counts is not depicting all these sides of ordinary existence as they appear in experience, but rather conveying enough of their detail to allow the depiction of exemplary conduct to have a worldly reality sufficient to sustain its due individuation. Otherwise, conduct becomes an abstraction, indifferent to its sensuous configuration.

The Differentiation of Alternative World Conditions

Incorporating these ubiquitous environmental dimensions is not the end of the matter, however, for the world condition is further distinguished in terms of two basic alternatives extending to all types of ethical conduct. The world condition may be one in which a sphere of conduct already exists, or it may be one in which what lies at hand is the struggle to bring it into being. In the former case, action takes place against a backdrop in which property relations, moral accountability, family rights and duties, social relations, and political institutions already exist in accord with their normative principles. This comprises a situation where individuals can act in observance of prevailing norms or commit violations of the sort endemic to the different ethical spheres themselves. In the latter case, action confronts a world in which the spheres of ethical activity have yet to be adequately realized. As a consequence, the ethical challenges of agents here lie not in conforming to recognized rights and duties and remedying violations of standing structures of normative interaction, but in counteracting invalid practices and replacing them with those in which ethical agency is at home. Both conditions unavoidably involve contingent circumstances indifferent to the ethical activities they precipitate. In this respect, both need imaginative reconstrual to present an appearance whose configuration is imbued with a significant meaning. Yet is there any ground for maintaining that one of these general states of affairs is more susceptible of aesthetic transfiguration than the other or even uniquely appropriate as a subject of artistic beauty?

Hegel, who duly examines the general backdrop of action as the first stage in his investigation of how ethical activity figures in art,[10] argues that one world condition is more suited to artistic incorporation, even suggesting that it alone provides a ready field for artistic beauty. This aesthetically privileged world condition is the state of affairs where the structures of right have yet to be founded. Calling this condition a heroic age, Hegel argues that in such circumstances of revolutionary challenge, where individuals can participate in overthrowing unethical practices and in founding legitimate forms of life, individual action can more readily be imbued with universal significance. In such a predicament, matters of the greatest import hinge directly on the individual efforts of agents. For where the system of right has yet to gain institutional stability, there are no prevailing institutions whose impersonal operation can be counted on to uphold the rights and duties of all. On the contrary, heroic action is the order of the day, action that aims at founding the very institutions of right that are of fundamental concern. Consequently, this world condition is one where what is of universal ethical significance is immediately affirmed in individual conduct and where the independent activity of individuals is most closely tied to the realization of right. For in the absence of law and settled governance, ethical conduct has little option but to rise to the occasion and be exemplary in deed.[11]

By contrast, Hegel maintains, the post-heroic world condition, where action takes place in a realm of established institutions of right, is an obdurately prosaic environment in which the unity of universal and individual never immediately appears. Where legitimate practices already prevail, the affirmation of right no longer hangs on what any one individual undertakes. Overcoming the subjective contingencies of personal temperament and initiative, the anonymous workings of the system of justice are the abiding guarantee for the realization of the good. On its own account, the action of an individual can only be of particular significance, restricted in meaning to a specific interest or locale. Even if an individual here acts from a position of highest public authority, it is the impersonal institutions of justice that hold sway, making the locus of concern the general prerogatives of office rather than the unique conduct of the officeholder. Precisely by carrying through the institutionalization of right, this world condition resists aesthetic appropriation.[12]

Hegel judges that modernity has given rise to the legitimate structures that constitute such a prosaic world condition. Accordingly, he can conclude that as the modern age brings valid ethical institutions toward their universal realization, it will be an increasingly inhospitable source for artistic inspiration.[13] One could, however, equally observe that modernity's introduction of valid institutions has not borne a world condition intractable to artistic construal. For, insofar as modernity remains a battlefield in which these developments remain partial and contested, the era for "heroic" action is far from over.

Leaving such historical debates aside, the more important theoretical issue is whether a heroic world condition has any aesthetic preeminence over its legitimized successor, let alone the exclusive suitability that Hegel's argument might suggest. A world condition in which ethical practices already prevail may well diminish the universal significance of any individual action in its immediate givenness. Yet even so, this cannot directly preclude such a world from being the object of artistic beauty. What counts is whether such an environment is susceptible of any aesthetically redeeming transfiguration that could infuse its incipient conduct with a sufficiently meaningful appearance. By the same token, what is here at stake regarding the heroic world condition is not simply identifying its structure, but determining how it can figure as an object of artistic beauty.

It must be kept in mind that the investigation of world conditions as elements in the content of artistic beauty is distinct from an inquiry into how different actual world conditions affect the production and reception of art. How and to what degree the existence of certain institutions influences what contents can be employed by the artistic imagination and appreciated by an audience does not impinge on the questions of what contents can be subject to aesthetic construal in general and how that construal transfigures them. In fact, the former issue presupposes the latter, insofar as the determination of what is inherent in the content of art must be present in whatever particular forms of art may be tied to certain historical conditions. At this juncture, it thus remains an open question whether the artistic construal of one type of world condition is in any way linked to the simultaneous existence of such an order. What instead lies at issue is the character of any such artistic construal itself.

The world condition of revolutionary challenge. To begin with, we must clarify the conceptual bounds of the world condition in which the institutions of right have not been fully realized.

Hegel himself could be suspected of giving too restrictive a characterization, indicated by his labeling this state of affairs a "heroic condition" and by his conspicuous reference to the Homeric epics as paradigmatic illustrations of its artistic employment. Within this framework, a world condition is a heroic age either by being prior to all legal enactment or by containing communities possessing no legitimacy to bind the action of their members. In either case, it serves as a backdrop for heroes whose individual character and deed can be the fountainhead of all justice, be it as founders of a state or as a law unto themselves. Given their unsettled and unjust surroundings, such heroic figures exhibit a self-reliant virtue that they possess as unique personal endowments, rather than as entitlements of a prevailing order. Yet, although this allows the personal glory of honor to figure prominently, the ethical worth of the heroes is directly united with the deeds they perform, deeds that are themselves completely at one with the ethical community that heroic action institutes and affirms. Accordingly, the heroic age is one whose heroes are held responsible for all consequences of their actions, without any distinction drawn between those results that were intended and those that were not. Indeed, their responsibility can just as well extend to the deeds of ancestors and surviving kin.[14] However, what explicitly secures the unity of individual effort and universal ethical significance is the presence of regimes of personal rule, allowing a leader's undertakings to be directly identifiable with the foundation or redemption of the ethical community. When the state of the world includes a class of rulers personally embodying the fate of the polity, acting in the absence of adequate laws and constitutional checks, heroic action is at its acme, immediately melding individual effort with what is of substantial ethical importance.[15]

Significantly, Hegel does not limit the heroic world condition to Homeric Greece, but extends it to the realms of Arabian fantasy and the sagas of European feudalism and knighthood.[16] Nevertheless, he sets the heroic world condition outside the modern present, as something best consigned to an age of myth. This is not only because modernity allegedly eliminates the space for heroic action, but because the past in general is a more hospitable arena for appearances that are to be imbued with universal significance. What makes the past specially fit for art is that it belongs to memory, whose reproductive imagination jettisons insignificant details to retain only what is worthy of remembrance. As a result, a world condition from bygone ages is one already purified in line with the requirements of beauty.[17]

Although Hegel's depiction of the heroic world provides the image of a condition in which the appearance of action can be joined to affairs of ultimate ethical significance, it must be amended on several accounts.

First, a world condition in which the institutions of right are not yet at hand need not be cast into a mythic past in order to have its content combine the individual and the universal. The recollection of past eras may already begin to filter out indifferent contingencies of detail, but the present can just as easily suffice, provided it is imaginatively transfigured rather than appropriated in its immediate givenness.

Similarly, although political deeds under conditions of personal rule may provide ready material for artistic construal, the same can be said of action addressing impediments to the various nonpolitical spheres of right. So long as the state of the world contains systemic infringements of the rights of person and property, of moral responsibility, or of family or social justice, individuals can make their immediate action count as the independent vehicle of a universal concern. Where, for instance, irrelevant natural factors of race, gender, sexual orientation, and birthright obstruct the legitimate opportunities of individuals in their disposal of property, marriage arrangements, childrearing, economic activity, and legal proceedings, they have ample room to engage in personal action that directly embodies the affirmation of right, even if they do not occupy the Archimedean position of a founder or master of the state. For this reason, a heroic age need not be ravaged by political upheaval or be home to princes or other such personal rulers in whose hands lies the fate of the nation.

Nor need its inhabitants be caught in a world in which the moral distinction between intended act and unintended consequences or between personal and collective guilt counts for nothing. Moral accountability may be acknowledged at the same time that other rights are flouted, leaving space for action of sufficient independent significance to be incorporated in art. So long as some of the structures of justice remain unrealized, there is abundant opportunity for individual initiative to manifest an unprosaic worth. The heroic age may well include the classical features Hegel emphasizes, but it may just as readily have a far wider scope. For this reason, it is perhaps more appropriate to describe the world condition in which institutions of justice are wanting as one of revolutionary challenge.

The world condition of established institutions of justice. The world condition of action suitable for artistic configuration may extend beyond the confines of a classical heroic era, but can it include a state of affairs in which impersonal institutions of justice duly enforce all the rights and duties of individuals in their capacities as persons, moral subjects, family members, civilians,[18] and citizens?

As we have seen, Hegel largely dismisses this latter possibility, taking as his cue the prosaic character he observes increasingly prevailing in modern life. The problem modernity presents to artistic construal, Hegel suggests, is that whatever individual action affirms as ethically significant is already embodied in standing institutions that impersonally secure all rights. Under such conditions, all that depends on the immediate effort of agents is the personal dimension of their activity, which here is of little more than private interest. Public leaders may contribute to ethically significant affairs by fulfilling their functions, but in so doing they merely act in accord with guidelines antecedently dictated by legislation and policed by impartial external authorities. All that derive from individual effort are the personal qualities that incidently clothe their public tenure. Otherwise, agents are cogs in a well-oiled machine of justice, who may act independently in disposing of personal property, in acting morally, in leading their family life, in entering the market, in pleading in the courts, or in engaging in self-government, but who never achieve anything of more than personal significance by power of their own action alone. One may here enjoy the status of a person entitled to respect and opportunity, but in one's conduct whatever good results is due as much to the efforts of others and established institutions as to oneself. The only focus of interest left is the purely particular matter of what happens to one in the course of one's life.[19]

Consequently, Hegel observes, modern artists are at pains to reintroduce a substantial element into modern action that can give their art a suitable content. They may try to resurrect a semblance of a heroic condition by appealing to individuals who break the bonds of existing law and order and assert themselves as independent avengers of wrong and oppression. Yet, so long as the institutions of justice still prevail, such scenarios can offer only deeds of insignificant scope and isolation, bordering on private revenge or on quixotic undertakings that are blind to their own absurdity.[20]

No doubt, Hegel has here touched on a genuine difficulty, reflected in how frequently modern art has turned to the margins of established institutions to find a suitable setting for action, be it in the "unsettled" frontiers of the Wild West, the exotic Orient, the high seas, and outer space, in the circumscribed crusades of crime fighters, or in the private recesses of romance and psychological confession. From the Lone Ranger to Dirty Harry, from Melville to Conrad, from time machines to star wars, and from Harlequin romance to Sylvia Plath, the coming of modernity has haunted art, high or low, with a common problem of finding some place where the individual retains an essential significance.

Yet, if we confront a world of just institutions from which there is no escape, a world that the modern age has yet to furnish, is the background for action as unyieldingly prosaic as Hegel prophesies?

Admittedly, with legitimate political institutions ensuring that democratic self-government sustains itself, that social welfare is publicly guaranteed, that laws are duly enacted and enforced by police and courts, that family relations are adequately regulated by the courts and public agencies, that moral responsibility is given its due to the degree that this can be externally upheld, that the rights of persons are maintained, and that in all its constitutive spheres freedom has been realized, it seems hard to find any action whose individual configuration commands exemplary importance, rather than lawful typicality.

The due exercise of one's property rights appears just as unaesthetically mundane as acting with rectitude as a spouse or parent, earning a living in the market, campaigning and voting in elections, or playing one's role as a civil servant or government official. In each case, what is unique to the agent is of little significance beside the worth of ethical practices that are independently maintained by the existing system of constitutional government in which freedom is realized.

Yet even within this pervasively prosaic state of affairs, there remains a sphere in which the personal character of action is wedded to normative validity. This is the sphere of morality, in which agents interact in terms of their accountability for the actions they have intended and the motives underlying their purposes.[21] In respect to the role accorded the personal dimension of subjective willing, moral interaction stands distinct both from the abstract right of property relations and from the concrete ethical community of the family, civil society, and the state.

In interacting as owners, persons do not make the particular content of their interests and intentions the focus of right. Rather, what matters as far as property entitlements themselves are concerned is simply that the embodiment of the will in an external factor be respected, whatever be the motives and preferences accompanying its exercise. When individuals put their personal interests first and thereby transgress the property entitlements of others, their affirmation of the particularity of their will is bereft of value, counting instead as a wrong that contradicts their own rights as persons. Although the committing of wrong might seem a good candidate for artistic appropriation, given how it revolves around the singular willing of the malefactor, under conditions of established justice criminal activity is demonstrated to be the nullity it is by the impersonal workings of the police and judicial system. Crime and punishment can here only borrow aesthetic suitability if the action can be made to resonate with some other ethical concern besides the prosaic proceedings by which juridical wrong is routinely handled.

Analogously, in the ethical associations of the family, civil society, and the state, the personal deeds of their members have a restricted normative significance, preventing a thorough melding of appearance and meaning. Although personal preferences can enter in as factors of right in regard to family affairs and economic activity, the rights in question never depend on an individual action for their realization. In each case, whenever participating individuals direct their action at goals of normative worth, these are already embodied in existing institutions that provide the context within which such aims can first be sought. Family members can only fulfill their obligations to their spouses, children, and parents if they belong to a household realizing the rights on whose existence such action is predicated. Similarly, members of civil society and the state can exercise their entitled economic, legal, and political roles only by belonging to a social and political order whose legitimate practices of regulated markets, courts, and self-government already sustain themselves independently of any one of the actions transpiring in their spheres.

By contrast, when individuals interact as moral subjects, their personal initiatives take center stage. In morality, agents hold each other accountable for acting with valid purpose and motive on behalf of one another's right and welfare. They do so in regard to a moral good that is not yet actual, but which depends for its determination and realization on the individual moral subject. Hence, whereas persons exercise their property rights with indifference to personal motive, and whereas members of ethical associations such as the family, civil society, and the state all aim at actualizing a good that is already embodied in the institutions making possible its pursuit, in morality, the individual willing of the agent is both fully constitutive of the moral good and uniquely responsible for its achievement.

As a consequence, morality provides an arena where the individuality of action can be wedded to universal significance even in a condition where property rights are upheld and the ethical institutions of family, society, and state already prevail. Although conscience cannot be sanctioned when it conflicts with the settled norms of these other spheres, moral action retains its place wherever practical dilemmas arise that escape resolution by the workings of the system of justice. These opportunities need not be rare, for at every level the particular realizations of right can depend on personal initiative above and beyond the preordained demands of rectitude. At these interstices, moral autonomy allows an otherwise prosaic condition of just institutions to serve as a backdrop for action worthy of art.

What distinguishes the role of morality under such settled circumstances is that it provides the exclusive domain of conduct suitable for artistic transfiguration. In contrast, under a world condition where ethical relations are lacking, all spheres of right can provide ready arenas for aesthetically serviceable action. In either case, however, the world condition is appropriable by art only by undergoing an imaginative transfiguration that makes it an environment whose boundaries and intensive detail obtain an appearance serving the significant action they encompass. By itself, the thus idealized world condition only provides a general setting. What next must be added to concretize the content that art can sensuously configure is the particular situation from which aesthetically suitable action arises.

The Precipitating Situation of Conduct as an Object of Art

The world condition presents the most general possibility for conduct susceptible of artistic appropriation, but it does not provide the specific predicament from which an individual course of action can emerge with an exemplary appearance. A particular situation must intervene to give a stimulus to such action. Given the considerable latitude characterizing the two basic types of world condition that art can utilize, what, if anything, necessarily pertains to the specific situation congruent with artistic beauty?

If we turn to Hegel for guidance, we find a proposal that again seems suspiciously restrictive for its close affinity with one form of art, the classical, and one genre of one individual art, tragic drama. Just as Hegel appeared to characterize the ideal world condition in terms specific to the Homeric epic, he now seems to conceive the particular situation following the pattern of classical tragedy. What Hegel argues is that the situation suited for artistic employment consists in an ethical collision arising from some act of violation eliciting an exemplary response. The collision in question may be the result of prior actions and, in that respect, may involve their portrayal as part of its own appearance. Yet, as a particular situation from which conduct follows, it comprises not an action suitable for artistic presentation on its own but rather an appropriate stimulus to aesthetically worthy action. Because it comprises a collision of opposing ethical forces, the situation reflects the rupture of a preexisting harmony and calls for action reestablishing that unity.[22]

In assessing the legitimacy of this outline of the situation of action ingredient in artistic beauty, the first issue to be decided is whether a situation warrants specification at all, subsequent to an account of the world condition and prior to an account of aesthetically suitable action. In order for action to have an exemplary appearance, it must involve the same concrete predicament generic to any ethical conduct. Not only must it be the act of living individuals inhabiting a world with a natural constitution, but it must imply reference to other agents, within the context of a historically given culture and institutional framework. No matter how much imagination may be responsible for determining the specific detail of this background, ethical conduct cannot fail to carry these accoutrements if it is to exist at all. Hence, the manifestation of conduct must always involve a world condition as well as the specific conjuncture in which any individual course of action arises. These two dimensions may be indicated with greater or lesser emphasis, but their presence cannot be denied without undercutting the reality of action. An account of how action figures in artistic beauty presupposes a determination of the particular situation, just as an account of the particular situation of conduct is predicated on a determination of the world condition to which the situation belongs. Hegel is therefore fully justified in maintaining that a prior determination of the situation is necessary for any account of the character of action as it figures as a content in art.[23]

However, must the situation consist in a collision of opposing ethical powers arising from an act of violation? Hegel seems to suggest that the presence of a situation full of collision may well be peculiar to only some arts, for as he points out, although dramatic art may easily incorporate ethical collisions in its subject matter, sculpture is hardly suited to portray any action at all, whereas painting can at best tackle a single moment of conduct.[24] Moreover, a collision that disrupts the unity and repose of conduct and ethical institutions may well manifest something so bereft of exemplary significance that it would be unusable by arts that can only portray one fixed content, without being able to advance to the overcoming of collision in which exemplary actions can be at hand.[25]

If these observations suggest that ethical collisions may be simply too specialized a matter for incorporation in the content of artistic beauty in general, Hegel adds complementary observations of how various historical art objects present agents removed from any particular situation, as well as in situations of complete repose. As he notes, ancient Egyptian and preclassical Greek temple sculpture will often present figures in an immobile, self-enclosed tranquility, suggesting, if anything, the absence of any situation. The same could be said of certain medieval portrayals of God the Father and Christ.[26] However, as Hegel admits, such examples primarily involve representations of the divine rather than portrayals of agents whose exemplary appearance is rooted in ethical value.[27] Might, then, the absence of situation be a possible option for devotional art, but not for secular artistry?

Yet even if a specific situation is a necessary ingredient in artistic portrayals that makes manifest exemplary character and action, can there not be situations devoid of hostile oppositions that are worthy of aesthetic appropriation? Is art to avoid bucolic settings, panoramas of peace and tranquility, gardens of play where no momentous issues require resolution, where no actions of special significance are called for, where no stimulus is provided for any exertion of inherently serious importance? If secular art is to sensuously configure exemplary conduct, then, indeed, such harmless situations offer at best settings to be left behind on the way toward conjunctures that challenge character and action to make a worthy appearance.[28]

A similar aesthetic deficiency afflicts situations that provide only an occasion for action, where what ensues has no determinate relation to the conjuncture from which it arises. In this case, even if the conduct that follows has an exemplary dignity, its lack of connection with its surroundings disrupts the unity of meaning and configuration, leaving the situation a prosaic residue devoid of aesthetic value. This does not signify, of course, that the wellsprings of action must lie outside the agent rather than in internal conflicts and yearnings. However, if inner struggles have no relation to their surroundings, the presence of those surroundings in the content of artistic beauty is unessential. Alternately, if the internal conflicts from which action arises bear no connection to the situation of the agent, it can be questioned whether they possess more than a subjective, arbitrary interest unworthy of artistic employment. In this respect, the withdrawal of lyric poetry into the inwardness of heart and feeling need not, and indeed, should not, signify a flight from all particular situation.[29]

Hence, situations of pure occasion are as inappropriate as idyllic pastorals. For if action transcends the insignificance of play only when it pursues aims of essential significance, and the impetus to such endeavor consists in situations where obstacles to the achievement of such goals must be overcome, then we must embrace Hegel's conclusion that corresponding opposition and conflict must be at hand in the situation of action.[30]

Nonetheless, must the opposition take the form of a collision of contending ethical powers arising from an act of violation? The answer can be decided, as Hegel proposes, by examining the basic possible types of collisions and eliminating those that are resistant to aesthetic appropriation. Broadly speaking, collisions giving a stimulus to action can be divided among those that involve purely natural conditions and those that originate in rational agency.

In the first category fall all situations where natural forces, such as tempests, droughts, earthquakes, disease, and wildlife, create a predicament where action must be taken to counter their consequences. Insofar as natural occurrences do not directly contain any ethical challenges, the action they independently elicit is of a purely technical kind, concerning the mastery of nature. Such activity has no ethical significance unless it is accompanied by a situation containing institutions and spheres of conduct where a natural misfortune affects these normative conditions so as to generate an ethical problem that calls for an ethically significant response. Consequently, purely natural collisions are too prosaic to provide a viable content for artistic beauty. At best, they elicit a particular exercise of a technical skill, which, by itself, is of no more significance than any other instance of that skill's employment. Only if natural forces become entangled with forces of convention can they figure in a condition specifically impelling exemplary conduct. In that case, however, the situation is not one of merely natural collision but one in which a conventional or, as Hegel would say, a spiritual opposition lies at hand owing to a natural circumstance.

Accordingly, of the two basic types of collisions, that resting on nature must be eliminated as a possible candidate for artistic construal. This leaves as a remaining option situations consisting in self-imposed collisions of rational agents. Since, however, natural conditions can enter in as a factor influencing conventional circumstances, the question arises as to whether such situations are as appropriate to art as those where natural forces play no role at all.

How suitable is a collision of rational agents that depends on natural conditions of some sort or other? To the degree that the powers of nature are not essential to the ethical conflicts of humanity, natural factors can only play a subordinate role as occasions from which ethical collisions break out in their own right.[31] Prominent examples of such collisions, as Hegel observes, are those where the natural fact of birth becomes a focus of ethical struggle, be it in conflicts over dynastic succession, inheritance, slavery, serfdom, caste, aristocratic privileges, racial and ethnic exclusions, or gender discrimination. In each case, an ethical response is elicited by a contradiction between conventional restrictions imposed on individuals in respect of their natural differences and the rights with which these individuals are endowed in virtue of their rational agency.[32]

Situations of this kind might seem particularly suited to artistic construal, given how a world condition of revolutionary challenge, so ripe for artistic rendering, is characterized by an underdevelopment of the institutions of justice where privileges rooted in natural difference prevail at the expense of rights. Yet, as Hegel points out, the dependence on natural conditions has its artistic liabilities. If, for instance, the bondage of an individual is beyond remedy and the only option of the oppressed is fruitless self-sacrifice or retreat into the purely personal liberty of choosing among the limited alternatives left at one's discretion, the situation is hardly pregnant with exemplary action. Conversely, if individuals assert their privileges of birth either in founding oppressive regimes or in conforming to existing institutions, their individual initiative cannot command any exemplary value either.[33] Nor are the conditions for artistic construal any better if some natural feature of an individual becomes the source of a personal passion colliding with ethical laws, for here again the conflict has a purely accidental origin, diminishing its significance.[34] In these respects, collisions of rational agents dependent on natural differences suffer from the same aesthetic weakness as collisions of purely natural origin: they each serve as occasions for conflicts that remain relative to an inherently contingent, ethically meaningless circumstance. As a result, the action they call for shares in their limitation, so long as it fails to free itself from them and they fail to become the point of departure for further collisions based directly on conflicting deeds.[35]

This leaves one type of situation unequivocally fit for artistic construal: a collision issuing from conduct independently of natural conditions. Natural factors may still enter in as occasions for the collision, but not as the determining elements deciding the shape of the conflict and the challenge it presents to rational agents. Here instead, the situation must be rooted in problems endemic to rational agency, posing tasks of importance that are not peculiar to avoidable holdovers of arbitrary circumstances. In that case, where, to paraphrase

Hegel, humanity is embroiled in a self-imposed collision concerning what is of intrinsic value,[36] artistic imagination has at its disposal a conjuncture from which exemplary action can be readily configured.

Because such a collision issues not from a natural occurrence but from an act of rational agency that produces a conflict over something of ethical or sacred importance, it makes perfect sense to characterize the impetus to further conduct as an act of violation. Unless some offense has created a genuine wrong deserving remedy, the situation has no link to the undertaking of an exemplary deed whose artistically transfigured appearance could provide a self-understanding of inherent importance.

This holds true for both types of world condition. Whether or not institutions of justice already prevail, collisions issuing from acts of violation remain a possibility. For this reason, the limited artistic suitability of collisions dependent on nature need not undermine the aesthetic viability of world conditions of revolutionary challenge, where agents confront a general predicament in which individual action can institute a whole new order of right. Even if such a predicament is replete with practices in which natural differences determine how individuals are treated, there is still always room for conflicts to arise based on actions independent of birth.

Given the structure of conduct, the situation of self-imposed wrong can take different forms involving varying degrees of responsibility. At one extreme, the offending deed can be performed in ignorance or inadvertently, setting in motion an unintended collision in response to which agents must react.[37] To have maximum aesthetic value, such a situation must involve the violation of something of inherent value, whose importance is consciously recognized by those who rise to the challenge of righting its wrong. Otherwise, whatever conduct ensues will fail to attain an exemplary dignity, due either to the insignificance of its goals or to the blindness with which they are pursued. Still, even if these conditions are met, this situation will be tainted, from an aesthetic standpoint, with an involuntary dimension diminishing the ethical challenge at hand.

This problem is avoided at the other extreme, where the act of violation is perpetrated in a premeditated manner, with full cognizance of the offense committed. In such a situation, the collision proceeds from a violation qualifying as a wrong in the fullest degree, since the offending act not only does injury to some implicit or established right but does so with malicious intent. Other accompanying circumstances being equal, the challenge to conduct is accordingly greater, giving impetus to deeds all the more exemplary.

In either case, the unity of meaning and configuration mandates that whatever content the situation has must be purged of irrelevant details and brought to that heightened shape where every aspect contributes to giving the action that ensues the exemplary significance required of artistic beauty. To achieve this, the situation must still retain its individuality and avoid reduction to a typical, all too familiar setting for predictable, trite activity.

Given the aesthetic possibilities specific to the two types of world conditions, these general dictates concerning the situation of conduct must be qualified in the following way. In a world condition of revolutionary challenge, where the institutions of right have yet to be realized in full, the situation eliciting exemplary conduct can involve a violation of right in either property, moral, family, social, or political relations, provided the sphere in question remains dependent on individual action for its enactment and safeguarding. By contrast, in a world condition of established institutions of justice, the only kind of violation that can call for an individual action commanding exemplary significance is an offense posing a distinctly moral challenge. Violations of any other form of right will be aesthetically problematic, since under conditions of established freedom, whatever individual response is undertaken will simply amount to a replaceable reflex in the self-ordering system of justice.

Beyond these qualifications, little else can be said in general about the situation of conduct as a content incorporated in artistic beauty. Within the basic limits of the type of situation where rational agents impose on themselves conflicts issuing from violations of inherently significant affairs, an inexhaustible variety of alternatives is possible under both types of world conditions.[38] Moreover, in each case, further variations may well enter in in virtue of the diverse modes of adaptation of which different forms of art and different individual arts may be capable.[39] What these turn out to be can only be determined after a systematic account has been given of the forms of art and the individual arts themselves.

At this stage of aesthetic inquiry, all that has been established are the general guidelines that decide what kind of a world condition and situation are suitable for artistic construal, guidelines that merely shape the type of collision from which aesthetically ideal conduct can commence. Since the situation performs its aesthetic duty by providing an impetus to exemplary action, what counts is how it moves the heart and mind of those agents whom it challenges to act.[40] Hence, the next matter to be determined are the features ingredient in any individual course of action that can ensue as a content for artistic beauty. Configuring the world condition and the situation within it are thus merely preliminary stages in the creation of the work of art. By themselves, they provide just the starting point from which exemplary action can finally make an appearance thanks to the transfiguring genius of artistic imagination.[41]

Conduct and Agency as Contents of Artistic Beauty

The determination of the world condition and situation of conduct susceptible of artistic construal has already provided certain strictures defining how conduct can be made a content for artistic beauty. To begin with, the conduct must issue as a response to an offense doing injury to affairs of inherent worth, and do so in cognizance of the significance of the violation. In the face of this challenge, agents must grapple with overcoming the violation and, in that respect, with reinstating the right that had been trampled. In a world condition of revolutionary challenge, artistically construable conduct can address any domain of right, whereas under conditions of established institutions of justice, such conduct will revolve around a moral dilemma. Beyond these basic dictates, what else must be true of conduct as a content for art?

If more can be said, it will pertain to the constitutive aspects of conduct as it unfolds from a particular collision in a world condition of one type or the other. The dimension that comes first, as something on which all others are predicated, is the passion with which the relevant agents are moved by the situation they confront, compelling them to react against the offense that has been committed. Then comes the action they undertake, together with the character they manifest in its execution. Finally, since the ensuing deeds are in response to an opposing ethically relevant power, they elicit reactions from that quarter, setting up the possibility of a resolution of the conflict that can bring closure to the course of action.[42] Without some such resolution, the action would come to a halt bereft of any inherent significance, contrary to the aesthetic unity of meaning and configuration.

In terms of these aspects of the course of action, its general point of departure will consist in the specific circumstances that necessitate the initial collision, impelling forward the subsequent action, reaction, and final resolution. However, there is an irreducible indeterminacy regarding exactly where this starting point lies, for the sources of the collision can be indefinitely extended either into a more and more spatially remote present or into a more and more remote past.[43] The unity of aesthetic form requires that this indeterminacy be overcome so that all that is conveyed of the circumstances be what is necessary to set up the action. This will be most clearly exhibited in relation to the immediate circumstances that lay hold of the passions of the central agents and precipitate their conduct.[44] For this reason, the point of departure of the action cannot simply be left as a prosaic fact, full of irrelevant and accidental detail.[45] It must rather be transfigured into the necessitating context that directly sets in motion the course of action, without reducing it to the typical product of an antecedently given law.

The action therefore begins in the response to a suitably proximate, imaginatively transfigured collision, a response first consisting in the cognitive and emotional reception of the collision on the part of the protagonists. Because the collision is only worthy of artistic construal if it concerns affairs of inherent value, it must involve competing forces that are universal in character. Yet, because the conflict is sensuously configured so as to elicit exemplary conduct, these forces have an individual existence in the protagonists and their deeds. As a result, it makes sense to follow Hegel in conceiving of three components in the course of action as a content of art: first, the universal forces for the sake of which the action unfolds; second, their realization in the actions and reactions of the protagonists; and third, the character of the protagonists as exhibited in their personal embroilment with the ethical dilemmas that set them at odds.[46]

The Universal Forces of Action

It might appear that the universal forces of action are nothing more than the conflicting sides of the particular situation that the protagonists confront. In that case, a separate account of these forces would be completely redundant and the course of action would contain only two components: the acts themselves and the character at play in them. However, once the situation figures as a stimulus to action, the powers in collision operate as motive forces entering into the resolve to act with which the course of action gets under way. What are now at stake, above and beyond determining the situation itself, are the generic features of these motive forces as they become internalized as guiding interests of the protagonists.

On the one hand, these interests must have the exemplary character required of the content of artistic beauty. Instead of exhibiting the contingent, local, private, arbitrary character of prosaic interests as they are immediately given in experience, the motive forces of artistically construable conduct must possess an inherent importance, a universal dignity reflecting their rationality and the justifiability this contributes. These, the supreme incentives to action, are those interests whose authority rational agents cannot fail to recognize. They are the essential cravings driving individuals to perform exemplary deeds: the perennial religious and ethical aims providing the content of art with its appropriate motive forces.[47]

However, as Hegel points out, these motives cannot enter into the content of art unless they meet two further requirements. First, they cannot already be institutionalized in positive legislation such that the impersonal workings of established legality render insignificant any individual action for or against their pursuit.[48] In that case, the conduct they elicit would be devoid of exemplary status.

Second, these motives must entail conflicts that are inherently compelling, rather than fortuitous and avoidable. If, on the contrary, a certain interest, however worthy, motivates conduct only on the occasion of some inherently meaningless circumstance, the resulting course of action becomes just as much a sham, undercutting the worth of its appearance. For this reason, Hegel, following Aristotle, is correct in maintaining that pure evil provides an inadequate motive force for eliciting exemplary conduct.[49] Unmitigated wrong is irreducibly prosaic because, in being devoid of all affirmative character, it presents a completely perfunctory challenge to conduct, a straw man whose overcoming is an empty exercise in which nothing of unique significance can arise. Individuals may well act out of sheer depravity and wickedness, but in doing so they behave without any compelling reason and thereby fail to generate a conflict of any abiding interest.

In other words, the aesthetic sin of pure evil lies in an inability to possess more than abstract universality. In being a merely negative scourge of all inherent worth, pure evil is devoid of specific content,[50] containing nothing affirmative by which determinacy could be sustained.[51] The motive powers of artistically construable conduct must, on the contrary, be essentially particularized and therefore contain positive and negative aspects at once. Otherwise, these forces remain abstractions, which can neither be sensuously configured nor be realized in an independent individual.[52]

Pathos and the Course of Action

Granted the general requirements of the world condition, the particular situation, and the motive forces eliciting aesthetically suitable conduct, what must hold true of the course of action itself as it figures in the content of art?

Already, a basic succession lies at hand, consisting first in the action elicited by an antecedent collision of ethical forces, then in the reaction of opposing powers, and, finally, in a resolution providing a unified closure to the course of action. Since, at each juncture, the opposing forces can only bring their universal content to sensuous life in the action of independent, individuated agents, the course of action consists in individuals taking action in their own right, from motivations arising out of their unique personal histories and emotional lives. The individuals in question can be divine or mortal, as well as human or nonhuman rational agents. In each case, it is essential that the inherently significant motives of action spring from within the individual heart of the agent involved. Otherwise, the ethical powers will remain abstractions, externally imposed on individuals, whose subsequent subsidiary actions will be rote motions, lacking the freedom and unpredictability of exemplary conduct.

Therefore, the aesthetic determination of individuals in action must come to revolve around what Hegel, following Aristotle, calls *pathos,* the motive force within the individual that combines an ethical power of universal significance with an emotive content internal to the individual life of the agent.[53]

Pathos is not present in each and every resolve to action, for when individuals act with motives of no inherent worth, their passion lacks the universal dimension that makes it suitable for inclusion in exemplary conduct. In those cases, the ensuing action is of interest only to those who may desire what it promotes or impedes or who may find

Conduct as an Object of Artistic Beauty   157

amusement in its spectacle. By contrast, when action is driven by pathos it cannot help but resonate in the heart of every rational agent, given how it concerns problems of unconditional worth.[54] No matter how unfamiliar may be the details of the general situation, the particular collision and the life histories of the agents involved, so long as pathos provides the wellspring of their actions, the latter's display is in principle of interest to all rational agents, irrespective of their personal desires and tastes.

Since action driven by pathos hereby becomes the focal point of the artistic construal of conduct, the world condition and the particular collision must be configured in service of framing the emergence of pathos in the heart of individual.[55] Extraneous external details must be set in the background, just as must emotions lacking any connection to the pathos at stake. In these respects, mimesis must once again be left behind, for conduct as it immediately appears is just as much caught in circumstances devoid of motivational significance as it is driven by folly and personal idiosyncrasy.

This is true even when given conduct is embroiled with those ethically important motivations involving love and friendship, fame and honor, and other private and public devotions. In all these cases, whatever pathos is at hand must be reconfigured according to the requirements of aesthetic form, purging extraneous details without reducing action and its motivation to common formulae. Above all, the pathos must be given a sensuous outward semblance, allowing it to manifest itself in an intelligible and moving way. However, in order for pathos to be concretely displayed, the background of the world condition and a particular collision must be supplemented by the appearance of the *character* of the agents who are driven to exemplary conduct. Because ethically significant action only appears as the work of individual agents with unique characters reflected in the drives their behavior exhibits, the artistic construal of conduct must depict personalities of corresponding suitability.

The Character of the Agents

Granted that artistically construed conduct must issue from pathos, where universal ethical powers appear as actual motivations of individuals, what implications follow for the configuration of the character of such agents?

To begin with, aesthetically appropriate character must be such as to act from pathos. The individual agent must be someone who is disposed to become engaged with the fundamental ethical problem that the pathos addresses. This is not simply a matter of possessing the capability of moral agency common to all persons. It rather involves possessing a specific personal constitution that places *this* individual in a position to be driven by *this* pathos in the unique way in which it gains actual existence. Otherwise, the pathos has no inherent connection with the individual it motivates, leaving that character a dispensable shell and rendering the pathos a universal passion devoid of any individuated reality.

Moreover, character must not just be disposed to acquire its pathos but must enter its thrall freely, through the agent's own decisions. If, instead, external forces foist it on the agent, the conflict that the pathos addresses will lack the self-imposed character on which its full ethical stature depends. The relation between personal initiative and resultant action will be absent, undercutting responsibility.[56] Accordingly, if fate or divine intervention are to play any role, it must be in line with what the character of the individual independently exhibits.[57] Otherwise, the response of the agent lacks exemplary character, deriving as it does from an external source that could conceivably act on multiple instances.

By meeting these requirements of being disposed to an essential passion and embracing it freely,[58] character comprises the unifying whole that brings pathos to actual existence in an individual agent.[59] In this capacity, character takes center stage in the exposition of exemplary conduct, providing the guiding vehicle of the course of action.

Yet in so doing, in what way is the character of the agent coextensive with its individuality? Despite how character must unite the individuality of the agent with the pathos that motivates exemplary conduct, that pathos cannot be the sole passion within the agent's heart. If it were, the agent would collapse into an allegorical embodiment of a particular ethical concern, relinquishing its own individuality. With a one-sided cipher as its protagonist, the course of action would thereby forfeit its own constitutive freedom and turn into a predictable, formulaic occurrence.[60] To avoid this dilemma, the character must be animated by a plurality of interests and desires, even if the pathos should figure as the enduring passion in whose pursuit the agent eventually decides. The demands of artistic content are met only when character contains such a differentiated inner life, uniting conflicting passions into the unique identity of an individuated subject.[61]

However, the variegation of content must not overcome empty stereotypes by going to the other extreme of relying on arbitrary, freakish, idiosyncratic details devoid of any connection.[62] The character of the agent must bind all its diverse passions into a single, intelligible self, whose every aspect contributes to concretizing the action under way. Then alone can the character exhibit the same concrete universality that underlies the entire artistic construal of conduct.

Once again, the demands of aesthetic value require more than mimesis. The concreteness of artistically construed character cannot be derivative of how character appears given in experience, replete with contingent features indifferent to the ethical conflicts that may embroil it. Character as an object of art is instead an idealized agency, constructed around the realization of some pathos in a context that is equally tailored to unite meaning and configuration. In this respect, such character must diverge from the prosaic norm, not only in being driven by a passion whose significance is anything but ordinary, but by being pared down to those appearances that contribute to realizing the course of exemplary conduct under way. Nevertheless, this concentration of the content of character must not make it one-dimensional; to count as an individual agency, it must exhibit a differentiated unity that distinguishes it from others. Character is therefore not just the universal substrate of all particular passions animating the agent, nor simply a unity of a certain kind. It equally retains its unique identity, which must remain self-identical in all its variegated content. Driven by its specific pathos, character may always be of a particular type, but it is no less individual.[63]

As Hegel notes by way of anticipation, different arts may only be able to convey character in varying scope, from the full panorama of situated action in epic literature, to the inner play of mood and emotion in music and lyric poetry, to the isolated, silent moment in sculpture. In each case, however, the governing limitation must not prevent the fullness of character from making itself manifest within those borders, allowing the pathos to have an adequately individuated realization, rather than a trite shadow of itself.[64]

Anticipatory Response to the Charge of Literary Bias

The determination of conduct as an object of artistic beauty has proceeded on the basis of factors that in themselves make no distinction between forms of art or individual arts. These factors are, on the one hand, the determination of ethical conduct itself, and, on the other hand, the determination of artistic beauty in general as the concretely universal sensuous configuration of truths providing fundamental self-understanding to rational agents. Nonetheless, at every stage along the way, from the general background of conduct, to the particular collision eliciting the course of action, and finally to the ideal transfiguration of conduct itself, the characterization of the content of artistic beauty has a scope and richness that appears to transcend the resources of many, if not most, individual arts.[65] Hegel himself explicitly acknowledges this predicament, observing that literature may be well suited to represent the complete process of conduct in which action, reaction, and resolution unfold from a particular situation within a world condition, but that arts such as figurative sculpture and painting can only present one moment of this process.[66] One could extend this premonition to other arts such as abstract sculpture and painting, or music and architecture, and wonder whether they can capture even one such moment. To be charitable, one might allow that these arts could give expression to the character at play in artistically construable conduct, either by sensuously configuring the inward struggles of the heart or by providing an environment whose appearance seems suitable for exemplary deeds.

Yet even then, how can the determination of aesthetically construable conduct lay claim to being ingredient in the content of art? Must it forfeit its universal pretensions and be relegated to a characterization of the possible content of certain individual arts? A negative answer is possible, provided the contents that pertain to the different forms of art and the individual arts can all be shown to borrow in varying degrees from the determination of artistically construable conduct in general. Then, the latter will maintain its universality, for every realization of art will derive its content within the parameters here laid down. Certain arts may only give fragmentary expression to this general content, some displaying only one portion of the course of action, some making manifest character in repose from action, and some exhibiting pathos in isolation from particular conduct and external circumstances.⁶⁷ Yet, this content can still remain the common basis of them all, providing the implicit whole in which their meaning ultimately resides.⁶⁸ The fact that the determination of conduct as an object of art has proceeded from factors that are not relative to particular forms of art or individual arts should already indicate that upholding this possibility need not be in vain.

Chapter 9

The External Reality of the Work of Art

The content of artistic beauty, determined in its special transfiguration of prosaic conduct and religious devotion, comprises only one side of the work of art. To express this content, the art object must equally give it an external configuration. The requirement of an outer shape holds true whether the work of art directly offers an aesthetic image to intuition or provides perceivable inscriptions from which the imagination can produce images on its own, be it for inner awareness, as in literature, or for outer appreciation, as in works performed from notation.[1] In every case, the artwork comprises an existing unity of meaning and appearance, which, in this dual capacity, thus retains a sensuous being of its own. Since this external facet of the art object enters into the reception and creation of art, as well as into every particular art form and individual art, it must be taken into account prior to their conception.[2]

However, that the work of art is not just the thing in which it physically consists does not render the artwork an allegory or a symbol that manifests something other than itself. Those, such as Heidegger,[3] who uphold this conclusion, only reinstate the discredited mimetic assumption that art embodies an antecedently given essence. They ignore that the work of art is a conjunction of meaning and expression, whose physicality may not be all the work is,[4] but which remains constitutively tied to a significance that still cannot be realized apart.

This inseparability of meaning and configuration might seem challenged by, on the one hand, the discrepancy in aesthetic value between fakes and original creations lacking perceivable differences, and, on the other hand, in "found" objects of art. How can beauty reside in the unity of form and content, if, as the case of fakes and originals suggests, there can be, to paraphrase Nelson Goodman, an aesthetic difference without a perceptual difference?[5] If an authentic work commands greater aesthetic value owing to the imaginative originality of its creation, for which the technical proficiency of a forgery can never substitute, the significance of an artwork seems eminently detachable from its sensuous appearance. Analogously, "found" artworks appear to have a double life, one in which they have a purely prosaic significance and one in which they acquire an aesthetic meaning without undergoing any perceivable alteration. If this is so, how can their configuration be tied to any aesthetic meaning, when the "found" object retains the same appearance whether it figures as a mundane tool or natural thing or as an art object?

Yet the difference in aesthetic value of an authentic work and its perceivably indistinguishable forgery does not bear on the connection of meaning and configuration because the beauty of original and fake equally depend on that connection. The difference hangs rather on the history of their respective productions, to the extent that this history is available to the audience.[6]

Similarly, the acquisition of aesthetic significance by a "found" object is not a matter of assigning an independently given meaning to it. Rather, whatever aesthetic meaning the object obtains in being exhibited as a work of art is a meaning that arises through the positing by which the artist makes perceivable to an audience that the object now stands as art awaiting aesthetic appreciation. If the meaning in question did exist in a phenomenal form other than that provided by that thing, it would lack the exemplary character required for aesthetic significance. Consequently, determining how a work of art exists in its thinglike presence necessarily involves taking into account the presentation of the sort of meaning susceptible of aesthetic display.

The Work of Art as an External Thing

Although the concrete universality of beauty ties together the form and content of the work of art, so that neither is given independently, the external configuration of the art object remains distinguishable from its meaning. If shape and significance were literally one, the outwardness of sensuous imagery would disappear into the purely logical unity of self-thinking thought, where what is thought is the same thinking by which it is conceived. Instead, the work of art has a double reality,[7] consisting, on the one hand, in the sensuously configurable content of sacred and profane conduct and character within a particular situation in a certain type of world, and, on the other hand, in the sensuous object that brings this content to appearance. Art thereby creates a new world of its own,[8] not only transfiguring the content of prosaic reality but also expressing this transfigured content in a sensuous embodiment distinct from mundane things.

This specificity of the sensuous existence of the object of art might seem challenged by how the work of art may be a thing of a completely familiar sort, a "found" object whose tangible being is indiscernible from objects of use or things given in nature. Yet, even in this extreme case, whose aesthetic viability may well be questioned despite the celebration of Duchamp and his epigones, the sensuous reality of the art object is set apart from its mundane clones by some perceivable convention, be it placement on a gallery wall (of urinals and bicycle handlebars), inscription on an audio medium (recordings of Cage's measured silences), or simply the addition of an identifying label.

Alternately, the contrast between content and external configuration in art might appear cast in doubt by how the expression of the work of art may be nothing more than a verbal embodiment of its content, as in a self-referring "conceptual art," where the work is nothing but a description of itself. Yet this case does not eliminate the distinction between the content of the work of art and its sensuous configuration, for the language that expresses the content still has a tangible appearance distinct from the meaning it conveys.

Given, then, that the work of art expresses its content in a distinguishable sensuous object, admittedly with hidden and incidental physical features of its own, what, if anything, necessarily pertains to that external reality, considered solely in respect to its tangible presence as an artwork, irrespective of the particular form of artistic expression or the individual medium involved?

Since the art object has an external existence, it will automatically exhibit the natural features germane to tangible things. It will accordingly possess those modes of external organization that came under discussion in deciding whether the configurations of nature could possess the concrete universality ingredient in beauty.[9] As a tangible object, the work of art can incorporate the homogeneity, regularity, symmetry, harmony, and lawfulness that provides unity to natural things. Indeed, as Hegel suggests, different forms of art and different individual arts may be capable of incorporating these abstract orderings in varying degrees.[10] Yet, just as the modes of natural form cannot sustain aesthetic value on their own, so the art object cannot be exclusively restricted to these external unities without forsaking the essential individuality of configuration needed to do justice to the content of art. As we have seen, regularity and symmetry provide only a lifeless geometrical ordering, which may lay hold of the quantitative dimensions of matter in time and space, but otherwise fails to capture the internal self-ordering of rational agency.[11] Harmony and lawfulness may extend their grasp to qualitative differences, but they too comprise an external unity that determines the outer shape of things but not the autonomous activity central to the content of art.[12] And the homogeneity of sensuous material can only offer an abstract oneness, lacking the dynamic differentiation that life and subjectivity involve.

Yet if the sensuous configuration of the work of art cannot simply be homogeneous, regular, symmetrical, harmonious, or lawful, the art object also cannot simply be a chaos of physical properties devoid of discernible organization. If it were, the physical existence of the work would be completely singular, lacking anything that could connect with the universality of its content.

Nor will it suffice for the reality of the artwork to consist simply in a living thing, or, more specifically, in the actual tangible activity of rational agents, as might be possible in the performing arts. Plants and animals may exhibit an organic unity, but religious and ethical problems are not matters of health. By contrast, the tangible presence of rational agents might seem to afford precisely the conjunction of sensuous configuration and humane meaning that artistic beauty requires.[13] However, the immediate givenness of persons and their actions always involves a plethora of contingent, singular details that are indifferent to whatever exemplary meaning is otherwise displayed. The sensuous configuration of the art object must thus involve more than the given appearance of individuals in their mundane affairs.

The problem is that although the work of art unavoidably has a tangible being, marked by the physical relations ingredient in any prosaic thing, it must equally manifest in these very same relations an exemplary meaning providing a fundamental self-understanding for rational agents. This supervenience of humane meaning on sensuous configuration cannot be achieved solely by physical properties, even when the artwork is tangibly unlike any natural thing or object of use. For any such sensuous originality will still be ordered by the same physical parameters that characterize perceivable things. The special significance of the art object can only be sustained through the employment of tangible appearances that are already associated with the type of content germane to artistic beauty. Whether these tangible appearances consist in modulations of sound, splotches of color, shaped masses of material, or performing agents, their aesthetic value will depend on such a connection.

However, this connection does not render the tangible reality of the art object a sign or a symbol. The sensuous configuration of the work of art cannot figure as a sign, because the sensuous appearance of a sign has, as such, no inherent connection to the meaning it expresses. The sign signifies its meaning in a purely conventional way, where all that ties it to its significance is the arbitrary fact of its being employed in this way. Consequently, there is no unity of form and content between sign and signified, and each is independently given, in violation of the aesthetic requirement that meaning and configuration be essentially related.

This requirement might seem better served by a symbol, since it, in distinction from a sign, possesses a sensuous configuration that does have an indwelling connection to its meaning. However, the connection lies in certain properties that are neither unique to the symbol nor exhaustive of its appearance. For instance, the figure of a lion may symbolize courage owing to the prowess and ferocity of its species. Yet the courage signified by the figure of the lion can be conveyed by other means, whereas the symbol's image itself contains other features that are indifferent to the meaning it expresses.[14] Because a symbol thus expresses a content that can appear independently and because a symbol always contains features that do not pertain to that content, it is incongruent with the unity of meaning and configuration specific to beauty. Consequently, the sensuous being of the work of art can no more figure as a symbol than as a sign.

Whereas this does rule out making either semiotics or symbolic representation the principle of artistic configuration,[15] it does not preclude signs and symbols from playing a subordinate role in art.[16]

Certainly signs and symbols can enter into the notational formulation of a piece of performance art, where, for example, the configuration of a score can be altered to a certain degree without affecting what the notation determines. However, even in arts that cannot be notated, such as painting, where no perceivable visual features of its aesthetic content[17] need be incidental to the meaning conveyed,[18] the subordinate role of signs and symbols may be iconographically crucial for enabling the sensuous appearance of the work of art to express its content. By incorporating images bearing relevant semiotic or symbolic meaning, the physical being of the art object can transcend the limitations of natural form and display the individuality of exemplary conduct.

Without addressing this dimension of how the sensuous configuration of the work of art is imbued with meanings dependent on the interpretive framework within which signs and symbols operate, there is little more to note than how the physical characteristics of the art object must avoid reduction to either formless heterogeneity or the abstract unities of homogeneity, regularity, symmetry, harmony, and lawfulness. Systematic aesthetics must therefore turn to conceive the external reality of the work of art in its being for its audience, for it is here, in its relation to its reception, that the configuration of the work of art can be more concretely determined.

The External Reality of the Work of Art as Determined in Its Relation to the Audience

The turn to consider how the external reality of the work of art is determined through its relation to its audience might appear to exonerate and reinstate the strategy of transcendental aesthetics, according to which the reception of beauty determines the features of the beautiful object. However, this turn actually serves as a refutation of the transcendental path, given how it is undertaken only *after* the beauty of art and the art object have been minimally determined without reference to their reception. To uphold the transcendental construal of aesthetics as a critique of aesthetic judgment, aesthetic experience must figure as an Archimedean point for constituting the character of aesthetic phenomena. On these terms, the work of art should have no specifically aesthetic determination prior to and apart from its reception. Yet this primacy of aesthetic experience has already been disqualified by how beauty in general and the content of art have been shown to have certain basic determinations independently of their reception by an audience.

Consequently, as much as the configuration and content of art now stand at the point of being further qualified in respect to aesthetic experience, this very juncture demonstrates how art's existence for its audience can only be addressed when beauty in general and beauty in art have been minimally determined in themselves. Unless beauty has already been identified, there is no way of assuring that a certain mode of experience is an aesthetic experience, just as unless the art object has been identified in terms of the general content and configuration it must possess, there is no way of certifying that the reception in question is a reception of art.

Nevertheless, just as the categories of metaphysical aesthetics can be subordinately employed in determining artistic technique and the art object's aspect as an artifact, the transcendental approach can now be partially assimilated into systematic aesthetics. For although the work of art has certain aesthetic determinations that independently underlie its being for its audience, the conditions of its reception do determine further aspects of both its content and its configuration.

Whereas natural things and objects of use have a being for other, that is, a relatedness, consisting in causal interaction, biological metabolism, and subordination to desire, works of art are specifically related to a public audience that has access to them, on the one hand, through perception of art's sensuous configuration, and, on the other hand, through an understanding of cultural meanings that are tied to tangible details of the work. This being for an audience of the work of art in regard to its meaning and its sensuous configuration has ramifications in both respects.

On the one hand, the work of art must be so configured as to manifest its unity of shape and meaning to the sense and imagination of its audience. Indeed, since the work of art is for the sake of this, its appearance, its physical being need serve nothing but this purpose alone. However, a complete subordination to this purpose is impossible, since the material of the artwork will always possess physical features that escape submission to the aesthetic unity of meaning and shape. Because the art object is not a pure appearance but has a physical being of some sort, it cannot fail to have some dimensions that remain hidden, and other aspects that show themselves but are incidental to the artistic configuration they accompany. For example, a painting will have innumerable physical attributes, such as a weight, temperature, chemical composition, electromagnetic charge, acoustic resonance, and a visual pattern on its reverse side and edges, that will ordinarily fall completely out of view with regard to its bearing of aesthetic worth.

Nevertheless, the subordination of the material of the artwork to its manifestation of beauty has both negative and positive ramifications for its physical being. Negatively speaking, works of architecture need have no ornament or design within structures that cannot be perceived, any more than sculptures need have concealed, internal details, paintings need have images on the reverse side of the canvas, or music need have notes whose pitch and volume transcend the limits of hearing. Positively speaking, art objects must present their configurations in ways that fall within the limits of perception of their audience, so that, for example, as Aristotle demands, the size and duration of works fit the limits of attention, or, as Hegel observes, the characters of a play speak so that they can not only hear one another but also be heard by the audience.[19] By the same token, literature and notated works of performing art must be inscribed in a language that an audience can, in principle, apprehend.

Moreover, the art object must manifest itself to those modes of sensation[20] that are sufficiently differentiated and "theoretical" to convey a concretely universal configuration imbued with humane significance without consuming the art object in the reception process of a single individual. Modes of sensation are "theoretical" to the extent that they sense their tangible object without degrading its reality. Regarding degrees of differentiation, smell and taste are most impoverished, sensing their objects in a relatively homogeneous way, whereas touch has an intermediary sensitivity, falling below the more comprehensive and discriminating scope of hearing and sight, which can apprehend their objects without the limiting condition of immediate contact. In this capacity, sight and hearing count as theoretical senses insofar as they apprehend visible and audible things without consuming them in the process, whereas smell, taste, and touch are more practical, relying on the decomposition or abrasion of the things they sense. When the object of sense is physically altered by its reception, the common identity of its appearance is undermined, rendering it something only available to a personal, singular experience, incongruent with the prescriptive generality of aesthetic judgment. For this reason, a putative work of art that is consumed in a single reception loses its constitutive universal relation to its audience, becoming a purely private experience of no possible communicability. Hence, it will be no accident that the work of art will most readily take a form manifest to the "theoretical" senses of sight and hearing, rather than rely on the more practical senses of smell, taste, and touch.[21] Hence, perfume design, cooking, and massage face an inherent obstacle in overcoming relegation as techniques for producing pleasing sensations, unfit for elevation to the pantheon of fine art.

Further, in manifesting itself to the appropriate senses, the work of art must tailor itself so that its appearance accords with perceptual experience to produce the intended effect. So, as Plato points out in the *Sophist*, visual artists must distort the actual proportions of their figures in function of their placement to the potential viewer in order to have them appear in proper perspective.[22] Hence, not only must the work of art have an external reality determined for the sake of its appearance, but its aesthetic properties will be what they are in conjunction with the process of their perception.[23]

On the other hand, the work of art must not only have an external configuration that manifests itself to its audience in accord with the requirements of perception, but it must do so in a way that permits its unique meaning to be understood by the public. This consideration affects the content as well as the configuration of art, since the requirements of concretizing sacred or profane action in a specific world condition and a particular situation introduce details that can be so culturally specific as to conceal their meaning from an audience unfamiliar with the significance of the usages and customs that are displayed. This is true even though the content of art has a universal dimension that guarantees that it can eventually be appreciated by any audience of duly informed rational agents.[24] For unless the individuated manifestation of that universal dimension is made intelligible to the audience, the work of art remains opaque, full of shape but lacking meaning. What is at stake is not merely securing a common language, for that may still leave obscurities owing to nonlinguistic conventions and contexts that determine the significance of the imagery. What is rather involved is attaining a perceivable presence that offers its audience the keys to its own intelligibility, providing access to the associations, usages, customs, and histories[25] that invest its images with sense.[26]

How must the work of art be externally configured to achieve this universal transparency, constitutive of its relation to its audience? And can the art object ever succeed in securing its manifestation without critics and art historians perennially providing a supplementary apparatus directed at the public of the day? Given the dual character of the work of art, the answer to these questions involves aspects of both content and configuration.

In regard to the content of the work of art, the challenge consists in ensuring that the specific world of action, pathos, and character be transfigured in accord with the demands of not only internal unity and exemplary significance, but also intelligible audience reception. Although the content of art revolves around devotional and ethical issues of importance to persons in all lands and eras, the individuality of its appearance necessarily introduces a historical specificity on two accounts. On the one hand, the artistic content displays aspects of exemplary conduct situated in some specific time and place. On the other hand, the artistic content stands in relation to a public that is itself located in its own age and locale. Consequently, the work of art cannot help but contain individuating details that are foreign to the audience of certain lands and centuries.

It may be that this estrangement will present challenges of varying scope in the different individual arts, owing to limitations on the content they can display.[27] Yet, even if such arts as architecture and music may offer only very restricted aspects of the world condition and the particular situation of exemplary conduct, they cannot escape a challenge rooted in something as basic as the relation of artistic configuration and meaning to the reception of the work of art.

In face of the predicament ubiquitously entailed by this relation, how should the setting of exemplary conduct be construed? Should the work display what is familiar to its own age to ensure accessibility to its contemporary audience? Should the work seek instead to distance itself from what is peculiar to its time by seeking refuge in the past? Or finally, should the work flee to a purely imaginary setting, equally removed from today as from yesterday or tomorrow?

As Hegel points out, fixation on the present offers no solution. The embrace of contemporary content can fall prey to an invidious parochialism, where the immediate appearance of the present and the local is ascribed an exclusive validity, conflating what is of current, personal, transient interest with subjects of abiding exemplary significance, while dismissing everything past and foreign as if the only artistically construable contents were hostage to the here and now. This can take the form of a modernizing anachronism in art, where everything of ages past and distant lands gets assimilated into contemporary custom and usage, destroying its objectivity by substituting an abstract sameness for the individuality of action in the world.[28] Either way, whether the present be made eternal or the past be transformed into a mirror of contemporary life, the exemplary individuality of the content of art is sacrificed at the altar of banal familiarity.

A similar outcome results if the past is canonized as the exclusive source for an objective, universally intelligible content of art. Indeed, the past may seem beyond impeachment as a parochial subject, being detached from fleeting, present interests by the passage of time. Yet, that formal detachment cannot alone guarantee its appropriateness, let alone privileged suitability, for artistic construal. Once again, a feature without any automatic connection with exemplary affairs is identified with the concerns of humanity, as if simply slipping from today into yesterday clothed action with an aesthetic sheen. This antiquarian devotion may well replace a modernizing anachronism with fidelity to the past, but this very exactitude falls prey to two complementary difficulties. On the one hand, it violates the demands of artistic transfiguration by mirroring prosaic life in all its given, meaningless detail. On the other hand, by so immersing itself in contingencies of no abiding significance, it undercuts the intelligibility of the work of art, filling it with details whose meaning can only be evident to connoisseurs of the historical period and place it so doggedly represents. In pursuit of objectivity, the avatars of historical authenticity thereby neglect the link to subjectivity, to the reception of the audience of art, which must also get its due.[29]

Attending to the audience is not, however, equivalent to catering to all its feelings and concerns, as if holding up a mirror to them. The truth art provides is not a matter of correctness, of confronting the audience with an accurate description of its own existence as it immediately appears. Affording that "self-understanding" is an utter redundancy of no aesthetic, let alone practical or theoretical, value. The self of the audience that must be spoken to is not the self in its subjective givenness but rather the true self,[30] the self that, without relinquishing its individuality and abandoning its world, is still engrossed with religious or ethical issues of conduct that transcend contingent desire and expediency.

To retain accessibility without sacrificing the exemplary dimension of artistic content, the work of art must thus navigate between the two extremes of privileging either the local and the present or the remote and the past at the expense of one another. Being concretely universal, the exemplary content of art is not limited by time and place, yet it must be historically specific to retain its individual dimension.

Admittedly, different eras and localities may be home to different types of world conditions. As we have seen, a world condition of settled institutions of justice tends to restrict exemplary conduct to the domain of moral action, whereas a world condition in which institutions of justice are lacking allows for exemplary conduct in those ethical spheres as well. However, since either case still leaves room for content fit for artistic construal, art can draw an appropriate setting from every past and every present in which rational agents engage in conduct.

Whether it be past or present, each such setting must combine enough fidelity to provide an individuated arena with sufficient transfiguration to capture universally significant affairs. In addition, it must attain an adequately intelligible expression, allowing access to audiences of today and tomorrow.

These considerations permit and indeed mandate a certain artistic anachronism, where aspects of departed eras are reconfigured in light of contemporary understanding, without foregoing enough historical specificity to destroy the internal objectivity of the artistically construed world.[31] Although the accuracy of historical details may be compromised in the process, this deviation from the naturalistic depiction of every idiosyncratic, accidental, transient fact serves the display of something unconditionally objective: the truly abiding pathos whose entanglement in affairs of universal importance gives art its valid content.[32]

The same underlying prescriptions hold true when an entirely imaginary time and place is made the content of art. So long as a fantasy world is imbued with enough individuating detail to display a convincing setting for action whose humane significance is accessible to the audience, it can serve art just as well as the past or the present.

Yet whether a work of art turns from the present to the past or to sheer fantasy, its accessibility to a contemporary audience will depend on the general culture of the time, with all the trappings of tradition and heritage in which it cultivates its members.[33] Thanks to one culture's perennial appeal to the tradition in which it sees itself nurtured, its members may be able to appreciate artistic contents drawn from places and times that another culture's members find alien and opaque. Moreover, given that what counts as tradition for a culture is subject to change over time, works of art that are immediately intelligible to a contemporary audience may become mysterious to a future public, or vice versa. Indeed, such diversity in accessibility can afflict members of the very same community, given differences in education, religion, and other cultural exposures.

These impediments to reception cannot be abidingly eliminated by any internal alteration of the content and configuration of the artwork, for they reside in differences of experience that are external to the work of art,[34] as well as in the temporal, transient aspects[35] that the work can never entirely expunge from itself. They do mandate changes in how works of performance art are mounted, in accord with the need to mediate the outlook and culture of the audience with those locally specific details of the work whose sense may not be intelligible without some modification.[36] Furthermore, these obstacles to accessibility dictate a perennial need for critics and art historians to supply skeleton keys to open the heart and mind of works as they fall in and out of the grasp of changing audiences.[37]

Nevertheless, what supplies the basis for all these labors of communication is the underlying intelligibility of the work itself, whose content and configuration must already be such as to allow for their success. The bedrock of this intelligibility remains the self-contained display of exemplary conduct, whose humane universality overrides any indeterminacy of translation, rendering a secondary accessory the historical, contingent aspect that its own individuality always brings along.[38] It may be somewhat of an exaggeration to maintain, as Hegel does, that artworks must be immediately intelligible without further study or instruction.[39] Certainly, repeated encounters with a work and with the appreciations of others can open deepened avenues of reception that were not at first apparent. Yet because the work of art provides the independent appearance of an exemplary course of action, whose universally significant meaning is bound to its own unique configuration, the art object possesses all the resources it needs to make itself accessible, provided the historical dimensions of its imagery are clarified in conformity with the historical cultivation of its particular audience.

For this reason, Danto is wrong in maintaining that certain artworks produced in one age cannot figure as artworks in another era even if things sharing identical perceivable properties can have a prosaic existence in that same epoch.[40] Admittedly, subsequent aesthetic appreciation of an artwork may depend on informing the current audience of the worldview and cultural meanings that were ingredient in the work's original aesthetic production and reception. However, such supplemental service can always provide for a new appreciation of the object as a work of art, both because the work must have had a self-contained universal, communicable significance to ever figure as art, and because no culture could even be identified as such it if were either closed to cultural transmission from without or a black hole from which no cultural productions could intelligibly emanate.

Consequently, beyond the ineliminable, yet subordinate details of translation, the significance of the work of art resides nowhere else but in itself, directly at hand. If, instead, art were treated as a metaphor, whose meaning were to be found only through the mediation of independent sources such as the presumed model for a work, author's intention,[41] or some other antecedently given factor, the dilemmas of metaphysical aesthetics would once again raise their weary head. Such factors can enter into the aesthetic unity of an artwork only to the degree that they help invest the artwork's configuration with a meaning that transcends and transfigures their own.[42] Then the given identity of author, subject, and prior art history (including the history of the work's own production) can be absorbed into the significance of the work of art, obtaining a new subsidiary role within the whole to which they contribute, a role guaranteed by the manifest conditions of the work's presentation.

Chapter 10

Artistic Creation

Artistic creation might appear to come first as a topic in aesthetic theory. If beauty is artistic beauty, existing only in the work of art, and the work of art issues from artistic creation, should not aesthetics begin by examining the process by which the art object comes into being? Admittedly, without the prior creation of works of art, the actual existence of artistic beauty can no more be experienced than can the phenomena of the reception of art. This is true despite the fact that artistic creation is never totally creative, but always involves an element of technique, where some given material is employed for the purposes of artistic imagination. Even where the artist does no more than select a natural thing or object of use and place it in the context that renders it an object of aesthetic appreciation, the work only arises as such for an audience subsequent to this creative act.

Moreover, the very identity of an object as an artwork depends not simply on its physical attributes, which can just as well be shared by a purely prosaic thing, but on how its appearance stands in relation to the context of meanings by which the artwork generically exists for its audience. Since this context includes a recognition that the work results from an act of artistic creation imaginatively configuring a self-understanding of humanity, do not, as Danto suggests, the conditions of production of an artwork play a constitutive role in its identity?[1] And if this is so, should not artistic creation be conceived prior to the concept of art?

The Place of Artistic Creation in Systematic Aesthetics

Yet how can artistic creation be identified in its own right without already introducing the concept of artistic beauty, whose *existence* in the work of art may well depend on the conditions of artistic production? As much as artistic creation is responsible for bringing into being artistic beauty in the work of art and making possible actual aesthetic experience, artistic creation does not generate the nature of beauty, nor that of the work of art or of the being of art for its audience. Not only can these all be determined without reference to an actual process of artistic creation, as the preceding argument has shown, but artistic creation cannot proceed or be identified as such unless it can incorporate in thought as well as in deed the categories that determine what counts as a work of art.[2]

To define art by seeking its source in the creative act of the artist would be to commit the same foundationalist mistake that undermines the parallel attempts to determine truth from the cognitive acts of a privileged standpoint and to determine what is ethically valid from the acts of will of individuals participating in a privileged choice procedure. In each case, a specific domain of normative validity (beauty, truth, and the good) is constituted by some privileged determiner, which, by standing prior to the domain in question, cannot already share in any of the normativity that its act is supposed to confer. Then, however, the justification of that prior determiner becomes an insoluble dilemma and the normativity of each domain becomes cast in doubt, given how it is relative to something that cannot share in its validity. For these reasons, how valid categories are known and spoken by real individuals can only be systematically conceived after the categories have been determined in their own right without reference to any standpoint of consciousness or linguistic competence, just as the genesis of justice can only be rigorously addressed after the structures of justice have themselves been conceived without appeal to any privileged procedures.[3] By the same token, artistic creation can be systematically determined only after the character of what it constitutively creates has been established.

However, the account of artistic creation in general must precede the examination of particular forms of art and of the individual arts. As long as there is anything common to the genesis of art, it must be determined prior to the particular and individual forms of art, whose determination can only add features that apply within their specific regions. When these particular and individual forms of art are at stake, artistic creation may well return as a theme, but only in respect to the further qualifications it acquires in these domains. What now stands at issue are not those features specific to the artistic creation of symbolic, classical, or romantic art, or of works of architecture, sculpture, painting, film, dance, music, or literature, but rather the determination of the creation of art that is ingredient in all its forms.

The Challenge of Purely Formal Artistic Creation: The Cases of "Found," "Primitive," and "Industrial" Art

What, then, is the minimal determination of artistic creation? Systematically speaking, the initial characterization of artistic creation must here be undertaken with no further resources than the preceding account of the work of art and the features of nature and rational agency that underlie it. Anything involving particular or individual forms of art must be excluded at this time, since they still await their own conceptualization.

As it stands, artistic creation minimally consists in the process whereby, without further qualification, a work of art gets produced by a rational agent or agents. Given the established character of the art object, what is at stake is determining how individuals produce something exhibiting the concrete universality with which a sensuous or imaginative configuration is wedded to a meaning providing fundamental self-understanding to rational agents.

Since artists are finite beings practicing their artistry as embodied selves inhabiting an independently given world, their activity must to some degree impose new form on a preexisting material and thereby contain an element of technique. However, since artistry is not simply craftsmanship, artistic creation must transform its material in a way that may incorporate, but must also transcend, the artisanal imposition of given form on given material. Moreover, given the limits of natural configuration and technique, this creative activity should be neither an involuntary occurrence nor just a purposive exercise of skill. Presumably, it should rather comprise a conscious undertaking driven by its own specifically artistic aims.

Yet are even these rudimentary requirements called into question by the origins of two recognized types of art: "found" art and "primitive" art? In the case of "found" art, the artist may well be driven by artistic aims, but the activity of the artist restricts itself to simply selecting a given object, be it a natural thing or an object of use, and merely displaying it as is, employing some conventional device to indicate that it is being put forward as an art object. Since the "found" object is not transformed in any discernible way but simply placed within a new context isolating it from mundane use and soliciting aesthetic appreciation, the creative activity of the artist seems devoid of any transformative action whatsoever. Although a Duchamp may wrench his urinal off its plumbing and stick it on a gallery wall, he otherwise leaves it be.

By contrast, "primitive" art may issue from an activity transforming preexisting material as much as does "nonprimitive" artistic creation, but the maker of the "primitive" work of art is thought to have produced it not as an art object but as a mundane utensil, a ceremonial object, or a fetish directly embodying a spirit. Here what is presumably lacking is the presence of any specifically artistic aims. The same absence of artistic intentions would apply to objects that may end up being appreciated as works of art yet are produced by the proverbial monkey at a typewriter or by the unintentional efforts of rational agents (who are not self-professed aleatory artists, like Cage, who employ chance for aesthetic effect). A similar situation might be thought to arise in objects of use whose "industrial design" is later made an object of aesthetic appreciation in its own right.

Do these cases dictate that the minimal determination of artistic creation must be sought independently of transformative activity and a conscious artistic purpose? To begin with, such examples of individual works of art cannot have any argumentative weight unless it is granted that they qualify as bona fide works of art. Appealing to the authority of the "art world," in the manner of institutional theories of art, only begs the question, for the aesthetic identity of the "art world" must itself be established. From a systematic point of view, justifying any assumption that such objects are artworks would require first separating the conceptual determination of such cases from their empirical appearance and then determining whether their conception specifies an option germane to artistic creation in general. Let it be granted, for the sake of argument, that "found" art and "primitive" art do qualify as fine art.

With "found" art, the positing of the given object within an aesthetically appropriate context comprises the sole creative act that can be identified. Yet, even here, that act plays a constitutive role in transfiguring the found object, removing it from mundane usage and informing its pure appearance with the burden of qualifying as art. This imaginative metamorphosis may be purely formal from a physical point of view, but it comprises some tangible alteration in regard to the being for an audience of the found object, attaching an aesthetic meaning in some perceivable way to its sensuous configuration. In this regard, it is enough that a Duchamp place his bicycle handlebars on a gallery wall or that a Cage bracket his period of silence sitting on a stage before a concert grand. Whether or not "found" art is adequate to support these artistic intentions, the artist who "authors" it has exercised a creative act that involves some facility in selecting and contextualizing the proper thing in a way that communicates its newly ascribed aesthetic status.

As for "primitive" or "industrial" art, where the art object has been produced with nonartistic ends in view, two alternatives are possible. On the one hand, the object may have been produced with artistic aims accompanying the nonaesthetic aims that make it a utensil, a ceremonial object, or a fetish. For if the object were produced with the concomitant intention of it being a *beautiful* utensil, ceremonial object, or fetish, this concern with creating something with aesthetic value would entail the same process at stake in the express creation of independent works of art. On the other hand, if the utensil, ceremonial object, or fetish were produced with no accompanying concern for beauty, the subsequent appreciation of the object's aesthetic worth would be predicated on the same process of contextualization from which "found" works of art originate. Then, the inadvertent "primitive" or "industrial" work of art would issue from a creative act taking an antecedently given artifact and informing it with an artistic aim made perceivable in the tangible contextualization conferred on it by, for example, some ethnomusicologist, architectural historian, dance critic, gallery collector, or museum curator.

On either account, these apparent cases of exception end up retaining the same transformative activity and artistic aim that they might be thought to exclude.

The Question of Creativity in the Performing Arts

The performing arts might appear to present a more stubborn challenge to the transfiguring originality of artistic creation. For, unlike other artistic activities, nonimprovisational performance seems committed to embodying antecedently given forms comprising, for example, the notated music, choreographed dance, or scripted theater that the performing artist brings to life. Indeed, if all that performance involved was realizing given artistic compositions in the way an artisan fulfills a blueprint, creativity would become an incidental quirk, contributing nothing significant to the life of the work. However, if performance is to be a fine art rather than a prosaic craft, the move from artistic composition to performed work will not be located in the mere reappearance of prior notations. The fidelity and identification of the performance may well depend on embodying the notated forms of the composition, common to any other recognizable performance. However, the artistry of the performance will lie beyond in an individual dimension consisting in how the performer takes the given form of the composition and transfigures it further, generating an original "interpretation" that treats the composition like any nonperformance art treats its material. Accordingly, no rules of craft can specify the move from composition to performance, even if the performance is distinguishable from improvisation by embodying the composition to a sufficiently recognizable degree. Although this creative gap frees performance from any slavery to a composer's alleged intentions, it does not free performance from meeting the objective requirements of art, requirements that the performance must meet on the same terms that apply to the original composition.[4] Far from impeding the conception of artistic creation, performing art thus only raises the problem anew.

The Constitutive Aspects of Artistic Creation

Granted that the work of art arises from an activity of rational agency involving a tangible transformation of given material following specifically artistic aims, how does this process necessarily operate? What more can be said beyond repeating that the activity includes but cannot be reducible to an artisanal production and that it results in the fashioning of an object bearing all the attributes that have so far been established to be constitutive of the work of art?

An obvious avenue for bringing artistic creation to a more concrete determination is to differentiate necessary stages in its process. To begin with, there is the subjective, inward activity of the artist's imagination where genius and inspiration might be thought to delineate the work of art in consciousness. Then, there would follow the objective dimension of the creative process, where the talent of the artist is set at work realizing the inspiration that genius has provided, giving it an external actuality available to an audience. Needless to say, appealing to genius and inspiration remains an empty gesture unless they can be characterized in positive terms that specifically account for the genesis of the work of art. Moreover, any such differentiation of artistic creation into subjective and objective stages risks either resurrecting the artisanal conception that must be transcended or falling into vacuous generalizations about the ineffability of genius and inspiration.

Hegel, for one, seems to be resigned to the latter difficulty, warning that the treatment of the subjective productive activity of the artist falls outside the domain of systematic analysis to the extent that demanding an account of artistic creativity is tantamount to the vain enterprise of seeking a recipe for making a work of art.[5] Yet, although Hegel ridicules any inquiry into the source of artistic creativity, he does admit that a few generalities can be given concerning the creative process itself.[6] He suggests three basic headings under which artistic creativity can be determined: first, the imaginative process defining artistic genius and inspiration; second, the objective aspect of creation, whereby inspired genius creates the actual work of art; and third, the genuine originality made manifest in the creation, uniting artistic imagination with its product.[7]

This division has, on the one hand, a certain plausibility. If artistic creation involves any transformation of given material guided by conscious artistic aims, what comes first is the imaginative process by which the artist determines some specific approach to the medium, followed by the working out in that medium of a sensuous configuration of aesthetic value, whose artistic originality is only intelligible by how the imaginative inspiration of the artist is revealed in the appearance of the creation. Yet, on the other hand, such a succession raises the suspicion that the creative process has been coopted by categories of technique, in terms of which genius provides an antecedent form that is then imposed on a given material. In that case, the generation of this form in the artist's imagination would comprise the only creative element in the process, rendering the art object a reproducible artifact devoid of originality and lending support to Collingwood's paradoxical claim that art creation actually resides in the imagination of the artist. To avoid this outcome, must the distinction between the imaginative process of artistic inspiration and the objective configuring of the art object be overcome, leaving the artist to create without any determinable artistic purpose, as if blindly possessed?

This either/or would condemn artistic creation to a mystery beyond the pale of thought. What makes it far from final is that it rests on the assumption that what artistic inspiration generates is a separable form that is then merely embodied in the fashioning of the actual work of art. This assumption can be circumvented in two coordinate ways. If, on the one hand, the artistic purpose of genius does not operate as a guiding form, but undergoes its own alteration in conjunction with the configuring of the medium of art, then the distinction between inspiration and objective shaping can be retained without sacrificing artistic originality. Moreover, the imaginative working of genius and inspiration need not then operate as a temporally prior stage preceding the objective transformation of the medium of the artwork. It can rather be a coeval aspect of the creative process comprising the subjective side of artistry accompanying the actual shaping of appearances from which the art object results.

This option provides a coherent way of conceiving artistic creation in accord with the individuality of artistic beauty. To complete the determination, due account must now be taken of the features of artistic beauty that already dictate with what the process of artistic creation must conclude.

The Subjective Side of Artistic Creation: The Imaginative Inspiration of Genius

In developing a concept of the subjective dimension of the creative process, imagination provides the rudimentary resource. Because artistic beauty resides in exemplary images given directly to sense or mediated by linguistic representation, the imagination must play a fundamental role in the creative activity of the artist. To create such exemplary images, the imagination cannot confine itself to the passive role of a reproductive imagination, reimagining antecedently given appearances in an exercise of memory. If art were simply mimesis, such reproductive labors might do, yet since the exemplary individuality of artistic beauty transcends the confines of given appearance, artistic imagination must be creative in character, transfiguring the given in a unique, unprecedented manner.[8]

However, imagining sheer novelty is not sufficient when the artistic transfiguration of given appearance must create not just unique images, but exemplary images contributing towards the self-understanding of rational agents. Not only does this require surmounting abstract generalities devoid of individuality, but it equally demands imaging religious devotion and individuated conduct in accord with all the established considerations pertaining to the background of action, the collision, and the character of agents. To the degree that meeting these demands involves incorporating or modifying elements of given appearances, the artistic imagination cannot dispense with the reproductive facility of memory, which gives it access to the given reality of past and present conduct as it appears externally, as well as to the inner life of individuals, and to how their inner life manifests itself in external appearance.[9]

Yet, whereas the reproductive imagination plays an essential role in providing for such appropriation of the internal and external reality of sacred and profane conduct, the artistic employment of such content requires more than the arbitrary transformations of unrestricted fancy. The artist must have a trove of received representations of humane reality and a facility of fantasy for altering these given images and inventing novel views and arrangements. Nonetheless, an artistically creative imagination can only generate exemplary images if it is further informed by an understanding of the truths that should be given sensuous configuration.[10] This requirement is not met by the possession of philosophical knowledge, which, by itself, lacks the element of sensuous individuality that remains crucial for art. What is needed instead is an understanding of the truths susceptible of exemplary configuration and an imaginative facility to shape them into individuated appearances. Since emotion and sense provide a source of individual content for imaginative construal, the artist must draw on feeling and sensibility provided these are informed by universal concerns, yet capable of animating those concerns with an imaged configuration.[11]

It would be idle to suppose that these subjective engagements could proceed independently of the actual transformations of a medium, be it color and figure, the movement of one's body, sound, language, or some special notation. For if they constitutively effect the interpenetration of meaning and configuration, it makes little sense to set them at work without already engaging the material side of artistic creation in some degree. Admittedly, a composer could conceivably compose music without yet committing it to a visible notation or an audible performance, just as a poet could create a poem within the recesses of the imagination without reciting or writing it out. Yet even in these cases, the internal activity of imaginative creation already involves a molding of a specific given medium, namely, the language or notational system that must be employed to shape meaning. Moreover, although the linguistic or notational formulation here provides the centerpiece of artistic creation, it still requires the further technical act giving these imagined representations a tangible existence for others, so essential to the objectivity of the work of art. Since no one but the artist can provide this service, the subjective dimension of artistic creation must involve not merely the generation of aesthetic images in the mind of the artist, but also the activity of giving them an external form. This activity may or may not be joined to the generation of exemplary images, depending on the medium in question, but it remains a ubiquitous element of artistic creation.

Consequently, genius, understood as the capacity for artistic creation, must consist in the general ability to create images uniting humane meaning with sensuous configuration as well as in the facility to bring these images to external expression.[12] The latter facility is a specific talent for mastering the particular features of the medium in question. Such talent has a technical character to the extent that it involves realizing the products of artistic imagination in a specific medium. Accordingly, it demands particular capacities that not all individuals may possess, yet may be taught to those who are capable of exercising its specific technical dexterity. By the same token, such talent remains merely an external skill devoid of aesthetic value unless genius links it with genuine artistic inspiration, issuing from the general ability to configure exemplary images.[13]

This latter capacity for creating aesthetic appearances is at a complete remove from technique, because it generates images of exemplary individuality that no antecedent given or definable procedure can originally determine. Once created, the art object can, of course, be duplicated by an exercise of technique. Yet its genesis must rely on a creative facility that cannot be acquired through instruction or by the experience of performing nonartistic activities.

Accordingly, genius appears as a "natural" gift, which manifests itself immediately once the artist has sufficient mastery of a medium to give external expression to his or her inspiration. Genius operates as a "natural" gift not in resting on a given nature, actualizing an antecedent potential, but in spontaneously generating an art object whose individuality escapes determination by any formula or recipe. This spontaneity of artistic creation indeed has as its prerequisite the general capabilities of autonomous imagination, reason, and will, but these constituents of rational agency do not of themselves guarantee, let alone necessitate, the exercise of genius by any particular individual. It is this very absence of any determining ground that renders the capacity for artistic creation something that operates immediately, not simply in the spontaneous imagining of aesthetic images but in the practical facility to immediately execute these images in function of the unity of inner production and external realization that characterizes the melding of meaning and shape in art.[14] The possession of technique may serve as a prerequisite for artistically shaping a medium into an aesthetic appearance for others, but once this talent is at hand the unique exercise of genius precludes dependence on any other intervening factor that could determine how genius proceeds. Admittedly, by having a productive imagination, the artist always retains the ability to rework and amend whatever inspiration arises within. Yet each stage of artistic elaboration will still exhibit the capability of immediately executing inner artistic imagination, for otherwise the path of artistic creation would follow a preordained order.[15] Consequently, artistic inspiration, joining creative imagination with technical execution, cannot be rooted in any prior ground, be it some sensation or emotion, a conscious resolve to create, or an external encouragement. Artists may well be moved by feeling and sense, or simply decide to produce a work of art, or answer the call of a commission, but all these are but incidental occasions that can neither guarantee nor specifically determine inspiration. In each case, whatever inspiration follows must arise with the same spontaneity of inner conception and objective execution that alone befits a unique creation.[16]

Similarly, any prosaic content that serves as a material for artistic transfiguration is equally devoid of any specific connection with the exemplary image it occasions. Since its artistic transfiguration cannot be defined by the application of any given procedure or principle to its given content, there can be no talk of any actual inspiration until imaginative construal is already under way. As Hegel observes, the artist may possess a natural gift, a given theme, and an external incentive, but only by seizing a content of fundamental significance and animating it in an exemplary configuration does the artist create with inspiration.[17]

The Objectivity of Artistic Creation

Although the process of artistic creation involves the subjective activities of imaginative construal and execution, it must attain an objectivity corresponding to the objective unity of the work of art. Just as the art object does not possess its aesthetic worth by representing the outer world or inner life of the artist in all the singularity and insignificance of its immediate appearance, so artistic creation must avoid copying mundane reality in its contingent and meaningless givenness or expressing each and every emotion with which the artist is afflicted. The true objectivity of artistic creation rather resides in imaginatively configuring what is essential to humane affairs, shaping the content generic to artistic beauty into an artistic form that is tied to its presentation.

Since, as we have seen, the individuality of artistic content introduces contingent elements that are not immediately intelligible to each audience, the artist must equally take into account the particular culture to which the work is immediately addressed to ensure the disclosure of its meaning. Insofar as the content of artistic beauty is inherently universal, the modifications at stake concern only the incidental details that necessarily clothe the individual configuration of exemplary conduct. As with all aspects of artistic creation, these considerations are dictated by the prior determination of beauty as it exists in the work of art.

Yet although this determination mandates objective features common to all artistic creation, the subjective dimension inherent in the production of art stamps artistry with an individuality that leaves its mark in the completed work. In order to possess its constitutive aesthetic worth, genuine artistry must unite the subjective individuality of the creative process with the objective requirements of realizing artistic beauty. It is this unity that comprises what, following Hegel, can be aptly identified as the genuine originality of an artist's creativity.[18]

The Originality of Artistic Creation

Whether or not a work of art is produced anonymously or through the cooperative labors of a plurality of authors, it remains the product of the unique inspiration of its creator or creators. This inspiration must indeed address fundamental concerns of humanity and shape them in a universally accessible configuration, yet all this still proceeds from the unique sensibility and imagination of the artist or artists, to which the novel appearance of the work stands tied. This connection does not consist in a perceivable relation between the artwork's appearance and the inner experience of the artist. If it did, the originality of the work would be only available to the introspection of the artist or to uncertain estimates of what the artist underwent in the process of creation based on testimony and conjecture. Since, however, genuine inspiration cannot remain hidden but must manifest itself in the work of art, the originality of an artistic creation will be ingredient in its appearance.

Since the originality of artistic creation is therefore at hand in the work of art itself, it might appear to fall outside the consideration of the creative process and into the determination of the existence of artistic beauty. However, because it connects the individuality of the work with the individuality of artistic imagination, the creative process will exhibit artistic originality in its own working.[19]

This aesthetically significant originality cannot consist in the singular, incidental idiosyncracies that accompany the production of a work of art without contributing to its melding of meaning and configuration.[20] Such features that may repeatedly mark the working of an artist comprise only a personal mannerism that is fundamentally distinct from the originality that unites artistic inspiration with the objectivity of its creation. Mannerism may interfere with the aesthetic achievement of artistry by substituting personal caprice and interest for the internal necessity by which the content of an artwork unites with its shape into an independent whole of exemplary humane significance. Yet, mannerism may equally accompany artistic creation without undermining the aesthetic unity of the work of art if it is confined to those incidental aspects of its appearance that can be indifferently varied. As Hegel suggests, mannerism of this benign sort is actually an unavoidable element, given the individuality of artistic configuration. It enters into both the treatment of the work, as evident, for instance, in the infinite variety of color and illumination by which painters can hardly help but differentiate their creations, and into how the treatment is executed, as visible, for instance, in differences in brushstroke and thickness of paint.[21] Hence, Rembrandt and Van Gogh may have their distinctive manner, without succumbing to the mannerism by which other artists reduce their creations to an idiosyncratic but repeatable formula (for example, late and lesser Picasso, Chagall, and Dali).

Conversely, artistic originality is to be distinguished from style, understood as a mode of artistic representation whose common patterns and rules differentiate genres of art within a particular medium.[22] As such, style does not match artistic originality's unity of the unique inspiration of the artist and the aesthetic objectivity of the work of art, for it cannot differentiate the individual creativity of artists who follow the same style. Moreover, since style is a factor distinguishing *groups* of artistic creations, it cannot be constitutive of artistic creativity or of the work of art in general. Because style rather presupposes whatever it is that makes for artistic creativity and a work of art as such, it properly becomes a theme only after the universal dimension of art has been determined and art's particular realizations lie at issue. Then, artistic creation will become further qualified in function of the particular modes of art. Accordingly, artistic originality lies between succumbing to a riot of personal idiosyncrasy and the rote adoption of rules of style. It involves laying hold of a meaning fundamental to the self-understanding of humanity and giving it an imaginative configuration freely spawned from the subjective inspiration of the artist, yet uniquely matching the significance it expresses. In this way, what is most individual in the artist's creation is completely immanent to the exemplary image of the work. Then, the subjective dimension of artistic creativity becomes one with the internal coherence of the work of art, upholding the concrete universality in which genuine originality resides.[23] Artistic originality is thereby identical with the true objectivity of the work of art[24] in two respects: first, in engaging in a subjective activity freely following out the internal necessity constituting the unique unity of shape and meaning that the work presents; and second, in becoming the imaginative corridor for a unique configuration of meaning providing an objectively true self-understanding to humanity.[25] Moreover, because the art object constitutively communicates its truth via the aesthetic reception of any duly prepared rational audience, the originality of the artist is conditioned upon producing an independently meaningful creation whose beauty is fully appreciable by those who lack the genius to make what they view.[26]

Due to these emblems of the dual identity of artistic creativity and art object, any thought of appealing to independently given artistic intentions to disclose or support the aesthetic worth of the work falls by the wayside as a superfluous ambition. Although such intentions may help unravel the iconography of a work, if the meaning of the work is not available in its configuration or lacks an objective, exemplary resonance, the aesthetic aspirations of its author are idle. As Hegel observes, to have no manner is to be truly original.[27]

Chapter 11

The Reception of Art

The absence of any discrete treatment of aesthetic judgment in Hegel's *Lectures on Aesthetics* might suggest that the dilemmas of transcendental aesthetics preclude any abiding position for the analysis of aesthetic experience. The individuality and truth of beauty may be subverted if the reception of art is granted a privileged role in determining the objectivity of beauty. Yet this does not signify that the reception of the work of art cannot be treated in function of the established features of artistic beauty and its reality in the work of art.

The Place of Aesthetic Judgment in Systematic Aesthetics

These features provide the systematic point of departure for determining aesthetic appreciation. This is because the reception of art is predicated on the constitutive elements of artistic beauty that must be recognizably perceived in order for art to be experienced as such. As Danto points out, insofar as one's comprehension that an object is a work of art, and not a natural thing or prosaic artifact, already plays a role in determining how one responds aesthetically to it, any attempt to define art in function of reception would fall into a vicious circularity.[1]

Yet, features of art in general need not be the only aesthetic factors determining aesthetic appreciation. If it turns out that reason can determine particular forms of art and individual arts, then the reception of art will be further determined after their specification in function of whatever relevant considerations may be introduced by their differentiation. However, at this juncture, where what is at stake is the universal structure of the reception of art and not the peculiarities of appreciating classical versus romantic art or of experiencing music versus poetry, all that enters in are the determinants of art in general. The question, then, is what is involved in appreciating the appearance of a work of art as a unique, exemplary presentation of a fundamental self-understanding for rational agents?

The Abiding Truths of Catharsis

Although the conceptions of aesthetic reception by metaphysical and transcendental aesthetics proceed from discreditable assumptions, some of their content can be reappropriated in answering this question.

Metaphysical aesthetics conceives the reception of beauty as a catharsis consisting in the twofold experience where the audience perceives a mimetic portrayal of an ethical conflict of fundamental significance, comprehends it to be just that, and thereby is emotionally moved by the plight portrayed. This experience is intended to have a salutary effect on the character of the spectators, confronting them with the difficulties encumbering valid conduct and training their desires by repeatedly associating the pleasures of beauty with the portrayal of the good.

Catharsis, as arisen in the framework of edifying mimesis, presents a puzzle. In order for the experience of art to have any value, it must cultivate the character of the audience. This cannot be achieved by simply producing an understanding of the predetermined forms of goodness that are imitated. Such a theoretical influence is insufficient given that weakness of will is possible and knowledge of the good is not equivalent to virtue. Furthermore, even if knowing what is right were identical with being predisposed to do good, the deficient cognitive contribution of sensuous imitation would undercut the value of edifying art. Yet if virtue involves doing right for its own sake and not for attendant pleasure, can character actually be improved through habitually experiencing aesthetic pleasure from the mimesis of good deeds? Habit may, as Aristotle claims, instill correct desires so that individuals are already inclined to do what is right without need of external incentives. However, virtue requires not just an ingrained inclination but one that is acted on expressly for its own sake, as something known to be right. Consequently, although art might produce correct dispositions through habitual training and thereby facilitate the pursuit of valid conduct, art could only fulfill its edifying role if a cognitive element entered into reception.

The need for a cognitive element applies equally to the force of catharsis. The emotive dimension of catharsis is tied to the work of art's sensuous individuality to which feelings constitutively respond. Yet the emotional release of catharsis no less necessarily depends on two concomitant cognitive recognitions. First, the audience must comprehend that the appearance before it is a work of art and not a prosaic happening. Second, the audience must comprehend the sacred and/or ethical importance of the course of action that the work of art presents in varying degrees of scope and intensity. Unless the audience can recognize such truths in what it perceives, the experience lacks the seriousness that can raise feelings from the level of mere pleasure and aversion to that where the heart is stirred in its humane depths.[2]

As we have seen, what keeps this cognitive element from condemning art to a second-rate, dispensable encounter with our central concerns is the exemplary individuality by which beauty displays something that cannot be given an independent expression, be it in conceptual thought or religious faith. This exemplary individuality also frees art from depending on edifying effects for its legitimacy. For art now possesses a nonderivative revelation of humane truth, providing unique access to what Aristotle described as the realm of particulars that are wholly infused with what is universal and necessary,[3] a realm that exists neither in nature or prosaic convention, but only in the imaginative creation of art.

If catharsis is to be ingredient in the reception of art, it must thus be shorn of the remnants of edifying mimesis that still retain the categories of craft so incongruent with the exemplary individuality of beauty. On the one hand, catharsis can no longer have its value reside in edifying effects on the character of the audience. On the other hand, the truth that enters into the cathartic experience can no longer lie in predetermined forms whose meaning can be exhaustively defined and comprehended in independently given expressions.

Given these exclusions, does the reception of art retain any cathartic dimension? The experience of art by an audience will involve an encounter with truths that touch on the most valued aspects of that or any other rational audience's own existence: the domains of religious or secular conduct as exhibited in character and action involving a pathos elicited in significant spiritual or ethical strife. Accordingly, reception will contain the cathartic element of a self-revelation that is effected in perceiving imaginative displays of exemplary conduct, implicitly or explicitly traversing the outbreak and resolution of a spiritual or ethical conflict. Moreover, since this experience of self-understanding occurs through sensuous appearances, either directly intuited or imaginatively represented, it enters into relation with the feeling and emotive life of the audience in a way in which concepts alone cannot.

However, the established character of the external realization of the work of art precludes catharsis from occurring the moment the artwork is perceived. The individuality of artistic beauty necessarily injects an element of singular detail into the content of art as well as into the conventions of its configuration whose significance will be immediately intelligible neither to every member of a particular culture nor to every cultural community. As a result, the experience of catharsis will be dependent on a concomitant cultivation that gives the audience access to the aesthetically significant form and content of the work of art before it, as well as on the active application of that cultivation on the part of the viewers who will otherwise be left unmoved.[4] In all these respects, the reception of art requires an act of judgment in which the audience moves beyond instantaneous intuition to a more discriminating experience.[5]

The Recovery of Aesthetic Judgment

The abiding role of catharsis in the reception of art might seem to preclude the cardinal features of aesthetic judgment so strongly emphasized by transcendental aesthetics' master thinker, Kant. In order to retain the specificity of aesthetic judgment, while avoiding all recourse to natural forms of objectivity, Kant was compelled to identify the experience of art as one in which the spectator perceived a representation in a completely disinterested, noncognitive manner while experiencing a communicable pleasure at the free play of imagination and understanding elicited by the perception.

Catharsis seems to contradict virtually every one of these features. Because catharsis involves a self-revelation rooted in a comprehension of the spiritual significance of the artistic appearance, it contains an inexpungable cognitive dimension. Moreover, because the emotive engagement of catharsis rests on a self-identification where the spectator recognizes in the work some truth of fundamental value to his or her own conduct, the spectator can hardly be viewed as completely disinterested. Although interests of a purely private matter are here irrelevant, interests of a moral and religious character are not. And owing to these cognitive and ethical or spiritual elements, whatever satisfaction is felt at the aesthetic value of the artwork cannot reside simply in an awareness of a free play of imagination and understanding. Although the exemplary individuality of the work of art precludes any law-governed, formulaic reception, aesthetic experience cannot be indifferent to humane truths and the unity of meaning and configuration. To appreciate the aesthetic worth of an artwork requires recognizing not only the significance of its meaning, which involves the active cognitive contribution of the audience, but also how that meaning is joined to the shape by which it is conveyed. The idea of "free play" may exhibit the negative freedom of liberation from unaesthetic, externally ordered unities of craft, but it fails to lay hold of the specific role that imagination and understanding must play to experience the beauty of art. Moreover, it completely neglects the role of reason, which Kant totally ignores, in line with his dismissal of determinate cognitive elements in taste. Since the content of art revolves around normative conduct and the unity of concrete universality, both of which are determinable by reason rather than by the descriptive labors of understanding, aesthetic judgment cannot be a matter of imagination and understanding alone.

Nevertheless, aesthetic judgment retains aspects of all these features of the transcendental conception of reception. First, the reception of art is disinterested in both a theoretical and practical way. Aesthetic experience is theoretically disinterested to the extent that the truth of art is neither given independently of aesthetic display nor subordinate to prosaic ends.[6] It is practically disinterested in that the ethical significance of the work is not the result of extrinsic agendas but internal to its own aesthetic demands of content. Appreciating the aesthetic worth of an artwork involves neither using the work to achieve any independently given aim nor employing it to obtain any perspectively limited satisfaction. Only by letting the work show itself on its own terms,[7] in respect to its exemplary individuality and its unique unity of meaning and shape, does aesthetic experience occur.

Second, the experience of artistic beauty does not involve the type of cognition consisting in judging given objects to be subsumed under universal forms. The exemplary individuality of art provides lessons of a different sort, whose intelligibility centers on comprehending the concrete universality exhibited in the work of art's display. Here the registering of the individual in sense and feeling plays a cognitive role,[8] joining in the rational awareness that grasps the universal dimension equally at hand.[9]

Third, the pleasure derived from the reception of art will be universally communicable, but not because of some sensus communis residing in a transcendent, noumenal self. Instead, aesthetic pleasure will enjoy universal communicability because, on the one hand, the art object will exhibit the universally constitutive features of artistic beauty, and, on the other hand, the aesthetic experience of these features will depend on the corresponding employments of imagination, understanding, and reason by which they are perceived.

Fourth, the appreciation of a work of art can provide an occasion for a free play of the imagination and understanding to the extent that the work cannot be reduced, in respect to either its meaning or shape, to an externally given rule or formula. However, such free play cannot exhaust the positive side of the reception of art, which brings to bear a self-understanding of humanity and an appreciation of how that self-understanding is given a novel and unique configuration in the appearance of the artwork. Such appreciation requires not merely sensing the physical appearance of the art object or applying timeless forms of understanding to its image, but also comprehending the cultural context within which that object figures as a work of art melding a specific meaning with its shape.

Indeed, it is this abiding positive dimension that stamps the reception of art as an engagement reflecting autonomy on all sides.[10] Because the work is aesthetically appreciated only by being recognized to provide an exemplary configuration contributing to the self-understanding of humanity, the spectator must bracket out all his or her contingent, singular desires and interests and equally view the artwork apart from all the external influences and contingencies that impinge on the reality of a prosaic thing in contrast to the autonomous connection of meaning and shape distinguishing an art object. To appreciate the aesthetic worth of a work of art is to recognize both the independence of the artwork from its mundane surroundings and one's own freedom to partake in an experience that transcends all particular epochs and locales precisely because it reveals how one's most central concerns have an intrinsic value.¹¹ Thus, by allowing the work of art to show itself in its own independent integrity, the spectator experiences a correlative freedom, a freedom only to be had by refraining from subordinating the art object to the external demands of personal or public edification. Only then does catharsis occur, incorporating a form of prudential and theoretical disinterestedness, communicable pleasure, and a play of imagination, understanding, and reason in which freedom is reaffirmed.

Interpretation and Aesthetic Judgment

As the recovery of catharsis and aesthetic judgment underscores, the appreciation of a work of art is not rooted in the perception of any specific physical properties but rather in the recognition of a concretely universal unity of meaning and configuration, where the meaning conveys a self-understanding of humanity. The latter recognition requires comprehending a perceivable cultural context that both sets the art object apart from prosaic things as something to be appreciated in terms of aesthetic categories and enables the work to communicate the significance of its configuration.

However, does the constitutive role of this contextualization reduce the work of art to a plaything of interpretation, devoid of any aesthetic features that are not arbitrary, subjective constructs of each viewer? Admittedly, as Danto never tires of emphasizing,[12] entities of the same physical appearance could conceivably figure as either a prosaic thing or a work of art depending on their cultural context. Moreover, the same entity could conceivably figure in either capacity according to the framework in which it was received. Further, the same entity could function in one context as an artwork of a certain significance and count in another as an artwork of an entirely different meaning. Analogously, physically indistinguishable things could comprise different artworks with different unities of meaning and configuration according to the framework in which they were perceived. Indeed, it is even possible for the same entity or for physically identical things to fall into different artistic forms or genres[13] depending on the context in which they are advanced and apprehended.[14] Does this signify, as Danto suggests, that with every new interpretation a new artwork is born, even if its abiding material body remains unchanged from its previously interpreted ensoulment?[15]

Indeed, in each case an element of subjective discretion cannot fail to enter in regarding what context to employ in aesthetically appreciating the putative artwork, which of its physical features to accept as part of its artistic configuration, and what meaning to associate with that shape. All of these judgments involve an inexpungable subjective dimension on two accounts. First, each one proceeds on a sensible perception of the work's appearance, a perception that, as such, is to some degree relative to the perspective and sensibility of the individual observer. In this respect, the "material counterpart" of the artwork, that is, its mere physical appearance, is itself something whose apprehension is relative to the subjective variances of empirical observation, for which a pragmatic consensus is the most that can be sought.

Second, each of these judgments involves a choice among alternative interpretations concerning what significance is tied to the physical being of the putative artwork. Moreover, as Danto suggests, what elements and structures of the material counterpart of the artwork are part of its aesthetic reality are equally determined by the interpretation that associates a meaning with it, for this interpretative act must distinguish those features of the artwork's physical appearance that are significant parts of its artistic configuration from those that are incidental accidents of its physical being.[16] The support for this interpretation of the meaning and configuration of the artwork must largely rest on characterizations of cultural contexts and associations that are given in experience, including what are perceived to be the artist's beliefs and intentions.[17] On account of this dependency on meanings culled from experience, the interpretation of the artwork is once more subject to the same uncertainties plaguing any empirical knowledge.

Although these endemic subjective conditions of art appreciation render art criticism of individual works a matter of corrigible, unquenchable debate, they only enter in in conjunction with all the systematically established determinations of the concept of artistic beauty and its realization in the work of art. As Danto points out, without interpretation there certainly can be no art appreciation.[18] Yet it is an exaggeration to conclude in idealist fashion, as Danto does, that the artwork's "*esse* is *interpretari*."[19] Without the objective determinations of the concept of art already at hand in the intersubjective reality of aesthetic appearance and available to the communicable thought of its audience, art appreciation cannot begin to engage in the act of interpretation whereby it leaves prosaic observation behind and instead apprehends the identity of the work of art by judging how the artwork joins meaning to its physical presence.

For this reason, there can be no question of aesthetic interpretation determining the concept of art.[20] On the contrary, the reception of art is defined in respect to the conceptually antecedent determination of artistic beauty and its realization in the work of art. Hence, although there may be no neutral way of judging the aesthetic character of a particular object,[21] any such judgment still stands in need of the neutral categories of art in general. They provide the only standard available for thinking the divide between the prosaic and the aesthetic, a standard to which art critics must appeal in evaluating the putative artworks before them. Hence, contra Danto,[22] even though encountering an individual artwork is predicated on various historical aspects of the environment of its production and reception, this does not preclude the philosophy of art from being an ahistorical theory.

The situation of art interpretation is thus not unlike that of a court of law. Judges only have the discretion to decide what the law means and how it is to be applied to individual cases within a legal framework resting on a settled recognition of what constitutes the body of law to be interpreted and applied and of how the identity and procedures of judicial authority are defined.[23] Unless their parameters are already decided, there is no law to be interpreted and applied, and no authority to engage in legal interpretation. Those who would absolutize interpretation by advancing a universal hermeneutics in which all discourse is plagued by the contingent contextuality of the hermeneutic circle ignore how interpretation always presupposes a given subject matter to interpret and a given interpreter. As such, the very identities of theme and interpreter are beyond interpretation. Interpretation is thereby left conditioned by factors determined independently of itself, precluding the hegemony of hermeneutic discourse touted so fashionably today.

This dependence of interpretation on terms insusceptible of hermeneutic reflection is exhibited in art appreciation by how the possibility of variously interpreting the artistic identity of some physical entity is predicated on the objective determinations of the concept of art, which supplies aesthetic judgment with the categories it needs to apply in assessing the character of any putative artwork. Whether a particular object counts as a certain work of art with a specific meaning and configuration is irrevocably a matter of interpretation, conditioned by the uncovered historical identity of the object and the cultural formation and subjective discretion of its audience. Yet what it takes to be, produce, and appreciate an artwork, either in general or in respect to a particular style and individual genre, all remain matters of aesthetic theory, dictated by reason independently of any particular interpretive standpoint.[24] Without employing these fruits of the nonhermeneutic discourse of systematic aesthetics, the interpretation of art cannot even certify its own identity as artistic interpretation.[25] It remains blind, deaf, and dumb, or full of sound and fury with no certainty of where to look for its prey or how to recognize it when stumbled upon.

Consequently, although the interpretation of art can never free itself of an element of subjective discretion, aesthetic judgment is always constrained by two sets of independently determined factors. On the one hand, art interpretation must seek its standards in the categories of aesthetics, which identify art in general, particular art forms, and individual genres independently of any subjective or historically relative standpoints. Accordingly, whenever an object is judged to be an artwork it must be interpreted so as to satisfy the general requirements of artistic beauty, which mandate the concrete universality of the unity of meaning and configuration, the type of content suitable for artistic construal, and the conditions for accessibility to an audience. Similarly, for an object to be judged an artwork of a specific form, the interpretation must identify how the putative artwork exhibits the particular mode of artistic construal constitutive of that form of art. And if the object is to be interpreted as an artwork of a certain genre, that interpretation must abide by that genre's rules.[26] Any would-be art interpretation that violates these guidelines dictated by the systematic concept of art condemns itself to incoherence, ascribing putatively aesthetic features to an object that fail to possess a properly aesthetic character.

On the other hand, art interpretation must guide its judgment of how to identify the meaning of a particular putative artwork by appealing to the given common associations that already underlie the cultural context and history of production of the object under scrutiny. Owing to the concrete universality of beauty, tying meaning and configuration together, none of these factors can individually or together comprise the complete significance of the work of art. If they could, the work would express a meaning that is given independently of its unique configuration, destroying its aesthetic value. Instead, these factors play a contributing, but not a determining, role in establishing the work's meaning. Yet, in this subordinate role they must be paid heed if the object is to reveal itself as a work of art.

Thus, although the perceived or hypothetically constructed intentions of the artist can enter into forming an interpretation of an artwork, they do so not by comprising its meaning but rather by helping to unravel aspects of its iconography, which, once unveiled, permit the work to speak in its unique, self-contained right. Accordingly, even if the interpretation of an artwork must cohere with the putative intentions of its maker, it would still be a mistake to commit the "intentional fallacy"[27] of understanding the meaning of the artwork to lie in the antecedent intention of the artist.[28] Moreover, although an artwork expresses a self-understanding of humanity, the exhibition of that viewpoint in the depiction of some content need not be fully apparent to its author. As art, the work expresses a worldview by how its configuration is imbued with meaning and not in virtue of what beliefs its creator may have had, even if these help decipher its significance.

Constrained by the categories of aesthetics on one side and by the historically given conditions of meaning on the other, art interpretation retains its due subordinate place in the reality of art. Incapable of establishing even its very own structure through the hermeneutic judgment in which it engages, art interpretation can only be grasped by the noninterpretive conception of systematic aesthetics. Yet, without art interpretation's acts of discretion, no audience can gain access to art, nor can any artwork manifest its unique beauty.

Postscript: The Abiding Tasks of Systematic Aesthetics

In determining the constitutive features of the work of art, artistic creation, and the reception of art, systematic aesthetics has provided an account of what is common and necessary in each and every aesthetic phenomenon. What certifies the completeness of this account is how each successive determination of art has incorporated those that preceded it without relying on any other aesthetic factors that have yet to be established. In so conforming to the strictures of immanent categorial development, the resulting theory of art in general has conceived a whole without any gaps, a whole whose unity resides in the integration of those elements by which it is constituted, a whole whose own content testifies to the nonarbitrary ordering of its conception. The minimal determination of beauty has finally vindicated itself as a starting point, demonstrating its own necessity by being contained in each and every further dimension of what is universal to art. Moreover, the factors privileged by metaphysical and transcendental aesthetics have been recast in their proper place, as subsidiary elements rather than determining principles of beauty. In all these respects, the systematic theory of art in general has done far more than satisfy the requirements of reflective equilibrium. By developing the categories generic to art without presupposing any prior aesthetic principles, systematic aesthetics has not only coherently united the notions perennially ascribed to art but has overcome any dogmatic reference to accepted intuitions.

Yet in bringing to closure the conception of what is universal to art, has systematic aesthetics exhausted its labors? By being universally constitutive, the features so far grasped must be at hand in any particular forms of artistic expression and in any individual art. However, simply by being universal dimensions of the reality, creation, and reception of art, they cannot serve to identify what distinguishes the particular art forms and individual arts from one another. Whereas any putatively universal determination of art would forfeit its universality if it were the identifying mark of any particular art form or individual art, each art form and art would lose its specificity if all it involved were generic dimensions of aesthetic reality.

This predicament could suggest that systematic aesthetics has here run its course, leaving analyses of how classical and romantic art forms compare or of how architecture and film have different aesthetic possibilities to the ever debatable interpretive judgments of art criticism. After all, if the particular forms of art and the individual arts are differentiated by more than the universal features of art, and if systematic aesthetics has no other resources than these that have been certified by reason, any further account of particular and individual dimensions of art would seem to depend on empirical contents derived from interpretations of art history.

As plausible as this resignation to corrigible interpretation might seem, it ignores a capital problem plaguing any attempt to conceive the particular art forms and individual arts on the basis of historical example. To begin with, no interpretation of the given reality of art forms and individual arts can establish which of the found features are genuinely constitutive without already taking for granted the identity of each art form and art. Moreover, any attempt to distinguish art forms and arts without employing the categories of art in general risks constructing boundaries whose defining borders are devoid of aesthetic significance. Art forms, for instance, could be divided according to formal features of configuration such as linear versus painterly, to take Wölfflin's famous example,[1] or as severe, ideal, and pleasing, as Hegel suggests in his introduction to the analysis of the individual arts.[2] Alternately, art forms can be grouped according to formal features of content, such as the religious, national, racial, class, or sexual identity of their creators and themes. However, constructing art forms under such headings cannot unite artistic phenomena in any aesthetically relevant sense, because these headings ignore the unity of meaning and configuration basic to art. Analogously, any attempt to identify individual arts by factors given independently of what is commonly constitutive of art will end up relying on differentia that have no relation to aesthetic concerns.

Consequently, if aesthetically meaningful differences are to be found among particular art forms and individual arts, these must rest upon an application of features already provided for in systematic aesthetics' determination of art in general, using these to qualify one another. Then the methodological requirement of categorial immanence can be upheld, arriving at irreducible new levels of artistic reality without relying on any constituents that have not already been determined. Therefore, systematic aesthetics has hardly arrived at its end simply by completing the conception of what is universally the case in art. Rather, systematic aesthetics has here reached the threshold for advancing to two further levels of artistic phenomena. If, for instance, the generic elements of meaning and configuration in art can be joined in different but conceptually determinate modes of unity, then the road to a systematic theory of the art forms lies open. Similarly, if the constitutive elements of the external reality of the work of art allow for diverse but conceptually defined artistic media, and these media offer different but conceptually determinate possibilities for configuring the content generic to art, as well as for realizing the possible particular modes of artistic construal, then systematic aesthetics can advance to a theory of the individual arts.

Although few historical thinkers have ventured in these directions, the exceptional example of Hegel's *Lectures on Aesthetics* presents at the very least a premonition of how a theory of the art forms and of the individual arts may fall within the grasp of philosophical reason.[3] Can systematic aesthetics succeed in these undertakings? No greater challenge than this confronts theorists of art today.

Notes

Introduction

1. For a further exploration of this problem in Wittgenstein, see Winfield, *Freedom and Modernity*, 16–18.

2. This Achilles' heel of Foucault is well diagnosed by Habermas in his *Philosophical Discourse*, 266–93.

3. The three modes of normative argumentation and the overcoming of the dilemmas of foundationalism by the identification of normativity and self-determination are analyzed at length in connection with epistemology and ethics in my *Reason and Justice, Overcoming Foundations,* and *Freedom and Modernity*. In *The Just Economy* and *Law in Civil Society* I conceive the principles of economic and legal justice in accord with the normative requirements of systematic philosophy. For parallel attempts to legitimate the project of a foundation-free systematic philosophy and ethics, see Maker, *Philosophy without Foundations,* and Berman, *Categorial Justification,* works inspired, like my own, by Kenley Royce Dove's interpretation of Hegel.

4. See Rorty, *Irony, Contingency, and Solidarity*.

5. For a devastating critique of the Rortian gambit and its postmodern analogues, see Rapp, "Coming Out into the Corridor," 533–52; Rapp, "Ideology and the New Pragmatism," 125–37; and Rapp, "Crisis of Reason," 261–90.

Chapter 1: The Immanent Critique of Metaphysical Aesthetics

1. I here freely draw from Michael B. Foster's analysis of ancient thought, developed in his *Political Philosophies of Plato and Hegel*.

2. Goodman, *Languages of Art,* 5.

3. In this vein, Susan Sontag observes how the perseverance of the mimetic

theory of art has condemned its followers to a perennial project of interpretation, for whose act of translation what always comes first is the search for the separable content of the work of art (*Against Interpretation*, 4–5).

4. For a somewhat comparable list, see Collingwood, *Principles of Art*, 20–26.

5. Admittedly, many particulars of the artwork remain indifferent to its aesthetic significance, such as the weight and chemical composition of a sculpture, the unobservable marks on the back of a canvas, or the typeface of a novel.

6. As Collingwood rightly emphasizes, Plato's appeal to imitative craft does not apply to the entire realm of art (*Principles of Art*, 46–51) but extends only to those arts that are representative, excluding, for instance, those types of nonrepresentative poetry that Plato also acknowledges on several occasions in the *Republic* (392d, 607a). Whether Plato has any other conceptual tools at his disposal to determine such nonrepresentative art is a question for speculation, since his aesthetic analyses are almost entirely directed at works of representative, mimetic art. Here, in any event, Plato provides a classic statement of the metaphysical approach to aesthetics, even if he never advances it as an argument addressing art in general.

7. Although Collingwood maintains that representation must be distinguished from imitation in that art as representative relates to something given in nature whereas art as imitative relates to another artifact (*Principles of Art*, 42), it makes more sense to regard imitation in Collingwood's restricted use as a particular type of representation, since artifacts and natural entities are equally susceptible of representation. On the other hand, since the imitative character of mimesis is commonly applied to its representative features in general, there is little reason not to allow the two terms to overlap. In any event, insofar as representation, broadly understood as the reimposition of given forms in given matter, remains bound to the categories of craft, which turn out to be unsuitable for determining aesthetic worth, Collingwood's claim that the aesthetic value of art cannot reside in its representative character (43) retains its validity.

8. Danto, *Transfiguration of the Commonplace*, 70.

9. Plato, *Sophist*, 264d–267d.

10. Or as Susan Sontag observes, the theory of mimesis sets art in need of a defense (*On Interpretation*, 4).

11. Plato, *Laws*, 667b–669b.

12. Plato, *Republic*, 598.

13. Ibid., 599.

14. Ibid., 601.

15. Ibid., 603, 605.

16. Ibid., 401d.

17. Ibid., 402a.

18. Friedrich Schiller appeals on these same grounds to the edifying role of art as a remedy for overcoming the indifference of freedom and necessity, or of duty and inclination (see the ninth letter in Schiller's *Aesthetic Education*, 59, 61).

19. Given that the life of the citizen provides the focal point of ethical conduct, it thus makes perfect sense to follow Allan Bloom in considering Aristotle's *Poetics* an appendix to his *Politics* (see Bloom, *Closing of the American Mind*, 72–73).

20. Plato, *Republic*, 398c–400d, 401d; *Laws*, 667b–669a; Aristotle, *Politics*, 1339b.

21. I have described the basic logic of the metaphysical approach to ethics in chapter 2 of my *Reason and Justice*.

22. Plato, *Republic*, 607.

23. Plato, *Laws*, 667b–669a.

24. Plato, *Republic*, 379a–382c.

25. Ibid., 386a–398b.

26. Plato, *Ion*, 532h–536b.

27. Kant, *Critique of Judgment*, no. 46, Ak. 307; 174–75.

28. Again, as with Plato, it must be borne in mind that Aristotle's advocacy of metaphysical aesthetics does not unambiguously extend to all of his remarks on art. As Collingwood points out, Aristotle, like his teacher, admits of a distinction between representative and nonrepresentative art, allowing for the possibility of a type of art to which the categories of imitative craft are inapplicable (*Principles of Art*, 50–52). Nevertheless, Aristotle's *Poetics*, at least in the fragmentary form in which it has survived, restricts its analysis almost entirely to the particular representative art that Aristotle finds exhibited in poetry, and in dramatic poetry in particular. In this limited domain, Aristotle's discussion does provide a classic elaboration of the implications of the metaphysical approach in aesthetics.

29. Aristotle, *Poetics*, 1448b4. Thus music, for example, supplies aesthetic enjoyment by imitating all the qualities of character in its rhythm and melody, fostering habits of feeling pleasure or pain at its mere representations that cultivate the power of forming right judgments and taking delight in good character and noble actions (1339b).

30. Ibid., 1449a20.

31. Ibid.

32. Ibid., 1452b.

33. See Brecht, *Kleines Organon*, 660–700.

34. Aristotle, *Poetics*, 1450b25.

35. Ibid., 1449a20.

36. Ibid., 1452a.

37. Ibid., 1459a.

38. Ibid., 1451b.
39. Ibid., 1452a.
40. Foster, *Political Philosophies of Plato and Hegel*, 201.
41. I am here following out the brief but extremely important points that Michael Foster makes on art in the course of his masterful critique of ancient political thought (*Political Philosophies of Plato and Hegel*, 185–87, 201).
42. For this reason, Collingwood can urge abandoning employment of the term "fine art" for aesthetic productions because it retains a residual vestige of the technical theory of art (*Principles of Art*, 36). However, so long as the term "art" is still employed to describe certain artisanal activities, "fine art" remains a helpful term provided it is used with cognizance of its incongruity with craft.
43. Foster, *Political Philosophies of Plato and Hegel*, 186.

Chapter 2: The Impasse of Transcendental Aesthetics

1. Collingwood goes so far as to claim that the problems afflicting any attempt to develop aesthetics on a "realistic" footing also preclude any retention of beauty as an object of aesthetic speculation. In the wake of the breakdown of the technical theory of art, Collingwood maintains, all "beauty" can be left to connote is the property of objects for which they are loved, admired, or desired (*Principles of Art*, 37–41). However, as the example of Kant demonstrates, the transcendental turn to aesthetic experience to which Collingwood subscribes has room for addressing beauty as a feature peculiar to taste and distinct from love, respect, and desire. Yet Collingwood's denial still has a prophetic ring, for transcendental aesthetics proves unable to provide any particular content for beauty without reverting to the metaphysical categories of the technical theory of art.
2. In indifference to the Kantian argument that aesthetic reception forfeits its specificity if it be tied to practical ends, Terry Eagleton expressly reduces aesthetics to rhetoric in his deconstruction of literary theory (*Literary Theory*, 205ff.).
3. Thus we find Kant introducing his *Critique of Pure Reason* as a propaedeutic that will pave the way for metaphysics of nature and of freedom, only to admit that these treatises of a priori knowledge consist in nothing but an explication of what is already analytically contained in the synthetic a priori truths of the *Critique*'s doctrine of the understanding and reason.
4. Hume, "Of the Standard of Taste," 229.
5. Ibid., 230.
6. Ibid., 231–32.
7. Ibid., 231.
8. Ibid., 227.
9. Ibid., 233.

10. Ibid., 232–34, 237, 240–41.

11. Ibid., 233.

12. Kant, *Critique of Judgment*, no. 31, Ak. 280–81; 143–44.

13. Ibid., no. 37, Ak. 289; 154.

14. Ibid.

15. Ibid., no. 36, Ak. 288; 153.

16. Kant is quite open about this indeterminacy. Not only does he acknowledge that the judgment of taste is based on an indeterminate concept, but he grants that this concept is the indefinite idea of the supersensible in us, which cannot be rendered any more intelligible, since its sources are hidden from our knowing (ibid., no. 57, Ak. 341; 213–14). Yet, if this is true, how can anyone be certain that one is experiencing the free play on which beauty is to be grounded, or that the appearance one contemplates should elicit an equally ineffable and indefinable response in others?

17. Ibid., no. 22, Ak. 241–43; 91–93.

18. Ibid., no. 12, Ak. 222; 68.

19. Ibid., no. 22, Ak. 240; 91.

20. Ibid., no. 14, Ak. 224–25; 69–70, 71.

21. Ibid., no. 14, Ak. 225; 71–72.

22. Ibid., no. 22, Ak. 242–43; 93.

23. Ibid., no. 51, Ak. 321; 190.

24. Ibid., no. 45, Ak. 306–7; 173–74.

25. Ibid., no. 48, Ak. 311; 179.

26. As Gadamer points out, when Kant conceives artistic beauty as dependent on a given concept, in contrast to natural beauty, which is free in virtue of not representing an object, he ignores the possibility that creative art could exhibit a freedom from the representation of given concepts that could still have its own special relation to truth. As a result, "nonsignificant" beauty, as in decoration and nature, becomes paradigmatic for Kant as the only abode for avoiding the cognitive pitfalls of mimetic craft (*Relevance of the Beautiful*, 18–20, 164).

27. Kant, *Critique of Judgment*, nos. 62–68, Ak. 362–84; 239–64.

28. Ibid., no. 59, Ak. 353; 228.

29. Ibid., no. 18, Ak. 237; 85.

30. This abiding indeterminacy is reflected in Gadamer's suggestion that the model of Kant's notion of free beauty is decorative art and natural beauty, both of which offer little more than pleasantness of form without connection to any determinate truths by which rational agents could obtain an aesthetically specific self-understanding (*Relevance of the Beautiful*, 18–20, 161, 168).

31. Kant, *Critique of Judgment*, no. 49, Ak. 314; 182.

32. Ibid., no. 57, Ak. 342; 215.

33. Ibid., no. 49, Ak. 314; 182.

34. Ibid., no. 49, Ak. 315; 183.
35. Ibid., no. 49, Ak. 316; 185.
36. Ibid., comment I to no. 57, Ak. 344; 217.
37. Ibid., no. 34, Ak. 286; 150.

Chapter 3: The Mandate of Systematic Aesthetics

1. This autonomy is already anticipated in the Platonic theory of forms, which, despite its appeal to an antecedently given realm of intelligible essences, acknowledges that the beauty of what is beautiful can reside in nothing but the presence of beauty.

2. This conflation of rational reconstruction and transcendental argument is committed by Klaus Hartmann in his "nonmetaphysical" rehabilitation of Hegel ("Hegel: A Nonmetaphysical View," 101–24) as well as by White in his *Absolute Knowledge*. For a more extended critique of this conflation, see Winfield, *Freedom and Modernity*, 19–32.

3. For a further discussion of the dilemmas of transcendental argument, see Winfield, *Reason and Justice*, Chapter 3; Winfield, *Overcoming Foundations*, Chapters 1–4; and Winfield, *Freedom and Modernity*, Chapter 2.

4. In *Hegel contra Sociology*, Gillian Rose maintains that Hegel's aesthetic theory is transcendental "because it assumes actual art-forms and individual arts as given and examines their possibility" (122) in light of specific historical and social preconditions. Although Hegel certainly engages in an interpretative discussion of actual artistic developments in relation to their historical backgrounds, his systematic argument could not exhibit the degree of categorial immanence that it does unless these empirical items served only an illustrative, rather than constitutive, role in moving from one determination to another.

5. Presuppositionlessness is secured provided the entire categorial development issues from indeterminacy and not from some given content. For a more extensive account of how a systematic philosophy without foundations can so proceed and of the role of rational reconstruction within it, see Winfield, *Reason and Justice*, Part 3, 117–55, and Berman, *Categorial Justification*, 67–128.

6. That the determination of aesthetic phenomena in general leads to a determination of the particular forms of art, and then to the categorization of the individual arts, presupposes that the concept of an object of aesthetic worth turns out to be that of an object of fine art, rather than a thing of "natural beauty." By exposing the limits of "beauty" in nature, Chapter 5 establishes that this is indeed the case.

7. Derrida, *The Truth in Painting*, 20–22.

8. For a classic statement of this fatal view, see Derrida's essay "Différance" in *Margins of Philosophy*, 1–27.

9. Hegel, of course, shows this at length in his analysis of determinate being

in the *Science of Logic*. For further discussion of the significance of this argument, see Winfield, *Overcoming Foundations*, Chapter 3, 55–75.

10. Heidegger similarly suggests that art is prior to both artist and work of art. Yet before art can be certified to be "the origin of both artist and work" (*Origin of the Work of Art*, 650), beauty must be shown to be ultimately artistic beauty. As it turns out, the identification of beauty as artistic beauty rests on the individuality and truth ingredient in aesthetic worth. Heidegger may well tie the nature of art to truth, but whether he does so in a way that distinguishes art from other vehicles of truth, such as religion or philosophy, is questionable. Unless this differentiation is achieved, an account of art in respect to truth fails to capture what is specific to the aesthetic dimension.

11. Hegel's own position on this score appears at first glance rather ambiguous. Although he begins the systematic argument of his *Lectures on Aesthetics* with an analysis of beauty in general under the heading of the idea of *artistic* beauty, he divides this discussion into three sections successively addressing the concept of beauty, the beauty of nature, and the beauty of works of fine art. This ordering suggests that the minimal determination of beauty does not yet bear any particular reference to art, and that natural beauty is just as much a species of beauty in general as is artistic beauty. However, at the same time, Hegel is adamant that aesthetics is properly the philosophy of fine art and that the concept of beauty can only be adequately realized by objects of fine art. Indeed, as we shall see, the whole point of his analysis of the beauty of nature seems to consist in showing how natural beauty is inherently deficient, such that beauty turns out to be in truth nothing other than artistic beauty.

12. As discussed below, this conformity need not be construed merely as a feature of propositions, in accord with the model of truth as "correctness," where concept and object are independent givens, logically incommensurable and related through a subjective connection. The conformity of concept and object can also be conceived as what Hegel calls the "Idea," where the connection is no longer subjective and the related terms are not incompatible.

13. Danto, *Transfiguration of the Commonplace*, 83.

14. Heidegger may be justified in claiming that "beauty is one way in which truth occurs as unconcealedness," yet he still fails to identify what is specific to art when he proceeds to claim that artistic creation reveals what is essential to an entire world (*Origin of the Work of Art*, 682). Since such revelation is hardly exclusive to art, the constitutive relation of truth and art must lie in something more.

15. Hegel, *Lectures on Aesthetics*, 1:111.

16. Hegel characterizes the correctness model as the subjective paradigm of truth, where an appearance counts as true simply because its reality matches one of *my* representations, rather than because its reality is adequate to the concept (ibid., 1:110–11). Like so many other contemporary thinkers, Danto embraces

the correctness model by maintaining that philosophy requires opening a gap between reality on the one hand and a discourse on the other that "contrasts in a global way with reality," leaving philosophy ultimately concerned with "the space between language and the world" (*Transfiguration of the Commonplace*, 79).

17. For Heidegger's deft formulation of the dilemma of the correctness model, see his *Origin of the Work of Art*, 678–79. To the degree that Heidegger makes appeal to *Dasein* as the given framework in terms of which being is given to knowing, he remains trapped in the correctness model, retaining a representational structure (*Dasein* in its relation to being) as the underlying premise for all determinacy. This problem remains when the analytic of *Dasein* is replaced by an appeal to poetic discourse as the locus for the disclosure of being.

18. For a discussion of how Hegel hereby overcomes the dilemmas of foundationalism afflicting metaphysical as well as transcendental philosophy, see Winfield, *Reason and Justice*, Part 3.

19. For a provocative account of how Hegel provides a solution to the problem of the differentia in the *Science of Logic*, see Halper's "Hegel and the Problem of the Differentia," 191–202.

20. Hegel himself introduces this qualification, noting how beauty's union of meaning and individual configuration is achieved in the sphere of imagination as well as in sensuous externality (*Lectures on Aesthetics*, 1:101).

21. Hegel himself points this out, noting how when beauty presents itself in an objective existent, what gives that entity its aesthetic value is only the pure appearance of the Idea that it displays (ibid., 1:111).

22. As Michael Mitias argues, interpreting Hegel's account in a way that highlights its conformity with Danto's central point, the art object cannot be identified with its physical being, for it is an object of spirit in two respects: both as a product of creative imagination and as an object of imaginative contemplation ("Hegel on the Art Object," 73–74).

23. Danto emphasizes this point in his *Transfiguration of the Commonplace*.

24. In this respect, Hegel and, in a derivative vein, Danto both suggest that art arises as such when works cease to be treated as immediate embodiments of divine or magical reality, and instead are removed from the sphere of the immediately real to stand as bearers of an appearance that sensuously expresses truths of fundamental importance. See Hegel, *Lectures on Aesthetics*, 1:316, and Danto, *Transfiguration of the Commonplace*, 76–77.

Chapter 4: The Individuality of Beauty

1. Hegel makes this argument at each level of his systematic analysis of the logical forms of universality, particularity, and individuality in the "Logic of the Concept" of his *Science of Logic*.

2. For a further exploration of the codetermination of universality, particularity, and individuality, see "On Individuality" in Winfield, *Freedom and Modernity,* 53–55.

3. Lukács draws this connection in his *Über die Besonderheit als Kategorie der Ästhetik,* 7–8.

4. Michael Foster suggests this point in his article "The Concrete Universal," 2.

5. Ibid., 1.
6. Ibid., 4, 9–10.
7. See sections 35–37 of Wollheim, *Art and Its Objects,* 74–84.
8. Ibid., 76ff.
9. Ibid., 77.
10. Ibid.
11. Ibid.
12. Ibid., 80.
13. Ibid., 82.
14. Ibid., 76.
15. Ibid., 82.
16. Foster, "The Concrete Universal," 1.
17. Ibid., 2.
18. Ibid., 17.

19. See "Reification and the Class Consciousness of the Proletariat" in Lukács, *History and Class Consciousness,* 83–222.

20. The logic of the growth and reproduction of the species of real organisms requires the introduction of further categories that need not be addressed in this context.

21. As William Desmond suggests, the autonomy ingredient in the concrete universality of beauty can also be ascribed the character of being an end in itself, self-grounding, self-articulating, and a world unto itself (*Art and the Absolute,* 9–10, 22).

22. Ibid., 3.
23. Foster, "The Concrete Universal," 19.
24. Ibid., 16–17.
25. Ibid., 17.
26. Ibid., 19.
27. Ibid., 21.
28. Ibid., 17.

29. Lukács, *Die Eigenart des Ästhetischen,* 2:195–96, 206; Lukács, *Über die Besonderheit als Kategorie der Ästhetik,* 224.

30. Lukács, *Die Eigenart des Ästhetischen,* 2:206; Lukács, *Über die Besonderheit als Kategorie der Ästhetik,* 214.

31. Lukács, *Die Eigenart des Ästhetischen,* 2:232–33.

32. Perhaps it is for this reason that Lukács evades the issue of establishing *how* particularity functions as the privileged mediating term by claiming that there is no universal criterion for precisely determining this function, as if this provided a philosophical foundation for the plurality of fine arts, styles, genres, and individual works. See Lukács, *Die Eigenart des Ästhetischen*, 2:256, and Lukács, *Über die Besonderheit als Kategorie der Ästhetik*, 218–19.

33. Indeed, this is evident in Lukács's critiques of socialist realism and naturalism, in which he condemns the former for sticking to a formal universality where typicality prevails at the expense of individuality, and dismisses the latter for embracing the individual in its immediate givenness without investing it with the universality and particularity that can make it aesthetically meaningful.

Chapter 5: Beauty as Such and Natural Beauty

1. As we shall see, this does not mean that the given sensuous *appearance* of rational agents directly exhibits concrete universality. If it did, beauty would extend beyond works of fine art to the "natural" being of individuals and to the immediate existence of their interactions.

2. Lukács makes this point in his *Die Eigenart des Ästhetischen*, 2:611–12.

3. Hegel, *Lectures on Aesthetics*, 1:116.

4. Lukács makes this point in his *Die Eigenart des Ästhetischen*, 2:607.

5. Hegel, *Lectures on Aesthetics*, 1:143, 144.

6. For an analysis of how the totality of logical determinacy (the Idea) stands in relation to nature, see Winfield, *Freedom and Modernity*, 33–50, and Winfield, *Reason and Justice*, 146–50.

7. Adorno, *Ästhetische Theorie*, 110.

8. Lukács makes this point in his *Die Eigenart des Ästhetischen*, 2:611–12.

9. Hegel discusses these relations in his *Lectures on Aesthetics*, 1:116.

10. Hegel discusses the aesthetic deficiency of these abstract forms at length in ibid., 1:134–41.

11. Ibid., 1:142–43.

12. This dilemma undermines any aesthetics of proportion, such as propounded by St. Augustine, Vitruvius, and Boethius. For a discussion of such conceptions see Eco, *Art and Beauty in the Middle Ages*, 28–42.

13. See Hegel, *Lectures on Aesthetics*, 1:117–18.

14. See Hegel's discussion of the aesthetic limitations of harmony in contrast to melody in ibid., 1:141.

15. Lukács makes this point in his *Die Eigenart des Ästhetischen*, 2:612.

16. Foster, "The Concrete Universal," 13.

17. Ibid., 14.

18. Hegel makes this point concerning the difference in form between a living

thing's internal organs and the extremities with which it interacts with its environment (*Lectures on Aesthetics*, 1:136-37).

19. This limitation undermines "the aesthetics of the organism" that Eco ascribes to Aquinas, whose accompanying functionalist theory of beauty falls victim to the dilemmas of the mimetic theory of embodied form from which it derives. For a brief account of Aquinas's aesthetic thought see Eco, *Art and Beauty in the Middle Ages*, 74-83.

20. See Hegel, *Lectures on Aesthetics*, 1:122.

21. Ibid., 1:124.

22. Ibid., 1:130, 132, 145. Nevertheless, the extent to which animal life brings nature closest to such an achievement makes plausible why Hegel can describe it as "the summit of natural beauty" (1:132).

23. See Lukács, *Die Eigenart des Ästhetischen*, 2:602.

24. Hegel, *Lectures on Aesthetics*, 1:149-50.

25. Ibid., 1:146.

26. Ibid., 1:150-51.

27. See Lukács, *Die Eigenart des Ästhetischen*, 2:655.

28. Hegel, *Lecture on Aesthetics*, 1:149-50.

29. Lukács, *Die Eigenart des Ästhetischen*, 2:581.

30. Hegel, *Lectures on Aesthetics*, 1:147.

31. Following Hegel, Lukács affirms this point (*Die Eigenart des Ästhetischen*, 2:581-82).

32. Adorno, *Ästhetische Theorie*, 103.

33. Ibid., 102-3.

34. See Kant, *Critique of Judgment*, sections 23 and 42, as well as Lukács's discussion of these passages in his *Ästhetik*, 4:46-47.

35. Lukács, *Die Eigenart des Ästhetischen*, 2:620-21.

36. Ibid., 2:624.

37. Adorno, *Ästhetische Theorie*, 110.

38. Lukács engages in an example of such interpretation in his *Die Eigenart des Ästhetischen*, 2:633ff.

39. Ibid., 2:636, 673-74.

40. Hegel, *Lectures on Aesthetics*, 1:123.

41. Danto, *Transfiguration of the Commonplace*, 96.

42. Danto, who suggests that the beauty of the material counterpart of a work of art creates a divide between the beauty of an artwork and that of a prosaic thing (ibid., 105-7), fails to recognize that the distinction between an artwork and its material counterpart need not demarcate the terms of their respective aesthetic value or of their respective aesthetic appreciation. In each case, the presence of beauty and its reception depend on a concretely universal

sensuous presentation of a meaning providing a fundamental self-understanding for humanity.

Chapter 6: Beauty as Artistic Beauty

1. Hegel calls this concretely universal unification the Idea, which is why he considers the Idea to be the category of truth.

2. Inklings of this privileged aesthetic role of rational agency in the form and content of beauty are to be found in Shaftesbury's ranking of the orders of beauty (see Shaftesbury, *Characteristics*, 251–53).

3. As Herbert Marcuse points out, the transfiguration effected by art always involves to some degree a given cultural material that is then imaginatively reworked. Otherwise, as he argues, "all communication would be severed" (*The Aesthetic Dimension*, 41).

4. Danto, *Transfiguration of the Commonplace*, 168.

5. As Chapter 10 will discuss, this positing of the appearance of beauty can involve the creation of a novel physical configuration out of given materials or simply the setting of a given thing within the recognizable context of aesthetic appreciation, as when an object of "found" art, industrial design, or "primitive" culture is removed from its given context of prosaic, magical, or religious employ and displayed in a museum or performance space.

6. The sense in which beauty is an expression rather than a mimetic representation does not lend support to the aesthetic theory according to which art expresses inner states of the artist rather than imitating outer appearances. Such a theory of artistic expression remains a captive of the craft framework of embodied form, since it conceives the work of art as the realization of an antecedently given feeling or emotion.

7. Marcuse, *The Aesthetic Dimension*, 9.

8. Ibid., 10.

9. Pater, *Essays on Literature and Art*, 72.

10. Admittedly, Pater does hint at the element of concrete universality by mentioning how art must sustain mind in style, achieving the greatest unity of subject and expression (ibid., 80, 88), just as he seeks to qualify the kind of view expressed as one that concerns what is most real to the artist (87). However, whereas the former qualification requires further precision, the latter qualification remains too personal.

11. Danto, *Transfiguration of the Commonplace*, 190ff.

12. Ibid., 189.

13. Ibid., 197.

14. Danto aptly uses this term to describe the representations of art (ibid., 172).

15. Along these lines, Danto observes that the artwork operates as a

metaphor for life in which the audience identifies itself with the work's transfiguratively represented subject (ibid.). What must be kept in mind, however, is that the relation between meaning and configuration within the artwork is not itself metaphorical, since the terms of a metaphor are given independently of one another, whereas the shape of beauty is inherently connected to its meaning. This inherent connection is at hand even when the configuration can exist apart as a prosaic thing. If it is to figure as an element of artistic beauty, the configuration must fit the meaning it expresses, not just as an undifferentiated particular embodiment of that meaning but as its exemplary individuation.

16. Danto makes these points in *Transfiguration of the Commonplace* (vii), but he tends to accept a formalist conclusion where aesthetics is left with little to say of a necessary character about the sensible features and the content of art, the modes of artistic construal, or the individual arts.

17. Kierkegaard makes this point in reference to the treatment of classical art (*Either/Or*, 1:48).

18. This artificial production can range from the relatively formal appropriation of given things, whose imaginative transfiguration consists solely in being labeled a work of art, to the material transformation of given material, creating a completely novel appearance.

19. That the relation of art and truth involves not just the form in which truth is aesthetically captured, but equally the content that is fit for art, remains commonly ignored, even among thinkers who uphold the cognitive dimension of art. Nelson Goodman is a case in point. He restricts his gaze to the issue of form by identifying aesthetic merit as cognitive excellence in the sort of symbolic functioning qualifying as aesthetic, distinguishing between art and science in terms of differences in which characteristics of symbols prevail in their respective domains, and defining the aspects of aesthetic symbolization as syntactic density, semantic density, syntactic repleteness, and exemplification (*Languages of Art*, 252–53, 258–59, 264).

20. Hegel, *Lectures on Aesthetics*, 1:105.

21. This deficiency is not challenged by the aesthetic worth of landscapes or poetic descriptions of nature, both of which not only present scenes of nature as mediated by the creative efforts of rational agency, but therein present a view about what is depicted that, to be artistically successful, sheds light on the predicament of rational agency itself.

22. Science is hereby employed along the lines of Hegel's usage to convey the autonomous, self-responsible, rational inquiry to which philosophy has aspired until recent times, when the conditioned cognition of positive science has been absolutized to wide, if incoherent acclaim. See Winfield, *Overcoming Foundations*, Chapter 7.

23. See Heidegger, *Origin of the Work of Art*, 666, 672, 674.

24. Hannah Arendt describes the exemplary validity of judgments in similar terms in her interpretation of Kant's *Critique of Judgment,* but, like Kant, fails to distinguish the particular from the individual (*Lectures on Kant's Political Philosophy,* 77).

25. Hegel, *Lectures on Aesthetics,* 1:99.

26. As we shall see, to achieve this relation to an audience universal in scope, art will require the perennial aid of critical interpretation to compensate for the differences in particular cultures that veil the meaning of art's sensuous configurations.

27. This does not mean that, as Danto suggests, art should not portray injustices that we are obligated to remedy because the distance at which art places its audience would here contradict our ethical obligations (*Transfiguration of the Commonplace,* 22). That "distance" does not pertain to how individuals interact with others in prosaic life, but simply to how individuals treat artworks. Consequently, the representation of ethical conflicts in art does not contribute to depriving these conflicts of their practical significance.

28. For an extensive development of this arguments see Winfield, *Reason and Justice,* Parts 3 and 4.

29. Hegel, *Lectures on Aesthetics,* 1:112.

30. Ibid., 1:112–13.

31. Ibid., 1:113.

32. Ibid.

33. Ibid., 1:114.

34. Arendt, *Between Past and Future,* 208.

35. As Arendt argues, to the degree that artworks can fulfill their independent value only by having a public space where they can appear, the very nature of art implies that some public provision be made to prevent art objects from remaining in private hands entirely concealed from the public (see ibid., 218). Although this need not preclude private ownership of art, it does suggest, granted that the value of art be publicly acknowledged, a political imperative to provide affordable public museums, performance spaces, radio and television, and other venues for art appreciation.

36. Ibid., 114.

Chapter 7: The Existence of Beauty in the Work of Art

1. Hegel, *Lectures on Aesthetics,* 1:153.

2. Ibid., 1:95.

3. Ibid., 1:96.

4. Hegel argues for this discrepancy between mimesis and artistic beauty in the section "The Relation of the Ideal to Nature" in ibid., 1:160–74.

5. Since, as Nelson Goodman points out, representation rests on denotation

but not on resemblance, the correspondence sought in mimesis is not simply a matter of achieving physical similarity. It is rather a matter of denoting, expressing, or exemplifying a content that is taken to be antecedently given. Even if Goodman is correct in claiming that reception and interpretation are interdependent and the innocent eye and the absolute given are correlative myths (*Languages of Art,* 5–10), the mimetic search for "correctness" is still not completely overthrown. For even if the meaning of an artwork is a construction predicated on a certain scheme of reference, it can still be regarded as something given independently of its unique configuration. The reversion by transcendental aesthetics to metaphysical categories of craft, analyzed at length in Chapter 2, already shows how this is possible. Only due regard for the concrete universality of beauty can put to rest the "correctness" model.

6. This argument lies at the core of Hegel's critique of the mimetic conception of art (*Lectures on Aesthetics,* 1:155).

7. Ibid., 1:155–56.

8. Ibid., 1:156, 163.

9. Ibid., 1:163.

10. Ibid., 1:162, 169–70.

11. For a further discussion of this problem see "On Individuality," Chapter 5 of Winfield's *Freedom and Modernity.*

12. For a recent statement of this argument, which is already at hand in Hegel's *Philosophy of Spirit,* see Strawson, *Individuals.*

13. See Hegel, *Lectures on Aesthetics,* 1:175.

14. Although Hegel does not discuss this option in his analysis of how the divine, as unity and universality, can figure in artistic beauty, he treats it at length in his conception of the symbolic form of art and in his application of this form to the interpretation of Oriental art.

15. Hegel, *Lectures on Aesthetics,* 1:176.

16. Ibid., 1:175–76.

17. Ibid., 1:176–77.

18. Ibid., 1:177.

19. Ibid., 1:244.

20. See Adorno, *Ästhetische Theorie,* 119; Bloch, *Subjekt-Objekt,* 285; Lukács, *Beiträge zur Geschichte der Ästhetik,* 115; Szondi, *Hegels Lehre von der Dichtung,* 361.

Chapter 8: Conduct as an Object of Artistic Beauty

1. "Humanity" refers, as throughout these chapters, to the community of rational agents, whatever may be their natural species, rather than exclusively to those homo sapiens who qualify.

2. I have attempted to develop this system in outline in my book *Reason and*

Justice, reconstructing and revising where necessary the argument of Hegel's *Philosophy of Right.*

3. See Winfield, *Reason and Justice,* for an account of why this differentiation of spheres of freedom is complete.

4. Hegel introduces the following three general features in the opening passages of his exposition of "The External Determinacy of the Ideal," rather than in his discussion of the world condition framing conduct. He suggests that these features enter in after the account of how action figures as a content for art because, through action, the Ideal sallies forth into the external world, posing the question of how this aspect of reality is to be configured in accord with art. This issue, Hegel maintains, has so far been avoided, because the analysis of conduct as a content for art only addresses action and character (*Lectures on Aesthetics,* 1:244–45). However, an account of action and character, not to speak of the institutional background and collision that elicits exemplary conduct, automatically presupposes the fundamental natural, technical, and conventional relations within which conduct always proceeds. For this reason, I have introduced these factors here into the discussion of the world condition where they properly belong.

5. Hegel, *Lectures on Aesthetics,* 1:254–55.

6. Ibid., 1:256.

7. Ibid., 1:257, 259.

8. Hegel mistakenly maintains that such a situation is only configurable in terms of a heroic age, where, in contrast to an idyllic age, individuals must exert themselves to survive, but where they satisfy their needs directly through their own doings, rather than submitting to the social necessity of the market system of a developed civil society, where nothing individuals produce or consume appears as their own work. Hegel claims that a market economy is irremediably prosaic because it leaves individuals dependent on others for their satisfactions and compels them to make their earning activity an increasingly rule-governed mechanical laboring (see ibid., 1:260–61). Even if such were the case, this would not prevent individuals from engaging in activity of a different character, such as in their capacity as person, moral subject, family member, civilian, or citizen, where matters of ethical significance can still hang on their personal initiative.

9. Ibid., 1:263.

10. Ibid., 1:178.

11. Ibid., 1:179–93.

12. Ibid., 1:183–84, 193–94.

13. This conclusion is an important element in Hegel's further, famous claim that with the advent of modernity, art has reached its end.

14. Hegel, *Lectures on Aesthetics,* 1:185–89.

15. Ibid., 1:192.

16. Ibid., 1:186–87.

17. Ibid., 1:189–90.
18. The term "civilian" is here employed to denote the entitled role individuals exercise as members of civil society.
19. Hegel, *Lectures on Aesthetics*, 1:193–94, 260.
20. Ibid., 1:195–96.
21. For an extended investigation of this mode of self-determination, see Chapter 8, "The Limits of Morality," in Winfield, *Overcoming Foundations*, 135–70.
22. Hegel, *Lectures on Aesthetics*, 1:196–217.
23. Ibid., 1:199.
24. Ibid., 1:205.
25. Ibid.
26. Ibid., 1:200.
27. Ibid.
28. Ibid., 1:200–203.
29. See Hegel's remarks on such lyric situations in ibid., 1:203–4.
30. Ibid., 1:201.
31. Ibid., 1:207.
32. Ibid., 1:207–9.
33. Ibid., 1:210–11.
34. Ibid., 1:212.
35. Ibid., 1:213.
36. Ibid., 1:214.
37. Hegel cites the tragedy of Oedipus as a case in point (ibid., 1:213–14).
38. Ibid., 1:216.
39. Ibid.
40. Ibid., 1:217.
41. Ibid.
42. Ibid.
43. Ibid., 1:217–18.
44. Ibid., 1:218.
45. Ibid., 1:219.
46. Ibid., 1:219–20.
47. Ibid., 1:220.
48. Ibid.
49. Ibid., 1:222.
50. Ibid.
51. For an analysis of the requirements of determinacy, see "Conceiving Something without Any Conceptual Scheme" in Winfield, *Overcoming Foundations*, 55–75.
52. Hegel, *Lectures on Aesthetics*, 1:223.
53. Ibid., 1:232.

54. Ibid.
55. Ibid., 1:232–33.
56. Ibid., 1:241, 244.
57. Ibid., 1:227.
58. Ibid., 1:242, 244.
59. Ibid., 1:236.
60. Ibid., 1:237.
61. Ibid.
62. Ibid., 1:238.

63. Hegel attempts to capture these aspects of character in terms of its universal, particular, and individual dimensions. In its universality, character is coextensive with the agent's individuality; in its particularity, character has a specific prominent feature determining its identity; and in its individuality, character unites the former, maintaining its salient trait in conjunction with all its other features (ibid., 1:236, 240).

64. Ibid., 1:238–40.

65. Szondi observes that Hegel's determinations of the Ideal of the general world condition, the particular situation, and the individual action only fully apply to ancient Greek sculpture and epic and dramatic poetry. Szondi wishes to mitigate this apparent inconsistency by suggesting that Hegel's concept of the Ideal of art is already historically determined and therefore need not apply equally either to all forms of art or to all individual arts (*Hegels Lehre von der Dichtung,* 361–62). If Szondi were right, then the Ideal should be developed as part of the determination of the classical form of art. Then, however, the common character that allows each particular form of art to qualify as a type of art would still be in need of an account, leaving the analysis of the forms of art hanging in midair.

66. Hegel, *Lectures on Aesthetics,* 1:219, 238–40.

67. Ibid., 1:239–40.

68. So, for example, Hegel observes that even in the unlikely case of landscape painting, the artistic construal of the environment will exhibit a feeling that properly possesses a pathos of some sort, allowing the scene to resonate as a background and reflection of significant character and action (ibid., 1:233).

Chapter 9: The External Reality of the Work of Art

1. Collingwood ignores the essential significance of this external aspect of the work of art when he privileges the imagination of the artist as the true medium of art, relegating the work of art to an activity of consciousness (*Principles of Art,* 300).

2. It remains to be seen whether the distinction between works of art that (1)

directly confront the audience with an aesthetic image, (2) present inscriptions from which the imagination produces images for inner contemplation, or (3) offer notations from which performances are created for outer intuition is one differentiating individual arts or one properly falling within the determination of art in general.

3. Heidegger, *Origin of the Work of Art*, 652.

4. For instance, a work of art that is representational is no more intrinsically a representation than any other entity that represents. Since, as Nelson Goodman observes, something can figure as a representation only relative to a symbol system (*Languages of Art*, 226), the physical being of the representational artwork commands aesthetic significance only in conjunction with the system of meanings that inform its appreciation by an audience, as well as with the creative process that brought it into being. However, although a representational artwork may denote its meaning relative to a symbol system, just like any other representation, the concrete universality of artistic beauty adds further qualifications tying the images it provides to the meaning they convey.

5. Goodman, *Languages of Art*, 108.

6. See ibid., 122.

7. Hegel, *Lectures on Aesthetics*, 1:247.

8. Ibid.

9. Ibid.

10. Ibid., 1:248–50.

11. Ibid., 1:247.

12. Ibid., 1:250.

13. It may well turn out that in certain arts the body of rational agents can play a privileged role. Yet, even here, the transfiguration required by artistic content will necessitate the introduction of purifying associations.

14. Hegel, *Lectures on Aesthetics*, 1:303–5.

15. Paul de Man ("Sign and Symbol in Hegel's *Aesthetics*") makes the mistake of interpreting Hegel's claim that beauty is the sensuous show of the Idea as if it rendered art a mode of symbolic representation. The fact that meaning and configuration can still be distinguished in art no more signifies that they stand in a symbolic relation than that the intentionality of thought entails that what thinking is about is an independent given, accessible in terms of the representational model of knowing.

16. In this respect, the role of symbolization in a particular form of art, such as Hegel ascribes to symbolic art, need not be dismissed out of hand, for a mode of artistic creation might involve symbolic relations without yielding sovereignty to them.

17. Since the artwork is not a mere appearance but has a physical presence with hidden and recalcitrant features incidental to its creative shaping by its artist, it will always contain physical features that are not tied to its aesthetic

significance. For example, even if all perceivable features of color and shape on the surface of a canvas may be tied to its meaning, this connection will be entirely lacking in regard to innumerable other features of the work, such as its weight, temperature, chemical composition, and whatever pattern covers its reverse side. It is this ineliminable residue that permits Danto to observe that artistic medium can never be entirely identified with the matter of the artwork (*Transfiguration of the Commonplace*, 159).

18. Goodman, *Languages of Art*, 116–17. However, certain features of the physical being of the work of art will be incidental, such as how much a painting weighs, where it may be at a certain point in time, and so forth (230). What counts is that the distinction between contingent and essential features of the work of art still does not allow the aesthetic significance of those essential features to be expressed apart from their configuration.

19. Hegel, *Lectures on Aesthetics*, 1:264.

20. At this stage in the argument, any further discussion of particular senses in their relation to art would be inappropriate, since it would introduce the differentiation of the individual arts, which must rather follow the accounts of the remaining features of art in general and the particular forms of art that the individual arts incorporate.

21. However, contrary to Hegel's blanket dismissal of touch, smell, and taste as vehicles of art, it is conceivable that even these senses could be aesthetically employed for communicating a language or performance notation, as already demonstrated by the use of braille for the blind and of the feeling of vocal cord sensations by the deaf.

22. Plato, the *Sophist*, 235 and 236a, cited in Eco, *Art and Beauty in the Middle Ages*, 65.

23. Eco, *Art and Beauty in the Middle Ages*, 72.

24. For this reason, although Danto may be right in observing how an object can count as a prosaic thing in one age and as a work of fine art in another, he is wrong to suggest that how an object has figured as a work of art in one age can be irrevocably beyond the comprehension of audiences of another epoch (*Transfiguration of the Commonplace*, 44–47). Subsequent aesthetic appreciation of the work is always possible, owing to the universal significance a work must bear to qualify as art and to the intelligibility a culture must possess simply to be recognizable as one by other cultures. These truths are ignored by the avatars of incommensurable conceptual schemes, the indeterminacy of translation, and dissemination.

25. The histories at stake can involve the history of production of the work of art itself. As Danto points out, unless some sense is conveyed of how the creator of the work both regarded and undertook its production, the audience will not be in a position to decide such aesthetically significant matters as whether a work is a forgery, an anachronistic borrowing, or an ironic quotation

of the styles and manners of past masters (*Transfiguration of the Commonplace,* 51).

26. Hegel, *Lectures on Aesthetics,* 1:264.
27. Ibid., 1:276.
28. Ibid., 1:265–68.
29. Ibid., 1:269–70.
30. Ibid., 1:279.
31. Ibid., 1:277–78.
32. Ibid., 1:279.
33. Ibid., 1:272.
34. As Goodman observes, the internal configuration of a symbol does not determine how it functions, for "what describes in some systems may depict in others" (*Languages of Art,* 231). Although the work of art is no mere symbol, its own relation to its audience is also inescapably mediated by the system of reference in which it figures for them.
35. Hegel, *Lectures on Aesthetics,* 1:277.
36. Ibid.
37. Joyce's *Finnegan's Wake* presents a different difficulty, for access to its intelligibility requires a skeleton key for members of Joyce's own cultural community, raising the question of whether it is problematically recondite from an aesthetic point of view. The meaning of a work of art can no more be private than meaning in language.
38. Hegel, *Lectures on Aesthetics,* 1:274.
39. Ibid., 1:273, 274.
40. Danto, *Transfiguration of the Commonplace,* 44.
41. Danto points to Borges's story "Pierre Menard, Symbolist Poet," to show how the relation of an artwork to both preceding art history and its author is constitutive in part of the work, contrary to the dictum of the intentional fallacy (*Transfiguration of the Commonplace,* 35ff.). Danto's example, however, is a poor one, since when Borges depicts how his fictional character Pierre Menard produces a novel work of art that is nevertheless a verbatim restatement of *Don Quixote,* Borges *includes* the creative intent of Menard and its reference to previous literary tradition *within* the story. Consequently, neither author's intention nor the location of the work within art history here figure as independently given factors to which an external reference must be made to permit the artwork to have its proper identity. Borges's story instead confirms how such factors must be perceivably internal to the work if they are to be ingredient in its aesthetic significance.
42. Thus, for example, that a work was created with the intention of quoting past styles may be a relation constitutive of it figuring not as a forgery but as a creative comment on past artistic history. However, that still does not alter the fact that the antecedent intention of the artist cannot operate as a predetermined

form comprising the essence of the work. To maintain the concrete universality of artistic unity, the work must still present a meaning that is tied to its configuration, a meaning that must therefore go beyond the artist's intentions, even if those intentions comprise an *element* in its significance.

Chapter 10: Artistic Creation

1. Danto, *Transfiguration of the Commonplace,* 64.

2. This point, which is implicit in the ordering of Hegel's aesthetics, as well as in that of most traditional philosophies of art, is more recently upheld by Heidegger in *Origin of the Work of Art,* 650–51.

3. For a development of these points see Winfield, *Reason and Justice,* Parts 2 and 3; and Winfield, *Overcoming Foundations,* Chapters 4, 6, and 12.

4. Indeed, since author's intention has no binding authority over the significance of an artistic composition, it can hardly lord over performance.

5. Hegel, *Lectures on Aesthetics,* 1:280.

6. Ibid.

7. Ibid., 1:281.

8. Accordingly, Hegel maintains that fancy, as he calls the general capacity for artistic production, is creative and not simply passively reproductive (ibid., 1:281).

9. Ibid.

10. Ibid., 1:282.

11. Ibid., 1:283.

12. Ibid.

13. Ibid., 1:284.

14. Ibid., 1:286.

15. Ibid., 1:287.

16. Ibid.

17. Ibid., 1:288.

18. Ibid., 1:291.

19. Because artistic creation therefore cannot be reduced to technique, Hannah Arendt is wrong to maintain that the mentality bringing artworks into being is the greatest threat to their nonfunctional existence and that art and politics are in ineluctable, irremediable conflict because artists exercise a functional, technical agency, whereas politics is concerned with action for its own sake (*Between Past and Future,* 217–18). On the contrary, the creativity of the artist involves a freedom from functional concerns that is completely compatible with the freedom from particular interest exercised in aesthetic appreciation and the autonomy of citizens. Conversely, Marcuse goes overboard in maintaining that the transcendence of art sets art and politics in inevitable conflict (*The Aesthetic Dimension,* 37). The truths of humanity

conveyed by art may well call into question current political practice, but they may equally confirm its validity if politics has correctly tackled the problems of justice.

20. Hegel, *Lectures on Aesthetics,* 1:291.
21. Ibid., 1:292.
22. Ibid., 1:293.
23. Ibid., 1:294.
24. Ibid.
25. Heidegger analogously observes how "in great art ... the artist remains inconsequential as compared with the work, almost like a passageway that destroys itself in the creative process for the work to emerge" (*Origin of the Work of Art,* 669).
26. Hannah Arendt makes this point in discussing the relation of the productive imagination and taste in Kant's *Critique of Judgment* (*Lectures on Kant's Political Philosophy,* 63).
27. Hegel, *Lectures on Aesthetics,* 1:298.

Chapter 11: The Reception of Art

1. Danto, *Transfiguration of the Commonplace,* 91.
2. In terms of the metaphysical conception, if mimetic art is to be edifying, the comprehension ingredient in catharsis need not be a principled knowledge of the good but merely an opined recognition of an ethical situation. This will allow such art to contribute to the ethical formation of those who lack a proper knowledge of the good and are not yet in a position to be instructed philosophically. In the case of an audience containing individuals possessing wisdom about the good, catharsis will still be edifying to the degree that it emotively trains their will to accord with reason.
3. Aristotle, *Poetics,* 1451b.
4. Consequently, catharsis does not proceed "as passive contemplation of the immediately given, direct apprehension of what is presented, uncontaminated by any conceptualization, isolated from all the echoes of the past and all the threats and promises of the future ... aesthetic experience is dynamic rather than static" (Goodman, *Languages of Art,* 241), which is why the experience of catharsis depends on the contribution of the audience in its comprehension of the work of art, bringing to bear the complex of meanings and understandings that can coherently be tied to the physical appearance before it.
5. As Umberto Eco informs us, Aquinas accordingly recognized that aesthetic reception cannot be thought of as a passive, instantaneous, effortless intuition, but rather as an active, judicious investigation of the work of art that questions it in terms of its designs, unity, and achievement (*Art and Beauty in the Middle Ages,* 82–83).

6. In this respect, aesthetic experience involves a disinterested inquiry in common not only with pure science, as Goodman observes (*Languages of Art,* 242), but also with philosophy.

7. Again, it must be remembered that letting the work show itself in its own objectivity requires an active contribution on the part of the audience, rising beyond passive contemplation, sensation, and private emotion, just as it demands the correlative labors of genius in the production of the work.

8. Goodman observes that emotion joins sense in helping discern "what properties a work has and expresses," such that "the work of art is apprehended through the feelings as well as through the senses" (*Languages of Art,* 248). Given the determination of the content of artistic beauty and of how the configuration of the work conveys that content, the cognitive role of emotion in aesthetic experience is itself mediated by the rational comprehension that first renders the work aesthetically intelligible, allowing an audience to be moved by something it recognizes to be of exemplary importance.

9. Medieval nominalists, such as Ockham, who viewed the individual as something devoid of universality, accordingly conceived aesthetic reception as an immediate intuition, ignoring the mediated cognition required to gain access to the universality ingredient in beauty's exemplary individuality. For a brief account of Ockham's aesthetic conception, see Eco, *Beauty and Art in the Middle Ages,* 88–89.

10. See Chapter 6 under "The Freedom in Artistic Beauty."

11. Hegel, *Lectures on Aesthetics,* 1:99.

12. See, for example, Danto, *Transfiguration of the Commonplace,* 104–7.

13. Danto makes this point concerning artistic genres in ibid., 136.

14. For instance, a page of text could be literature or a piece of "conceptual" visual art, just as virtually any work of symbolic or classical art could be reappropriated as a "found" object of romantic art.

15. Danto, *Transfiguration of the Commonplace,* 125.

16. Ibid., 119–25.

17. Ibid., 129–31.

18. Ibid., 113.

19. Ibid., 125.

20. Ibid., 113.

21. Ibid., 119.

22. Danto upholds the contrary view (ibid., 175), despite his repeated recognition of the priority of the concept of art over artistic interpretation.

23. H. L. A. Hart powerfully argues this point in refuting "rule-skepticism" in his *The Concept of Law,* 121–50.

24. Thus, even though, as Danto observes, one may be forced to revise one's views of the aesthetic qualities of a work due to the acquisition of new knowledge of its historical context and origins (*Transfiguration of the Com-*

monplace, 111), what aesthetic qualities are in their own right remains something determined independently of historical knowledge and interpretation.

25. Ibid., 135.

26. Ibid., 138.

27. For the deservedly classic statement of this fallacy, see Wimsatt and Beardsley, "The Intentional Fallacy," 367–80.

28. Danto, for one, ignores this (*Transfiguration of the Commonplace,* 130).

Postscript: The Abiding Tasks of Systematic Aesthetics

1. Meyer Shapiro describes a variety of such efforts in his essay "Style," 151ff.

2. Hegel, *Lectures on Aesthetics,* 2:615–21.

3. For attempts to critique Hegel's theory of the art forms and remedy its shortcomings, see Winfield, "Rethinking the Particular Forms of Art," Winfield, "Hegel on Classical Art: A Reexamination," and Winfield, *Stylistics: Rethinking the Artforms after Hegel.* Among the more prominent attempts to develop aspects of the theory of the art forms as realized in individual arts are Adorno, *Philosophy of Modern Music,* Benjamin, *The Origin of German Tragic Drama,* Lukács, *The Theory of the Novel,* and Szondi, *Theory of the Modern Drama.*

Bibliography

Adorno, Theodor W. *Ästhetische Theorie*. Frankfurt am Main: Suhrkamp, 1973.
———. *Philosophy of Modern Music*. Translated by Anne G. Mitchell and Wesley V. Blomster. New York: Seabury Press, 1973.
Arendt, Hannah. *Between Past and Future*. New York: Viking, 1968.
———. *Lectures on Kant's Political Philosophy*. Chicago: University of Chicago Press, 1989.
Aristotle. *Poetics*. In *The Complete Works of Aristotle*, vol. 2, edited by Jonathan Barnes. Princeton: Princeton University Press, 1984.
———. *Politics*. In *The Complete Works of Aristotle*, vol. 2, edited by Jonathan Barnes. Princeton: Princeton University Press, 1984.
Benjamin, Walter. *The Origin of German Tragic Drama*. Translated by John Osborne. London: Verso, 1985.
Berman, Robert Bruce. *Categorial Justification: Normative Argumentation in Hegel's Practical Philosophy*. Albany: State University of New York Press, 1996.
Bloch, Ernst. *Subjekt-Objekt: Erläuterungen zu Hegel*. Frankfurt am Main: Suhrkamp, 1972.
Bloom, Alan. *The Closing of the American Mind*. New York: Simon and Schuster, 1987.
Brecht, Bertolt. *Kleines Organon für das Theater*. Vol. 16 of *Gesammelte Werke*. Frankfurt am Main: Suhrkamp, 1967.
Collingwood, R. G. *The Principles of Art*. New York: Oxford University Press, 1958.
Danto, Arthur C. *The Transfiguration of the Commonplace: A Philosophy of Art*. Cambridge, Mass.: Harvard University Press, 1981.
de Man, Paul. "Sign and Symbol in Hegel's *Aesthetics*." *Critical Inquiry* 8, no. 4 (Summer 1982): 761–775.

Derrida, Jacques. *Margins of Philosophy.* Translated by Alan Bass. Chicago: University of Chicago Press, 1982.
———. *The Truth in Painting.* Translated by Geoff Bennington and Ian McLeod. Chicago: University of Chicago Press, 1987.
Desmond, William. *Art and the Absolute: A Study of Hegel's Aesthetics.* Albany: State University of New York Press, 1986.
Eagleton, Terry. *Literary Theory: An Introduction.* Minneapolis: University of Minnesota Press, 1983.
Eco, Umberto. *Art and Beauty in the Middle Ages.* New Haven: Yale University Press, 1986.
Foster, Michael B. "The Concrete Universal: Cook Wilson and Bosanquet." *Mind* 40, no. 157 (January 1931): 1–22.
———. *The Political Philosophies of Plato and Hegel.* Oxford: Oxford University Press, 1968.
Gadamer, Hans-Georg. *The Relevance of the Beautiful and Other Essays.* Translated by Nicholas Walker. New York: Cambridge University Press, 1986.
Goodman, Nelson. *Languages of Art.* Indianapolis: Hackett, 1988.
Habermas, Jürgen. *The Philosophical Discourse on Modernity: Twelve Lectures.* Translated by Frederick Lawrence. Cambridge, Mass.: MIT Press, 1987.
Halper, Edward. "Hegel and the Problem of the Differentia." In *Essays on Hegel's Logic,* edited by George di Giovanni. Albany: State University of New York Press, 1990.
Hart, H. L. A. *The Concept of Law.* Oxford: Oxford University Press, 1961.
Hartmann, Klaus. "Hegel: A Nonmetaphysical View." In *Hegel: A Collection of Critical Essays,* edited by Alasdair MacIntyre. Notre Dame: University of Notre Dame Press, 1976.
Hegel, G. W. F. *Lectures on Aesthetics.* 2 vols. Translated by T. M. Knox and W. Miller. Oxford: Oxford University Press, 1975.
———. *Philosophy of Mind.* Translated by William Wallace and A. V. Miller. Oxford: Oxford University Press, 1971.
———. *Philosophy of Right.* Translated by T. M. Knox. New York: Oxford University Press, 1967.
———. *Science of Logic.* Translated by A. V. Miller. New York: Humanities Press, 1976.
Heidegger, Martin. "The Origin of the Work of Art." In *Philosophies of Art and Beauty,* edited by Albert Hofstadter and Richard Kuhns. Chicago: University of Chicago Press, 1976.
Hume, David. "Of the Standard of Taste." In *Essays: Moral, Political and Literary,* edited by Eugene F. Miller. Indianapolis: Liberty Classics, 1987.

Kant, Immanuel. *Critique of Judgment.* Translated by Werner S. Pluhar. Indianapolis: Hackett, 1987.
Kierkegaard, Søren. *Either/Or.* Vol. 1. Translated by David F. Swenson and Lillian Marvin Swenson. Garden City, N.Y.: Doubleday/Anchor, 1959.
Lukács, Georg. *Ästhetik: In vier Teilen.* Neuwied and Berlin: Luchterhand, 1972.
———. *Beiträge zur Geschichte der Ästhetik.* Berlin: Aufbau-Verlag, 1954.
———. *History and Class Consciousness.* Translated by Rodney Livingstone. Cambridge, Mass.: MIT Press, 1971.
———. *The Theory of the Novel.* Translated by Anna Bostock. Cambridge, Mass.: MIT Press, 1971.
———. *Über die Besonderheit als Kategorie der Ästhetik.* Neuwied and Berlin: Luchterhand, 1967.
———. *Werke 11 & 12: Die Eigenart des Ästhetischen 1. & 2. Halbband.* Neuwied and Berlin: Luchterhand, 1963.
Maker, William. *Philosophy without Foundations: Rethinking Hegel.* Albany: State University of New York Press, 1994.
Marcuse, Herbert. *The Aesthetic Dimension: Toward a Critique of Marxist Aesthetics.* Boston: Beacon Press, 1978.
Mitias, Michael H. "Hegel on the Art Object." In *Art and Logic in Hegel's Philosophy,* edited by Warren E. Steinkraus and Kenneth I. Schmitz. Highlands, N.J.: Humanities Press, 1980.
Pater, Walter. *Essays on Literature and Art.* London: Dent, 1990.
Plato. *Ion.* In *The Collected Dialogues,* edited by Edith Hamilton and Huntington Cairns. Princeton: Princeton University Press, 1961.
———. *Laws.* In *The Collected Dialogues,* edited by Edith Hamilton and Huntington Cairns. Princeton: Princeton University Press, 1961.
———. *Republic.* In *The Collected Dialogues,* edited by Edith Hamilton and Huntington Cairns. Princeton: Princeton University Press, 1961.
———. *Sophist.* In *The Collected Dialogues,* edited by Edith Hamilton and Huntington Cairns. Princeton: Princeton University Press, 1961.
Rapp, Carl. "Coming Out into the Corridor: Post-Modern Phantasies of Pluralism." *Georgia Review* 41, no. 3 (Fall 1987): 533–552.
———. "The Crisis of Reason in Contemporary Thought: Some Reflections on the Arguments of Post-Modernism." *Critical Review* 5, no. 2 (Spring 1991): 261–290.
———. "Ideology and the New Pragmatism." *Modern Age* 31, no. 2 (Spring 1987): 125–137.
Rorty, Richard. *Irony, Contingency, and Solidarity.* New York: Cambridge University Press, 1989.
Rose, Gillian. *Hegel contra Sociology.* Highlands, N.J.: Humanities Press, 1981.

Schiller, Friedrich. *On the Aesthetic Education of Man in a Series of Letters.* Translated by Elizabeth M. Wilkinson and L. A. Willoughby. Oxford: Oxford University Press, 1986.
Shaftesbury, Anthony Ashley Cooper. *Characteristics.* In *Philosophies of Art and Beauty,* edited by Albert Hofstadter and Richard Kuhns. Chicago: University of Chicago Press, 1976.
Shapiro, Meyer. "Style." In *Aesthetics Today,* edited by Morris Philipson and Paul J. Gudel. New York: New American Library, 1980.
Sontag, Susan. *Against Interpretation.* New York: Doubleday, 1990.
Strawson, P. F. *Individuals: An Essay in Descriptive Metaphysics.* London: Methuen, 1979.
Szondi, Peter. "Hegels Lehre von der Dichtung." In his *Poetik und Geschichtsphilosophie,* vol. 1. Frankfurt am Main: Suhrkamp, 1974.
———. *Theory of the Modern Drama.* Translated by Michael Hays. Minneapolis: University of Minnesota Press, 1987.
White, Alan. *Absolute Knowledge.* Athens: Ohio University Press, 1983.
Wimsatt, William K., Jr., and Monroe Beardsley. "The Intentional Fallacy." In *Philosophy Looks at the Arts.* 3rd ed. Edited by Joseph Margolis. Philadelphia: Temple University Press, 1987.
Winfield, Richard Dien. *Freedom and Modernity.* Albany: State University of New York Press, 1991.
———. "Hegel on Classical Art: A Reexamination." *Clio* 24, no. 2 (Winter 1995).
———. "The Individuality of Art and the Collapse of Metaphysical Aesthetics." *American Philosophical Quarterly* 31, no. 1 (January 1993): 39–51.
———. *The Just Economy.* New York: Routledge, 1988.
———. *Law in Civil Society.* Lawrence: University Press of Kansas, 1995.
———. "Natural Beauty and the Philosophy of Art." *Journal of Speculative Philosophy* 9, no. 1 (March 1995): 48–62.
———. *Overcoming Foundations: Studies in Systematic Philosophy.* New York: Columbia University Press, 1989.
———. *Reason and Justice.* Albany: State University of New York Press, 1988.
———. "Rethinking the Particular Forms of Art." *Owl of Minerva* 24, no. 2 (Spring 1993): 131–144.
———. *Stylistics: Rethinking the Artforms After Hegel.* Albany: State University of New York Press, 1996.
Wollheim, Richard. *Art and Its objects.* 2nd ed. Cambridge, Mass.: Cambridge University Press, 1989.

Index

abstract art. *See* non-representational art
abstract expressionism, 127
abstract right. *See* property rights
Adorno, Theodor W., 103, 132, 229n. 3
aesthetic idea, 53–54
aesthetic judgment, 2, 3, 8, 18, 35, 37, 44–50, 103, 170, 191–92, 194–201, 209n. 16. *See also* aesthetic reception
aesthetic reception, 3, 7–8, 18, 35–36, 45–50, 61–62, 70, 102–3, 120, 122–23, 162, 167–68, 173–75, 189, 191–201, 227nn. 4, 5, 228nn. 6, 7, 8, 9
aesthetics, 7, 15, 70–71, 77; as an a priori theory of taste, 38, 43–55; as a critique of taste, 8, 35–36, 37, 56, 61; as an empirical theory of taste, 38–43; as the philosophy of art, 70–71, 93, 111–12, 211n. 11; metaphysical, 7, 10, 15–33, 34, 36, 49, 52, 55–57, 61, 70–71, 126, 132, 168, 175, 192, 202, 206n. 6, 207n. 28; origin, 15; starting point of, 62, 67–68, 70–71, 121; systematic, 7, 9–10, 62, 66–67, 94, 132, 167–68, 200–201, 202–4; transcendental, 7–8, 10, 34–57, 61, 70–71, 103, 123, 167–68, 191–92, 194–95, 202, 208n. 1, 219n. 5
aesthetic value. *See* beauty
agency, as an object of artistic construal, 153–59
aleatory art, 179
allegory, 32–33, 158, 162
anachronism, in artistic construal, 172–73, 224n. 25
Aquinas, Thomas, 215n. 19, 227n. 5
archeology, 16
architecture, 24, 28, 77, 132–33, 160, 169, 171
Arendt, Hannah, 218nn. 24, 35, 226n. 19, 227n. 26
Aristotle, 11, 23–24, 26–28, 80, 83, 114, 127, 155–56, 169, 192–93, 207nn. 19, 28
art: autonomy of, 9, 29, 33, 62–63, 68, 86, 105, 117–20; descriptive and prescriptive dimensions, 1–3; distinction between useful and fine art, 18–19, 31–32, 170, 208n. 42; for art's sake, 128; individuality of, 2, 9, 19, 31–34, 37–38, 49, 52, 56, 71–72; originality of, 19, 30–33, 78, 115, 182–83, 187–90; teaching of, 32, 185

235

art appreciation. *See* art criticism
art criticism, 1, 18, 20, 25, 30, 33, 41–42, 55–57, 66, 171, 174, 198, 201, 203, 218n. 26. *See also* aesthetic reception
art forms, 67, 68, 110, 116, 122, 124, 128, 133, 152, 160, 161, 162, 165, 177, 178, 189, 191–92, 197, 200, 203–4, 210 n. 6; *See also* symbolic, classical and romantic art
artifact, 16, 30–31, 52, 78, 125, 168
artist, in contrast to artisan, 19–20, 25–26, 33, 181
artistic beauty. *See* beauty
artistic creation, 1–3, 19, 30, 32–33, 70, 122–23, 125, 153, 162, 176–90, 226nn. 8, 19; as conceived by the empirical theory of taste, 41; as conceived by transcendental aesthetics, 37; conceived as an imitative craft, 7, 18, 26, 29–30, 56, 125; in the performing arts, 180–81; role of technique in, 32–33, 62, 168, 176, 178, 182, 185
artistic genius, 2, 33, 53–55, 181–86
artistic style. *See* art forms
art work, 3, 70, 110, 117, 119, 122, 177, 189, 191; as conceived by transcendental aesthetics, 36–37, 123; as determined in its relation to the audience, 167–75, 218 n. 26, 225nn. 34, 37; conceived as a metaphoric exemplification, 109; conceived as an imitative artifact, 7, 16, 17–20, 208 n. 1, 216 n. 6; conceived as an edifying imitative artifact, 7, 20–23, 36, 61, 89, 132, 227 n. 2; external reality of, 162–75, 224 n. 18
art world, 39, 43, 65, 179
Augustine, 214n. 12
author's intention, 175, 190, 201, 225nn. 41, 42, 226n. 4. *See also* intentional fallacy
autonomous reason, 6
Beardsley, Monroe, 229n. 27
beauty, 2–3, 15, 35–36, 38, 40, 43, 45, 51–52, 62–63, 69–70, 168, 208n. 1, 211n. 11; artistic, 36, 51–52, 70, 77–78, 91–93, 104, 108, 111, 122–24, 128, 167–68, 176–77, 191, 198–200, 209n. 26, 211n. 11; as self-understanding, 107, 109–12, 115, 127, 134, 166, 172, 189, 194, 196, 201, 209n. 30; autonomy of, 86, 93, 108, 115, 196–97, 210n. 1, 213n. 21, 218n. 35; as exemplary, 52–53, 89, 92, 111, 114–17, 121, 128, 152, 155, 163, 165–67, 172–74, 185, 193, 195, 228n. 9; concrete universality of, 85–86, 90–91, 93, 106–7, 109, 119, 125, 164, 173, 189, 196, 200, 216n. 10, 223n. 4; content of, 87; individuality of, 76–778, 83, 187; minimal determinacy, 120–21, 202, 211n. 11; natural, 10, 36, 51, 70, 77, 91–105, 111–12, 126, 209nn. 26, 30, 210n. 6, 211n. 11; relation to an audience, 76, 86, 90–92
Benjamin, Walter, 229n. 3
Berman, Robert Bruce, 205n. 3
Bloch, Ernst, 132
Bloom, Allan, 207n. 19
Boethius, 214n. 12
Borges, Jorge Luis, 225n. 41
Brecht, Bertolt, 27

Cage, John, 164, 179–80
caste system, 150
categorial immanence. *See* immanent categorial development
catharsis, 25, 27, 29, 192–95, 197, 227nn. 2, 4
Chagall, Marc, 189
character, artistic representation of,

24, 135, 155, 157–59, 160, 193, 207n. 29, 222n. 63
civil society, 114; as an object of artistic construal, 143–45, 220n. 8
class: logical (*see* universality); social, 8, 126, 203
classical art, 67, 132, 146, 217n. 17, 222n. 65, 228n. 14
Collingwood, R. G., 182, 206nn. 6, 7, 207n. 28, 208n. 42, 222n. 1
conceptual art, 164, 228n. 14
concrete universality. *See* universality conduct, as an object of artistic beauty, 24, 26, 30, 102, 112–14, 129, 131–61, 171–74, 220n. 4; general background of, 135–46, 171–74; precipitating situation of, 135, 146–53
Conrad, Joseph, 143
conscience. *See* morality
content and expression in art, 124–26
convention, as an object of artistic construal, 137
craft, 16–20, 31–33, 62, 68, 123, 195
crime, as an object of artistic construal, 144

Dali, Salvador, 189
dance, 75, 180
Danto, Arthur C., 21, 72, 76, 105, 108–9, 175–76, 191, 197–99, 211n. 16, 212nn. 22, 23, 24, 215n. 42, 216nn. 14, 15, 217n. 16, 218n. 27, 224nn. 17, 24, 25, 225n. 41, 228nn. 13, 22, 24, 229n. 28
Darwin, Charles, 87–88
deconstruction, 9, 69
de Man, Paul, 223n. 15
Derrida, Jacques, 8–9, 68–70
Desmond, William, 213n. 21
Dickie, George, 8

differentia, problem of, 74, 106
dissemination of meaning, 69, 224n. 24
divine, as a content of artistic construal, 25, 129–31, 148
Dove, Kenley R., 205n. 3
drama, 27, 75, 147, 169, 180; tragic, 146
Duchamp, Marcel, 105, 164, 179–80

Eagleton, Terry, 208n. 2
edification, as the rationale for imitative art, 23–26, 207n. 18
efficient causality, 80, 97–98, 103
Entfremdung, 27
epic, 159
epistemology, 3–5
ethics, 2–5, 62, 134–35, 155, 160. *See also* conduct
evil, as an object of artistic construal, 155–56
expression, in art, 21, 108–9, 216n. 6

family, as an object of artistic construal, 141, 143–45, 152
fiction, 21, 27, 109
forgery, 110, 163, 224n. 25, 225n. 42
formalism in aesthetics, 55–56, 61, 103, 217n. 16
Foster, Michael B., 87, 98–99, 205n. 1, 208n. 41
Foucault, Michel, 5, 8–9, 205n. 2
"found" art, 17, 96, 104–5, 110, 127, 163–64, 178–80, 216n. 5, 228n. 14
foundationalism, 5–6, 74, 177, 212n. 18; foundational epistemology, 7, 65
freedom. *See* self-determination

Gadamer, Hans-Georg, 209nn. 26, 30

gender, 8, 101, 126, 141, 150, 203
genius. *See* artistic genius
genre. *See* individual arts
genus. *See* universality, as generic
Goethe, Johann Wolfgang von, 114
good, 3, 23, 45, 52, 69, 192
Goodman, Nelson, 17, 109, 163, 217n. 19, 218n. 5, 223n. 4, 225n. 34, 228nn. 6, 8
Habermas, Jürgen, 205n. 2
habit, 192
Halper, Edward 212n. 19
harmony, 97–99, 165, 167
Hart, H. L. A., 228n. 23
Hartmann, Klaus, 210n. 2
Hegel, Georg Wilhelm Friedrich, 11, 66–67, 70, 73–75, 83, 89–91, 95–96, 104, 111, 113, 117, 123, 126–27, 129–32, 138–40, 142–43, 146–50, 154–56, 159–60, 165, 169, 171, 174, 182, 186, 188, 190–91, 203–4, 210n. 4, 210n. 9, 211nn. 11, 12, 16, 212nn. 20, 21, 215n. 22, 216n. 1, 217n. 22, 219nn. 6, 12, 14, 220nn. 4, 8, 13, 222nn. 63, 65, 68, 223nn. 15, 16, 224n. 21, 226nn. 2, 8, 229n. 3; *Lectures on Aesthetics,* 11, 66, 191, 204, 211n. 11
Heidegger, Martin, 68, 115, 162, 211nn. 10, 14, 212n. 17, 226n. 2, 227n. 25
hermeneutics, 68–69, 199
heroic age. *See* world condition: of revolutionary challenge
highest good, 5
historical individual, and the concrete universal, 87–88
history, in contrast to art, 28–29
Hitler, Adolf, 24
Homer, 140–41, 146
household. *See* family
humanity, 111; *See also* rational agency
Hume, David, 8, 11, 38–44

iconography, 42, 167, 190, 201
Idea, 73–76, 90, 95, 111, 211n. 12, 212n. 21, 216n. 1
Ideal, 91, 108, 123, 126–27, 129, 220n. 4, 222n. 65
ideology, 5
imagination: role in aesthetic reception, 49, 75, 120, 162, 168, 195–97; role in artistic creation, 30–31, 33, 53–54, 102, 127–28, 138, 182–87
immanent categorial development, 63–64, 66, 94, 118, 124, 202, 204, 210n. 4
individual arts, 63, 67–68, 70, 104, 110, 121, 124, 128, 133, 152, 159–61, 162, 165, 171, 177–78, 191, 197, 200, 203–4, 210n. 6, 222n. 2, 224n. 20. *See also* architecture; dance; drama; literature; music; painting; performing arts; sculpture; visual arts
individuality: of art, 2, 56, 71; logic of, 70, 72, 78–79, 88–89, 129, 212n. 1
industrial art, 178–80, 216n. 5
institutional theory of art, 43, 65, 179
intellectual intuition, 87–88
intentional fallacy, 201, 225n. 41, 42
internal realism, 37
international relations, 114
interpretation, 18, 56–57, 68, 71–72, 82, 167, 197–201, 206n. 3, 228n. 24

Joyce, James, 225n. 37
judges, 199
justification, logic of, 3–4

Kant, Immanuel, 11, 26, 38, 43–55, 56, 83, 103, 194, 195, 208nn. 1, 2, 3, 209nn. 16, 26, 30, 218n. 24; *Critique of Judgment,* 38, 43
Kepler, Johannes, 98

Kierkegaard, Søren, 101, 217n. 17
knowledge, as the purpose of art, 22

landscape painting. *See* nature, as incorporated in artistic beauty
language, in art, 32, 96. *See also* literature
language games, 5
liberal theory, 4–5, 7
life, 52, 85, 99–100, 165, 213n. 20
literature, 24, 28, 32, 75, 90, 96, 130, 132, 159–60, 162, 169, 228n. 14
Lukács, Georg, 83, 88–90, 103, 132, 214nn. 32, 33, 215nn. 31, 38, 229n. 3
lyric poetry, 133, 148, 159

Maker, William, 205n. 3
mannerism in art, 90, 188–90
Mao Zedong, 7, 25
Marcuse, Herbert, 109, 216n. 3, 226n. 19
Marxist aesthetics, 89, 90, 103
Marxist-Leninism, 23–24
meaning and configuration, unity of in art, 19–20, 29–31, 61, 71–72, 76, 78, 83, 86, 107, 110, 115, 120, 124, 134, 148, 152, 154, 159, 162–64, 168–69, 195, 203, 217n. 15
Melville, Herman, 143
metaethics, 2
metaphor, 109, 175, 217n. 15
metaphysical aesthetics. *See* aesthetics, metaphysical
metaphysical philosophy, 4, 15–16, 35
mimesis, 7, 20, 27, 49, 52, 54, 61, 70, 89–90, 95, 108, 115, 126, 128, 132, 157, 159, 162, 183, 192–93, 206nn. 6, 7, 209n. 26, 215n. 19
Mitias, Michael H., 212n. 22
modernism, 90

modernity, 101, 139, 141–43, 220n. 13
morality, as an object of artistic construal, 141–42, 144–45, 152–53
music, 24, 28, 75, 77, 98, 132–33, 159–60, 169, 171, 180, 184, 207n. 29
nature, as incorporated in artistic beauty, 96, 104–5, 136, 149–50, 164–65, 217n. 21, 222n. 68
naturalism, 126, 173, 214n. 33
Newton, Isaac, 98
Nietzsche, Friedrich, 101
nominalism, 79, 228n. 9
non-representational art, 77, 160, 206n. 6, 207n. 28. *See also* abstract expressionism

Ockham, William of, 228n. 9
organic unity. *See* universality
originality, of art. *See* art

painting, 28, 132, 147, 160, 167, 169, 188
passion, as an object of artistic construal, 153–54, 156–59
Pater, Walter, 109, 216n. 10
pathos, as an object of artistic construal, 156–57, 158–60, 173, 193, 222n. 68
performing arts, 17, 75, 81–83, 162, 165, 167, 174, 180–81, 223n. 13, 226n. 4
personhood. *See also* property rights
philosophy, 117; of art, 55, 62, 199; of logic, 62, 95, 113; of mind, 62, 113; of nature, 62, 94–95, 113; of spirit, 94, 113; problematic character of, 1–2; quarrel between philosophy and art, 2; relation to art, 2, 28–29
physics: "new" modern, 98–99; "old" modern, 98–99
Picasso, Pablo, 189

Plath, Sylvia, 143
Plato, 7, 11, 17, 20–26, 79, 95, 170, 206n.6, 207n. 28, 210n. 1
pleasure, as a rationale for art, 22; in aesthetic reception, 26, 39–41, 47, 196
poetry, 25, 28, 184–85, 207n. 28
politics, and art, 109, 226n. 19; as an object of artistic construal, 141, 143–45, 152
post-heroic world condition. *See* world condition, of established institutions of justice
postmodernism, 5–6, 8
praxis. *See* ethics
praxis theory. *See* teleological ethics
"primitive" art, 178–80, 216n. 5
privileged determiners, 4–5, 8, 118; appeal to in aesthetics, 7–8, 10, 56, 62; appeal to in ethics, 4–5, 8, 177; appeal to in theoretical philosophy, 4–5, 8, 177
privileged givens, 4, 7, 118; appeal to in aesthetics, 7, 10, 56, 62; appeal to in ethics, 4; appeal to in theoretical philosophy, 4
procedural ethics, 5, 7–8, 177
Prokofiev, Sergei, 24
property rights, 114, 144; as an object of artistic construal, 141, 143–44, 152
psychologism, 8

quality. *See* universality
quantum mechanics, 98–99

race, 8, 101, 141, 150, 203
rational agency, 84, 94, 98, 111, 219n. 1; as the proper domain of beauty, 87, 92, 100–2, 106–7, 111, 119, 150, 165, 216n. 2
rational reconstruction, 63–66, 68, 210nn. 2, 5
realism, 127
reason, role in aesthetic reception, 120, 195–97; role in artistic creation, 186
reflective equilibrium, 65–66, 202
relativism, 15
relativity theory, 98–99
religion, 117; as a content for artistic construal, 112–13, 155
Rembrandt van Rijn, 188
representation, and imitation, 17, 20–21, 72, 206n. 7, 219n. 5, 223n. 4
representational model of knowing, 72, 74, 106, 223n. 15
rhetoric, and transcendental aesthetics, 36, 208n. 2
rock and roll, 24
Rockwell, Norman, 89
romantic art, 67, 132–33, 228n. 14
romanticism, 101
Rorty, Richard, 9, 205n. 5
Rose, Gillian, 210n. 4
rule skepticism, 228n. 23

Saussure, Ferdinand de, 69
Schiller, Friedrich, 207n. 18
science, as a content for artistic construal, 112–13
sculpture, 28, 132, 147, 159–60, 169
self-determination: in art 29; and the concrete universal, 85–86, 92; logic of, 85–86; and normative validity, 6, 118
semiotics, 166
senses, in relation to art, 169–70, 224nn. 20, 21
sensus communis, 54, 196
sexual orientation, 126, 141, 203
Shaftesbury, Anthony Ashley Cooper, 216n. 2
Shapiro, Meyer, 229n. 1
Shostakovich, Dmitri, 24
sign, 166–67
slavery, 150
socialist realism, 25, 214n. 33
society, as an object of artistic construal, 141, 143–44, 152

Sontag, Susan, 205n. 3
Speer, Albert, 24
Stalin, Josef, 24
state, 114, 117
Strawson, P. F., 219n. 12
style, 189. *See also* art forms
symbol, 162, 166–67, 223nn. 15, 16, 225n. 34
symbolic art, 67, 132–33, 219n. 14, 223n. 16, 228n. 14
systematic philosophy, 6–7, 210n. 5
Szondi, Peter, 132, 222n. 65, 229n. 3

taste, 2, 8, 37, 39, 42–43, 195
techné. *See* craft
technique. *See* artistic creation; craft
technology, as an object of artistic construal, 136–37, 149
teleological ethics, 4
tragedy. *See* drama, tragic
transcendental aesthetics. *See* aesthetics, transcendental
transcendental philosophy, 4–5, 8, 35, 37, 50, 65
transcendental conditions, 4–5, 65
transfiguration in art, 26–31, 102, 104, 107–8, 124, 126–28, 132, 134, 136, 139–41, 146, 153–54, 164, 171–72, 179–81, 183–84, 216n. 3
truth, 3, 6, 23, 29, 45, 64, 71–75, 118; of art, 71–72, 184; in beauty, 71–73, 75–76, 91, 106–12, 128, 172, 193, 209n. 30, 211nn. 10, 14, 217n. 19; as correctness, 73–74, 127, 172, 211nn. 12, 16, 212n. 17, 219n. 5; as the Idea, 74–75, 216n. 1
type and token. *See* universality, as type and token
universality: abstract, 71, 73, 76, 80–83, 85, 87, 92, 109, 115, 156; as class, 79, 82, 83, 109; concrete 10, 28, 29, 32, 72, 83–88, 92, 98–99, 106, 159; as form, 80; as generic, 80–81, 83, 85, 87, 92; as organic unity 84–85, 92, 99–100, 165; as quality, 79; as type and token, 81–83

Van Gogh, Vincent, 188
visual arts, 24, 77, 104, 170
Vitruvius, 214n. 12

White, Alan, 210n. 2
will to power, 5, 8
Wimsatt, William K., Jr., 229n. 27
Wittgenstein, Ludwig, 5, 8–9, 65, 205n. 1
Wölfflin, Heinrich, 203
Wollheim, Richard, 8, 81–82
world condition: as object of artistic construal, 137–40, 147, 152, 173, 220n. 4; of established institutions of justice, 138–39, 142–46, 151, 152, 153, 173; of revolutionary challenge, 138, 139, 140–42, 145–46, 150, 151, 152, 153, 173

Zhdanov, Andrei A., 25

For Product Safety Concerns and Information please contact our EU
representative GPSR@taylorandfrancis.com
Taylor & Francis Verlag GmbH, Kaufingerstraße 24, 80331 München, Germany

www.ingramcontent.com/pod-product-compliance
Lightning Source LLC
Chambersburg PA
CBHW061440300426
44114CB00014B/1765